Modern Dog Parenting

Also by Sarah Hodgson

Modern Dog Parenting

**RAISING YOUR DOG OR PUPPY TO BE
A LOVING MEMBER OF YOUR FAMILY**

Sarah Hodgson

ST. MARTIN'S GRIFFIN ✿ NEW YORK

MODERN DOG PARENTING. Copyright © 2016 by Sarah Hodgson. Foreword copyright © 2016 by Stanley Coren. All rights reserved. Printed
in the United States of America. For information, address St. Martin's
Press, 175 Fifth Avenue, New York, N.Y. 10010.

www.stmartins.com

Library of Congress Cataloging-in-Publication Data

Names: Hodgson, Sarah, author.
Title: Modern dog parenting: raising your dog or puppy to be a loving
    member of your family / Sarah Hodgson.
Description: First edition. | New York: St. Martin's Griffin, 2016. |
    Includes index.
Identifiers: LCCN 2016007621| ISBN 9781250095541 (trade pbk.) |
    ISBN 9781250095558 (e-book)
Subjects: LCSH: Dogs—Training.
Classification: LCC SF431 .H733 2016 | DDC 636.7/0835—dc23
LC record available at https://lccn.loc.gov/2016007621

Our books may be purchased in bulk for promotional, educational, or
business use. Please contact your local bookseller or the Macmillan Cor-
porate and Premium Sales Department at 1-800-221-7945, extension
5442, or by e-mail at MacmillanSpecialMarkets@macmillan.com.

First Edition: September 2016

10 9 8 7 6 5 4 3 2 1

For my Saint, who answers to the name of Roman and is known to all as my husband. Thanks, honey—I could never have discovered so much joy (or picked up so much dog poop) without you.

CONTENTS

FOREWORD

Sarah Hodgson has been a friend and colleague of mine for many years and we've worked on several projects together. She's an insightful and compassionate dog person and a warm and engaging people person—a lucky combination indeed. I was pleased when she asked me to write a foreword to her upcoming book.

When she sent me the manuscript for *Modern Dog Parenting* I knew right away that Sarah was onto something. Millions of dog owners feel deeply connected to their canine companions and it's clear that dogs can respond in kind. Through careful research and copious examples, Sarah shows that even though we aren't our dogs' actual parents, recent human psychological data and our expanding understanding of the canine mind suggest that we may as well be. Sarah wants us all to embrace our inner dog parent.

Don't be embarrassed if you go a little overboard with your dogs. A survey of one thousand people conducted by Kelton Research revealed that 81 percent of respondents considered their dogs to be equal in status to children. More than half (54 percent) refer to themselves as pet parents rather than pet owners. Even more (58 percent) use common parental nicknames like Mommy or Daddy when speaking in reference to their dogs. There's a pretty big number of people (35 percent) who call their dogs children and 10 percent celebrate Mother's and/or Father's Day with their dogs.

Do you talk to your dog? You're in the majority. Seventy-seven percent of pet owners talk to their dogs and most of us use the same language and rhythms that we use when we talk to our kids. Brain scans show that certain emotional centers are activated in the brain when we talk to our children and guess what? When we talk to our dogs, the same areas are triggered.

And there's more. Many dogs have the same rights and obligations of children. Nearly 72 percent of dog owners who have (two-legged) children apply the same disciplinary standards to the dogs as they do to their kids and most dog parents provide their dogs with their own chair, sofa, or bed.

Can we justify these attitudes towards our dogs? In *Modern Dog Parenting*, Sarah presents evidence that suggests that your dog's mind is roughly equivalent to a human two- to three-year-old child when it comes to problem solving, language use, and emotional behavior. And even more compelling, dogs tend to respond to their owners in very much the same way that human children respond to their parents. Our dogs are already treating us as parents! Sarah feels it's not only justified, it's imperative.

Any sort of parenting is hard sometimes. Shortly after my daughter Rebecca gave birth to my first grandchild she called me in an emotional state. "Daddy," she said, "I don't know if I know how to be a real parent. I feel like I'm making mistakes or at least not using best practices with my baby." I knew that my daughter was a wonderful mother and I reassured her as best I could but I couldn't fully answer her when she asked why, since parenting was so important, our brains were not pre-wired with an instruction manual.

Dog parents often feel this same frustration. You stare down at a vulnerable, dependent creature and wonder if you're doing things right. You'll ask yourself "Am I raising this dog correctly? Am I teaching my dog how to communicate properly? How do I teach my dog to be a responsible citizen and a good family member? Can I expect the same kind of adolescent rebellion from my dog as I experience with my children? And where the heck is the instruction manual?"

Puppies don't come with owner's manuals and our brains are not hardwired for dog parenting but the book that you hold in your hand is a pretty good substitute. In addition to providing some understanding about the way dogs think, and their similarities to human kids, this book covers the broad spectrum of issues which any dog owner is apt to run into when they are integrating a "furry child" of the canine variety into their family. Whether you are beginning with a new puppy, adopting an adult or older dog, or simply helping your present pet dog navigate through the various stages of its life, this book will provide a readable and practical set of guidelines. It will help you raise a well-mannered dog without major problems, and most importantly, a dog that is happy with its life and well integrated into your family, which could make you a happier person (or is that a happier dog parent?).

—Stanley Coren, Ph.D., DSc, FRSC, bestselling author of
How Dogs Think and *How to Speak Dog*

Introduction

I want you to know that I do get it: Living with a dog can be overwhelming. Raising a dog is a project, but—with the right approach—can be a fun adventure.

Dogs are so trusting, after all. From the minute they waddle into our hearts and homes, they follow our gestures and, when raised with people, will often prefer our company to that of other dogs. Like toddlers, they are eager to explore, play, and problem solve.

Throughout this book, you'll discover recent studies by well-respected scientists and behaviorists that show that dogs learn more quickly and effectively through positive reinforcement rather than negative, which is just fancy talk for the popular idiom: "You attract more bees with honey than with vinegar!" Or as I like to paraphrase it: You teach more with rewards than with retaliation.

No matter where you are in the process—just starting out with a puppy or adopting an older dog—I'll help you figure everything out. We'll begin with a little perspective—your dog's mistakes may be easier to forgive once you understand where they're coming from. After you've determined their emotional IQ (and yours!), we'll start lessons, then shift to problem-solving strategies. Throughout each chapter you'll find boxes and games that'll help you to jump-start your Happy Dog Adventure Story today!

It All Starts with Forgiveness

Maybe, like a lot of dog lovers, you've gotten mad—really mad—at your dog, and you've done things you regret. Forgive yourself. Not only do I understand this, but I've been there. Life can be really stressful at times. Having a dog doesn't make it any easier.

Perhaps you've been lured by the dominance myth, listening to or hiring someone who convinced you that cruel is kind. Cruel is not kind. People who use negative reinforcement are intimidating. This is more than ineffective—it can be dangerous. People who jerk, shock, or bully dogs into submission teach their pets by example. Dogs often retaliate by targeting a less assertive grown-up or child.

The good news is this: Your dog is not interested in a hostile takeover. Trust me. He just wants to know how to fit in. I'll help you teach him. Some adolescent dogs enjoy testing the limits of what they can get away with, not so unlike I did when I was a teenager; maybe you did, too. Think back. Have empathy.

Modern dogs need our support now more than ever. Living inside, they're expected to comply with our schedules and limitations and adhere to home rules that, from their vantage point, make little sense. We want them to listen when we speak, respect our stuff, and busy themselves when we're preoccupied.

Dogs aren't pets anymore—they're children! Fortunately, the timing is right—81 percent of dog owners polled consider their dog "family." Parenting dogs isn't such a bad idea after all.

A Bit About Me and My Philosophy

As an applied animal behavior consultant with more than thirty years of experience coaching dogs and their people, I've helped dog lovers get a handle on everything from housetraining and destructive chewing to impulsive issues like leash pulling, running away, anxiousness, and aggression. Dogs are a lot less mysterious once you discover what inspires them.

There are few things I love more than seeing relationships go from frustration and chaos to laughter and fun. You don't need an advanced degree to have a good relationship with your dog. Sure, I'm a respected dog teacher and and a friend and colleague to many stars, veterinarians, and shelters, but I'm also just a mom. A busy, pet-obsessed mom in a multispecies household. Experiences in my own life help me identify my clients' concerns and provide me with the insight I need to offer solutions that are easy to understand and master. After all, we really just want to feel safe, understood, and valued. It's a universal truth that everyone can appreciate.

Here are a few stories from my teaching book—see if you can relate!

Sandy, mom of two toddlers, thought it'd be fun to add a puppy to the mix. Little did she know! Housetraining a puppy is challenging enough without two diaper-clad human poop machines careening about the floor. I helped Sandy create a foolproof plan that worked on all three of her "puppies"! Discover similar housetraining routines in chapter 7.

Dave came to my studio with Samson, an aging eleven-year-old Jack Russell terrier who had suddenly developed extreme

separation anxiety. What Dave thought was spite was actually anxiety, triggered by a neighbor's construction project and then intensified by Dave's anger. Learn about your dog's emotions in chapter 1, and then check out chapter 8 for tips on how to be supportive when your dog gets stressed.

Raising three teenagers is a big project, even without a maturing puppy to squabble over. Called in as their last hope, I met with the Goodman family and their friendly, overexcited Labrador retriever, Pansy. A frantic, leash-pulling, counter-surfing, jumping whirl of enthusiasm, she had managed to convince her family that she was a lost cause. But in just one lesson, they learned that Pansy's manic routine was a call for help. Discover positive techniques for tackling these and other intrusive behaviors throughout part two.

As you read, you'll be hard-pressed to find the word "training." While chapter 6 takes you through a vocabulary list of important words—including all the basics like Sit, Stay, and Come—think of yourself as a teacher and parent rather than a trainer. Understanding happens faster when you appreciate that your dog is learning a second language. Be patient and supportive.

My goal is to help you feel clever, capable, and strong. Stay in

DON'T HAVE YOUR DOG YET?

If you're stressed at the starting line, you're not alone. Many people reach out to me before bringing their dog or puppy home. There are so many early decisions: Rescue or purebred? Puppy or mature dog? What food and toys should you buy and how can you puppy-proof your home ahead of time? Check out my blog at ModernDogParenting.com to find the best match and get your home ready for a new four-footed family member!

touch and share your stories and testimonials. Let's create a community of dog lovers who consider their dogs family.

If you need a visual or a quick lifeline, connect with me online at ModernDogParenting.com, where you'll find instructional videos and blog posts that bring these lessons to life.

PART ONE

Like Dog, Like Child

Modern dogs are lucky: They finally have science on their side. In the past, dogs were caught under the thumb of people who said our dogs are like wolves beneath the skin and should be subordinate at all times. Not only is that not true, but it's sad. Dogs revel in self-expression, fun, and laughter. They thrive where empathy reigns. Dogs, as researchers now insist, act more like young, preverbal kids than they do wolves. And isn't it just better to treat dogs more humanely? To help them fit in?

At the end of the day, all your dog wants is a loving scratch behind the ear, a bone or toy to help him pass the time, and a full belly. Lessons will come in handy, too—dogs like to know things.

The only glitch is that your dog isn't preprogrammed to understand speech. You might think he understands you, when he doesn't. Dogs do love to communicate—they just have a different style. Dogs use subtle movements of their tail, face, and posture to convey their moods and intentions—a language I call Doglish. They're eager to understand you but will learn better when you can understand them, too. In the chapters ahead, I'll help you make sense of it all.

If you really love your dog, get to know him. Discover the message coded in his mischief. Look at life from his perspective. I'll show you how to redirect aggravating habits into more sociable routines and organize lessons that will teach your dog to enjoy listening when you speak. Changes happen, often overnight.

1

Dogs, Reconsidered

Be kind, for everyone you meet is fighting a hard battle.
—IAN MACLAREN

Sometimes, I wonder why we still have dogs. With five of my own, I'm hardly one to talk, but still. It's not like we need them as we did fifteen thousand years ago around the campfire. Back then, we benefited from their foraging and waste-management skills—instincts we now discourage, much to our dogs' dismay.

Moseying along through evolution, it would seem we need dogs less and less. Few shepherding dogs ever see a farm, retrievers rarely retrieve more than a ball or a wayward slipper, and when was the last time you hitched your husky up to a sled? Impulsively, we tell alert dogs to be quiet, terriers not to dig, and protection dogs to stay behind a gate or door. What is a dog to do?

Why dogs are still so popular when we don't actually depend on them is perplexing to a lot of people. What propels us dog lovers to willingly reschedule our lives—and often our vacations—to cater to our dogs' needs? Dogs—who may at least initially disrupt the flow of everyday life—clearly have some value, but what is it?

For those of us who cannot imagine life without them, dogs kindle faith in the certainty of everyday life—faith in the promise that just showing up for someone counts. As science continually reminds us, loving a dog is healthy, and people who share their lives with dogs feel more optimistic and happy than people without them. Since most of us often live apart from our friends and families, relying on handshakes instead of hugs, we let our busy schedules and insecurities hold us back from new adventures. Making a new friend isn't just scary, it's hard. But not so for dogs. Dogs don't register our self-doubt, and they don't hold back. Standing at our side, dogs delight in every shared experience. They beg us to care for them, to reassure them with an unconditional presence—like kids who need their parents—and yet, just by being there, we are perhaps the ones who feel most fulfilled.

Living with People

Of course, living with people isn't always easy. We ask a lot of dogs, often with little regard to how they're feeling. Have you ever felt frustrated when your dog didn't stop and race to you the second you called for him? Are you mad at your puppy for demolishing your vintage LP collection or aggravated by the paw prints on the kitchen counter and the mysterious disappearance of your breakfast bagel? I hear you. But dogs will be dogs, and until they sense a real connection with you, they're not going to prioritize your opinion.

Wait—you want a dog who prioritizes your opinion? That's a different story, what I call the Happy Dog Adventure Story. It's about a relationship built on fun and understanding. I can help you with that. But the first step doesn't start with a leash or collar or even a tasty dog biscuit. The first step begins with a change of heart.

To transform your relationship into something beautiful and long lasting, you'll need to set aside the myth that your dog is closely related to the wolf and thus needs to be controlled, man-handled, or dominated. Dogs have as much to do with wolves as we do with monkeys. I encourage you to see your dog as science now defines him: an individual capable of devotion, respect, and strong attachments.

The Understanding Movement

Before we go any further, I want to take you back in time to 1873 to see how this understanding movement got started. Back then, both dogs and kids—and wives, too—were considered property, and many were treated like objects. They were put to work, isolated, or simply ignored.

Less than a decade after the American Society for the Prevention of Cruelty to Animals (ASPCA) was founded, Henry Bergh, its first president, received word about Mary Ellen. Mary Ellen was a malnourished little girl with deep scars across her back from being routinely beaten with rawhide.

Mr. Bergh took a stand. He argued that if Mary Ellen—who was just nine years old—were a dog, horse, or cat, his association would have every right to get involved. The following year a trial was held, and—in the spirit of the ASPCA—the New York Society for the Prevention of Cruelty to Children was created. Children were gifted the same rights as other citizens, protected until their eighteenth birthday under the eyes of the law.

Dogs, on the other hand, are still considered property, and few but the most monstrous acts against them are ever enough to prompt a trial for the perpetrator. But times are a-changing. Scientists from around the globe are now promoting dogs as emotional,

DOGS ARE DESCENDED FROM THE GRAY WOLF

The latest research shows other, now-extinct species along the dog's evolutionary path. The gray wolf has as much in common with dogs as apes do with people. Since psychology books don't reference great apes for rules about raising kids, let's put an end to the dog-as-wolf concept and get on with a new trend of loving our dogs like members of the family.

thinking animals who need lawful protection. In some countries, they are getting it! Dogs think. Dogs feel. Dogs love.

Losing the "D" Word

Some celebrity trainers and self-proclaimed professionals still preach dominance and all the philosophy that goes along with it. These "trainers" may have only recently bought into an internationally marketed franchise and may have little to no experience with dogs and the growing science of animal behavior.

I'm often called in to fix the emotional trauma of dogs who've been bullied in the name of "dog training." Nearly half the dogs I work with on the East Coast and 95 percent of my phone consultations begin with dog lovers who've been brainwashed into believing the only way to reach their dog is through negative reinforcement and punishment. Who came up with the idea that to raise a happy, well-mannered dog, you have to scare him first?

The truth? Dogs are adaptable. They'll try to fit in and learn in any way they can. Can you teach a dog with an electric shock collar, a quick slap, or a leash correction? Yes, definitely. Just like you can teach a toddler by jerking or pinching his arm. But the question is, what are you teaching them?

Children who are pinched or slapped won't suffer too greatly in the moment, but they'll remember the punishment and the punisher. Kids—like dogs—are smart. But will they blindly obey? No—that's highly doubtful. Have you ever yelled at your dog for putting his head in the trash or slapped him for jumping on the table? How has that worked for you? If your dog is like most others, he might look sheepish when you yell, but try leaving the room and he'll be right back at it, guaranteed.

Kids and dogs raised by punishment might learn to avoid any wrongdoing when the punisher is around, but all punishment really teaches is deceit. When the parent's away, the kids and dogs will play! Threatening dogs when they've already misbehaved not only doesn't make sense, but it doesn't work.

Ruh-Roh

Maybe you're feeling like you've already blown it with your dog, even though you really didn't mean to. I hear you—this happens all the time—but don't get too distressed. Dogs are immensely forgiving. Read over the following checklist with a pencil in hand. See what resonates. Then forgive yourself, turn a new page, and try a different approach. Whether you've been coached by a trainer to engage in the following activities, been inspired by media personalities, or are just repeating what you witnessed in your childhood, a lot of people start out with assertive training methods only to find out that they backfire. It's easy to move on, and your dog will be happy when you do.

TABLE 1.1

☐ *You use the word "dominant" a lot.*
   "My dog is dominant." "She's just being dominant." Or the ever popular: "My dog is trying to dominate me/my spouse/my kids."

☐ *You throw things at your dog to interrupt bad behavior.*
   While I get this, it's doubtful your dog will. Imagine being bonked from behind by some flying object while you're in the middle of

an important talk. Discover more effective ways to redirect problem behavior in chapter 7.

❏ *You use remote-control shock or vibrating collars to train your dog.*
Electricity takes all the joy out of being a dog. I can spot an e-collar-trained dog a mile away. They're stiff, terrified, manic, or depressed.

❏ *You stare your dog down, trying to intimidate him.*
Staring at dogs scares them. Scared dogs worry. Worried dogs act out.

❏ *You chase, hit, or kick your dog.*
Imagine a big gorilla chasing you, waving his arms in the air and making noises that make no sense. Although he understands what he's doing, you don't. You're terrified, feeling threatened, and confused.

❏ *You scream at your dog.*
Shouting sounds like barking to dogs. When you shout at a barking dog, he thinks, "Woo-hoo, bark party!"

❏ *You clamp your dog's jaw shut to discourage barking or nipping.*
This makes no sense to a dog. If they don't bite the squeezer, they're learning to clamp down hard when mad. Abused dogs become self-defensive. They may not snap at the squeezer, but they are more assertive with other people and/or with children.

❏ *You "pop" your dog's leash or hang him by his collar.*
Gagging your dog is terrifying to him, and while it will stop any behavior in the moment, the only thing your dog learns is to avoid you.

❏ *You shove your dog's face into his pee or poop to correct house-soiling accidents.*
Flooding your dog with the smell of his own excrement isn't an effective housetraining exercise. Your dog may stop going at all when you're around or just go undercover and poop somewhere you're less likely to discover, at least right away.

Although the thought of instant control might seem inviting, scientific studies show beyond a shadow of a doubt that punishment isn't effective in the long run. If you want to live in the real world with a loving, happy dog, set aside the remote control and drop the dominate-or-be-dominated attitude. Is that really you, anyway? No one—dog or person—wants to be dominant all the time. Learning takes time, patience, unconditional love, and consistency. Batteries not included.

PETER THE PIG

Lessons on life and dog loving can come from anywhere—even from a guinea pig. I first met Peter the Pig at a pre-puppy staging session at a house near my home in eastern New York.

As I was setting up the puppy's zones (for play, quiet, potty, feeding, and sleep), I stumbled on an anxious-looking guinea pig caged in a corner of the kids' playroom. "What's up with the pig?" I asked. Ruth, the mom, told me her family had long ago given up hope with Peter—they'd somehow failed him, and no one paid much attention to him anymore.

"Sad for the pig. I can help." Pausing our session, I lifted Peter in my arms. "He seems nice enough—why do you think that he doesn't like you?"

I watched as Ruth demonstrated how they carried Peter, fed him treats, and petted him. "All he does is squeal and squirm and try to get away from us."

Well, yes. I could see why. "Guinea pigs don't like being carried by their underarms—few animals do. Try carrying him like this," I said as I showed her the proper technique for resting a pig flat on her chest or arm. Next, I explained that while I'm sure Peter would love the dried mango treats she'd bought, what she was really doing was shoving them up his nose. I showed Ruth where his mouth was and encouraged her to feed Peter with a flat palm under his chin. Finally, I praised her for her loving pats—which would be perfect for her puppy—but poor Peter is an Abyssinian pig with cowlicks twirling his fur this way and that. I showed her how to stroke each twist of fur independently. In seconds, Ruth said she had felt Peter relax. Feeding him small treat squares from below his chin, I explained how this small effort would couple people-smells with positive, loving interaction—a technique that works with puppies, too.

When I visited the next week to meet their puppy, Ruth's daughter, Susie, greeted me at the door, the puppy playing with her shoelaces and Peter resting in her arms. Not only was the pig comfortable with the kids, but he was curious about the puppy, too! Peter went from being an isolated, sad pig to one who chirped when his people approached.

Who'd have thought that a six-month-old guinea pig could be so totally capable of trust and affection? Dogs are the same way— uniquely sociable, sentient beings who will give you their hearts gladly if only you learn how to ask.

Cool Science

Brain chemistry is a hot topic these days. For example, research on strong emotional reactions in mammals shows remarkable similarities in how neurotransmitters mediate hormone levels in dogs and people. Dopamine, the happy hormone, spikes when mammals play; oxytocin, the love and attachment elixir, flows with nurturing touches; and adrenaline and cortisol, the stress hormones, take charge when a dog or person is startled, threatened, or panicked. Fascinated? Flip to the bibliography (page 289) to find a list of books and articles on the topic.

WHAT ABOUT INVISIBLE FENCES?

I consider shocking/vibrating collars and underground electric fences to be in two separate categories. Shock training can transform even the kindhearted dog lover into a power-hungry, remote-wielding bully who randomly shocks their dog to "correct" behavior. When the remote is in your hands, your dog is powerless and won't learn from unpredictable and unavoidable shocks. In the end, the only connection your dog makes is between you and the remote. The shocker becomes the shock; trust is hard, if not impossible, to restore.

Electric fence collars, on the other hand, are self-activated devices that cue a dog to stay within a specified boundary. An underground fence shock is not random and can be avoided so long as the dog stays within the flagged fence perimeter. While hard fencing is my preference, it may not always be an option. Although not 100 percent effective, electric fences have proven to be a necessary evil, saving dogs from the dangers of wandering—from confrontations with other wildlife to car accidents and unintentional poisoning. A dog who is mindfully trained to respect the fence will rarely need more than a shock or two to learn the zone.

Recent research has also changed our understanding of how dogs learn. It all began with Stanley Coren, Ph.D., who was the first modern thinker to explore the similarities between dogs and young children. In his book *The Intelligence of Dogs*, he writes: "When it comes to the way that they think, dogs are just young kids in fur coats." This revelation began a revolution, setting scientists on a journey to discover how dogs learn and communicate. Their research confirms what we dog lovers have always known—dogs really do understand us, can handle simple problem solving, and can signal us for help.

Matching Emotions

Dogs, it turns out, experience a lot of the same emotions people do. Unexpected reactions cause similar shifts in body chemistry, too. Imagine the surge of adrenaline when a sudden loud noise wakes us in the night—dogs feel that, too. Both dogs and people startle if suddenly approached by a stranger. We both relax when we're happy, cringe when we're frightened, and tense up when we're mad or threatened. Sure, we lack a wagging tail and rotating ears, but short of the external clues, we're practically twins when it comes to expressing ourselves.

The most relatable emotions that motivate dogs and people include:

- ❏ **Curiosity**
- ❏ **Excitement and Play**
- ❏ **Fear**
- ❏ **Frustration and Rage**
- ❏ **Panic**

I was inspired to learn about a dog's emotional life when I read *Animals Make Us Human* by Temple Grandin and Catherine Johnson. Early on in the book, Grandin refers to a study by neuroscientist Jaak Panksepp. Dr. Panksepp cites seven Blue Ribbon emotional systems at the root of all mammalian behavior: seeking, play, fear, frustration, panic, lust, and caring. While they're important and interesting, lust and caring have to do with reproduction and—I hope this goes without saying—don't really come into play when teaching dogs.

Following Ms. Grandin's lead, I'm going to elaborate on how these concepts influence our understanding of dogs and how I use them to help clients on both ends of the leash.

CURIOSITY

Dogs love to sniff around and explore their world. They're curious about everything, from people walking in the street to piles of deer poop. But exploring is never only for exploring's sake—your dog's learning, too. He learns what's safe and pleasurable and what's not. You can see this emotion in motion all the time in actions like:

- ❏ **Sniffing street corners, aka reading the morning pee-mail**
- ❏ **Knocking over wastebaskets**
- ❏ **Rifling through grocery bags**
- ❏ **Running into the dog park to meet a new friend**
- ❏ **Crotch sniffing**

Curiosity can lead your dog to all kinds of adventures and habits—both good and bad. Praise and reward your dog when he Sits for attention, chews his toy, and greets guests on all four paws. Of course, you can encourage bad behavior just as easily if you focus on your dog when curiosity draws him to the kitty litter tray or food on the countertop. It's your attention he's really after: negative or positive, it doesn't matter.

If your dog's learned a bad habit or two, don't worry. It's easy enough to redirect him once you understand his instincts. Phew! He's not such a bad dog after all.

EXCITEMENT AND PLAY

Before we look at your dog, think of a hobby or sport you enjoy. What gets your metaphoric tail wagging—cooking, gardening, basketball, TV? When time allows you to get involved, you find other people who enjoy it, too. So here's the clue . . .

If you want to bond with your dog, find out what he likes to do and do it with him. If your dog has a passion for digging, running around, or tugging, do it together. Few things will make your dog happier than shared fun. Use routine words—like "Come," "Catch," and "Carry"—to signal a game, as your dog connects togetherness with happy memories.

Self-control and good manners can be taught, too, without your dog ever noticing he's learning anything new. Personally, I'd rather play with my dogs than do formal lessons—many of the exercises I'll teach you in chapter 6 begin with games, puzzles, and prizes.

The next three emotions—fear, frustration, and panic—may seem dark by comparison, but healthy levels of fear and frustration ensure a dog's survival. Fear of fire or cliffs is a good thing. But when fear or frustration becomes overwhelming—when someone yells at, shocks, or hits a dog—those normal instincts may morph into panic or rage. That's not good. When dogs experience these emotional tidal waves, they have no other option but to use aggression in self-defense. Bad dog? No. Insanely stressed dog? Yup.

FEAR

I'm no stranger to this emotion, and I don't like it. Whenever I feel fear, I look for a solution or displacement activity to distract me. I find one of my dogs, nibble on some chocolate, or reach out to my unflappable husband . . . sometimes all three at once. It usually works.

When your dog is afraid, he may express some or all of the reactions studied by Panksepp. Fearful dogs retreat, posture submissively, and/or avoid situations. Some people unintentionally scare their dogs by shouting or chasing them to discourage bad behavior. Yes, a dog may look guilty and stop the behavior by running away or rolling over onto his back, but really he's just worried for his own safety.

I had a client who firmly believed that his dog loved it when they roughhoused together . . . until the dog bit him. When they

AGGRESSION IN DOGS IS INCURABLE

No—dogs that use aggression are showing intense emotion. Just like people, a dog will defend himself from unbearable levels of fear or frustration and have different tolerance levels for these emotions. Aggression isn't good or bad; it just is. Read more about helping aggressive dogs learn better coping skills in chapter 8.

reenacted this behavior in my office, it took all my professional restraint not to shout "STOP" and put the man in a full-body hold. I videotaped the encounter to show the dog's fear—how he tried to run off and finally rolled over when caught. It took a modern, technological approach to get his parents to back off and see the world from his perspective.

Many professional dog trainers still use negative reinforcement to instill a fear of consequences and change behavior. They preach that dogs should be corrected whenever they misbehave and use a variety of punishments (e.g., kneeing, jerking, or electric shocks) to discourage misbehavior. This type of training can be immediately effective, but it breaks down over time. It doesn't help the dog learn what he should be doing instead. Personally, I would do anything to avoid pain and fear. Wouldn't you?

FRUSTRATION AND RAGE

Frustration and rage are closely related. A dog who can't do what he wants may experience frustration. A dog held against his will may feel equally frustrated or, if pushed, experience rage. If you've ever lost your keys or been mystified by your computer, you've felt frustration. It's less likely that you've been held against your will, but imagine it: That's rage.

Dogs express their frustration through postures, vocalizations,

HOW'S YOUR DOG'S FRUSTRATION TOLERANCE?

- ❏ Put your dog on a leash.

- ❏ Ask a friend to hold a treat or toy six feet in front of your dog, at his nose level.

- ❏ He may strain or bark in frustration. Be calm, but hold the leash steady.

- ❏ When he settles down, encourage him to sit and/or look up to you by calling his name.

- ❏ If he refuses, use a more savory treat or beloved toy.

- ❏ Once your dog quiets and looks to you, reward and release him to get the goodies!

- ❏ To see this move in action, check out my video on teaching self-control on ModernDogParenting.com/ProblemSolving.

and reactive behavior. A dog might pull, bark, or pace when frustrated. If he is not able to self-soothe, a dog's frustration might escalate to rage. When restrained or held tightly, he may nip or thrash around to free himself.

Frustration is not always the enemy, though. I often use moderate levels of frustration to encourage good behavior, like withholding a treat until a dog is calm or waiting to release a dog to greet a visitor until he looks to me, grabs a toy, or sits calmly.

PANIC

Panic is fear on steroids. This emotion relates to early attachments and is the reason baby animals fuss when separated from their caregivers. As puppies age, other situations may spark panic, especially if they first experienced the frightening situation alone. Storms, separation anxiety, and extreme stranger anxiety are just a few examples.

Emotions in Motion: Why Sparky Lost His Name

Sparky, a rescued eighteen-month-old springer spaniel, tiptoed into my heart one snowy winter morning when he came to my dog school. After peering around the door, he raced into my open arms like he'd known me his whole life. It was love at first sight.

Each week at training class, Sparky shined—fixating on my hand signals and watching every move I made. Margie—his new mom—was frustrated, though. "He never looks at me this way. He won't play with my son. He just sits by the window and barks if he sees a bird, or runs circles in the yard. We can't even have a bird feeder anymore!"

That was puzzling. All we knew of Sparky's history was that he'd been returned to his breeder at fourteen months. I called the breeder to get more information.

The breeder had failed to mention to Margie that Sparky's first owners crated him for ten hours every single day. This news was hard to take in. After listening to his original owners complain that Sparky barked all night, destroyed the furniture, and was prone to patterned pacing, the breeder offered to rehome Sparky.

Then the breeder added that Sparky's previous owners had confessed to medicating the dog with sedatives in an attempt to calm his hyperactivity and restless sleeping patterns. Yikes! After a two-month detox at the kennel, the breeder had placed Sparky with Margie and her family and hoped for the best.

I felt anxious just thinking about Sparky's chronic neglect. The first year of life is a dramatically formative time—dogs are eager for company, new experiences, and adventure. What Sparky endured instead was hour upon hour of complete social isolation. And yet he held out so much hope for love—that much I knew to be true.

I agreed to do a home visit. After a flush of excitement in the driveway, Sparky circled the yard in the ritualized path Margie had described to me over the phone. Professionals call any routine behavior triggered by a transitional event (e.g., my arrival) a stereotypy. What seems random can calm strong emotions. Margie was able to short-circuit his laps around the yard with a toy, which, once grabbed, was used to bait a dog-led game of Can't Catch Me. Pulling a treat cup from my bag, I shook it hard and gave Sparky a big handful for coming over and letting me clip a leash to his collar.

Inside, Sparky took up his post by the picture window. "Sparky!" I called. He glanced back, licking his lips, his body and tail lowered in submission. I shook the treat box and called him again. He ran over, took a treat, and returned to his window. His family got the same reaction when they called him.

That was telling. Home should be comforting for dogs—a place of love, bonding, and relaxation. Not so for Sparky. Home was a prison—a weird zone of isolation and dazed states.

I ordered a name change on the spot, as Sparky seem to have only negative associations to hearing his name called. "Rosco" was agreed upon, and we began pairing his new name with food and walks. His meals were fed to him by hand for two weeks.

Two months later, I made my final house call. Rosco met me with his ball, tail up and eyes sparkling. He retreated to his happy place resting on his bed, but now instead of barking and avoiding touch, he faced the table and wagged his tail when anyone entered the room. His gazing and barking happened less and less. Rosco was home.

Can you identify the emotions that came into play in this case?

FEAR	Rosco was unsure of people, and nervous when his original name was used.
FRUSTRATION	Rosco could only bark at the birds outside the window.
CURIOSITY	We used food to encourage interaction and allowed Rosco to chase the birds he'd only been allowed to watch.

PLAY   The whole family began play training Rosco, making positive associations to words and establishing a loving connection.

Your Dog's Daily Needs

Emotions aren't the only thing that dogs and people have in common. Our days revolve around the same needs, too. Every day we need to eat, drink, rest, exercise, play, and go to the bathroom. Ever try ignoring a need? How do you feel if you're tired, hungry, or sitting in a traffic jam when you need a bathroom? If you've raised a child, you'll notice the similarities. Ever hung out with a tired or thirsty kid? Imagine that kid with big, pointy teeth.

No matter what your dog's age or where you are in your Happy Dog Adventure Story, take a closer look at each of your dog's needs and create a consistent routine, if you haven't already. Dogs—like people—are a lot calmer when they know what to expect. Below you'll find a Daily Needs Chart to help keep you on track. Teach your dog words and routines for each need, and try to stay on schedule. Within a week, maybe sooner, your dog will know the routine and prompt you when it's time to take care of a need.

TABLE 1.2 Daily Needs Chart

NEED	WORDS/SIGNAL	ROUTINE
Eat	"Food"	Unless you're feeding by hand, use a bowl to portion your dog's food. Use each feeding to reinforce patience and other directions like Sit, Down, and Wait.
Water	"Water"	Assign a place for the water dish. Wait until your dog sits to add more or lower the dish.

TABLE 1.2 (continued)

NEED	WORDS/ SIGNAL	ROUTINE
Sleep	"Go to Your Mat"	Encourage your dog to nap in a quiet room or crate. Place mats around as resting spots.
Elimination	"Outside" or "Papers"; "Get Busy"	Follow the same path to your dog's potty place, inside or out. Say a word to get you to the area, like "Papers" or "Outside." Assign a word or short phrase to the action, like "Get Busy," and reward your dog with praise or a treat when he's done. More on housetraining in chapter 7.
Play	"Ball," "Tug," "Catch Me," "Toy," "Bone"	Dogs love to play and will willingly learn all kinds of games. Say a word like "Ball" or "Squeaky" as you identify a toy, and pair active games like Tug and Catch Me with words, too.

Tailor the chart to your lifestyle by using words that come naturally to you, and share it with everyone in your household.

EATING

The fastest way to show your dog affection is to feed him, preferably by hand. Yes, you read that right. Tuck the food dish in the cupboard, use rubber gloves or a spoon if feeding anything other than dry kibble, and strategically place hand sanitizer around the house. I once fostered a dog straight off the boat from China—it's a long story. Suffice it to say, no one in China had shown emotion to this dog, nor brought him inside. In fact, he spent a good part of his adolescence locked in a dark warehouse with dogs he couldn't interact with. I wrote his story in a Huffington Post blog post titled "Why I Gave My Dog Diarrhea," which details the many benefits of hand-feeding new dogs. Whether a puppy or an adult,

RETRAINING THE RESCUE DOG

If you've rescued a dog, remember that everything in your life might be new, startling, or exciting to him. What do you know about his previous life? Did he come from a safe environment surrounded by love, other dogs, or littermates? Did you adopt him from a shelter or rescue organization where the routines and people were comforting, but the stress was high? No matter what happened before, establish safe, predictable routines and stay calm. Watch as your rescued baby blossoms right before your eyes!

To keep your dog out of the toilet, close the lid and keep a water dish in each bathroom!

rescue dog or nurtured one, hand-feeding ensures they'll feel safe and focus on you from day one.

DRINKING

Dogs hate being thirsty. Panting is a big clue; so is standing by the water dish. Young puppies pace around or nip when they need to drink. A human baby would cry.

Keep clean water out at all times. If you're housetraining your dog, portion his water throughout the day, and keep track of his drinking habits. What goes in, comes out!

SLEEPING

Here's a life-changing fact: Dogs sleep a lot more than you do. According to research, the average dog rests 50 percent of the day, lolls around in a quasi-calm state 30 percent of the day, and has 20 percent of high-activity time. Big dogs sleep more than little dogs; sporting breeds conditioned to run and work sleep a little less; and when ill, a dog will sleep either more or less than normal. Sleep is a good indicator of overall health, too.

IT IS RARE FOR A DOG TO HAVE ADHD

ADHD is rare in dogs, according to Dr. Nicholas Dodman, a veterinarian, professor at Tufts University, and co-founder and chief scientific officer for the Center for Canine Behavioral Studies (CCBS). In his book *The Well-Adjusted Dog: Dr. Dodman's 7 Steps to Lifelong Health and Happiness for Your Best Friend*, he reports that, "Dogs with attention deficit/hyperactivity disorder are in almost perpetual motion. The classic presentation is that of a dog on the go, who is exuberant beyond all usual limits . . . and 'mentally noisy.'"

A proper diagnosis is needed to rule out thyroid problems, lead poisoning, and dietary deficiencies, which can play into this condition.

What does this mean to you? Plenty! You can stop arranging your dog's social calendar or worrying that he doesn't have a day job. Since his most active times are early morning and near dusk, organize some special doggie-'n'-me time then. Best of all, feel good about giving your dog some well-needed downtime while you work. In fact, if you concentrate on overstimulating instead of sleep training your dog or puppy, he'll be a living nightmare.

The Guiding Eyes for the Blind, a nonprofit group that trains dogs for blind people and autistic children, has an ideal schedule for their canine candidates. The day starts at 7:30 A.M., and includes time for play, school, and naps before the dogs are back in their kennel at dusk.

If you really want your dog to be happy and well mannered, make sure he's getting enough rest. Problems start when puppies don't get enough sleep. Puppies, like babies, need an early bedtime to help them grow. And don't overstimulate him with constant activity, or he'll have a hard time settling down.

POTTYING

If you'd like to get your dog to go potty in the same spot, even on command, show him to the door (or the papers). Follow the same route out of your home, use one door initially, and consider using a bell so he can indicate his needs to you when you're not close by. Follow the tips laid out in chapter 7, and within a few short days you'll notice improvement!

PLAYING

Play with your dog from the second you meet him, and don't stop. Dogs need play like fish need water. Remember Sparky's story on page 23? As a puppy, he couldn't make a connection in his first home because no one had time to play with him. His previous owners' solution to puppy mischief was sedation.

In chapter 5, you'll learn how to use play to teach your dog all life's major lessons, like Come and Stay. For now, teach your dog words to go with different toys. Say "Ball" when playing with round objects and "Squeak" when tossing toys that do. Figure out what gets your dog's tail wagging, and make up some games to go with it. Dogs play whenever they feel safe—it's a great gauge.

Dogs Are Pretty Smart, Too

Back when I started my dog-training business in 1989, the general consensus in educated circles was that dogs did not, and moreover could not, have independent thoughts. While dog lovers insisted that dogs had feelings, scientists shot us down every time.

Times are a changing, however. Studies from across the globe confirm that dogs think, feel, and reason! At Barnard College, researcher Alexandra Horowitz, Ph.D. (author of the *New York Times* bestseller *Inside of a Dog: What Dogs See, Smell, and Know*), is leading a team of scientists in tracking and recording the gestures dogs use when they play at the park.

In Europe, ethologists József Topál and Ádám Miklósi teamed

up with respected trainer Claudia Fugazza to show that dogs are capable of delayed imitation and declarative memory—fancy terms for Monkey See, Monkey Do. They tested many dogs and showed that not only can dogs imitate people when rewarded for doing so, they have long-term memory, too. Neat!

At Duke, Brian Hare, Ph.D., coauthor with Vanessa Woods of the *New York Times* bestseller *The Genius of Dogs: How Dogs Are Smarter Than You Think*, studies dogs' reactions to hand gestures and expressions. Hare and his team have classified five types of canine intelligence, which they list as empathy, communication, cunning, memory, and reasoning. In a movement he calls Citizen Science, he invites dog owners to test their dog's cognition online, where the results will be shared and used for research. Explore the growing science of dog intelligence and take part by visiting Dognition.com.

Here, there, and everywhere, the world is waking up to the fact that dogs are more than mere domestics put on the planet to do our bidding. Now, more than ever, dogs are brought inside where they stay—quite literally—at our side, under our dining tables, and, more often than not, quietly alongside us in our beds. Maybe it is because of these changes to our modern lifestyles that we're taking a closer look at dogs, how they view us, and how we can best live together happily.

Think of your dog as a part of your family, with similar wants, needs, and emotional and intellectual capacities. Take care of him like you would a curious, preverbal child. Apply empathy, wit, and understanding, and watch as your relationship blooms. Kids and dogs raised with kindness and respect grow up happy!

2

Welcome to Doglandia

Dogs do speak but only to those who know how to listen.
—ORHAN PAMUK

Before you travel to a foreign land, you learn a few key phrases: "Where's the bathroom?" "Does this train go to Paris?" "Can I get fries with that?" With a few simple words, you can communicate with the locals clearly, politely, and effectively. Without the right words, you're on a bus to who knows where.

Dogs are caught in a similar predicament. Without a translator, your dog is on that bus: a furry, four-footed tourist, bumping down the road of life without a tour guide. If you want a great relationship with your dog, learn how to speak her language, keep her safe, and surround her with things that make her happy to be your dog.

For starters, I'll walk you through a lesson in Doglish—the sounds and postures that make up your dog's communication playbook. Once you've learned her native tongue, you'll be surprised by how much she'll understand and respond to you. To help you remember, I've added lots of illustrations and links to my site, where you can find videos and downloads for additional help. If you're half the enthusiastic learner your dog is, you'll pick it up in no time!

At the end of the chapter, we'll go shopping with your lovely baby in mind. When you're more aware of what lifts her tail, you'll be able to focus your purchasing decisions on getting just what she needs and likes.

Doglish 101

One of the biggest differences between dogs and people is our communication styles. People talk way too much. Dogs, on the other hand, rely almost exclusively on body language. You may be listening when you should be *watching* your dog talk. Don't be overwhelmed, though: Dogs and people react and move in remarkably similar ways.

Consider, for example, how you act in these situations. Circle your answer:

What do you do when you're excited or happy?	RISE UP	GO TO BED	SLUMP	HIDE
What do you do when you're scared?	RISE UP	GO TO BED	SLUMP	HIDE
What do you do when you're tired?	RISE UP	GO TO BED	SLUMP	HIDE
How about when you're sad?	RISE UP	GO TO BED	SLUMP	HIDE

Dogs synchronize their movements in much the same way, but they use their face, tail, ears, and posture. To learn how to communicate with your dog, see if you can button your lips and just watch her for a while—you might see things you've never no-

To you and me, nothing says "friendship" faster than meeting eye to eye and exchanging a quick hug. We humans are pretty unusual, though. To dogs and the rest of the animal planet, face-to-face isn't friendly. Tooth-revealing smiles can be read as growls, and our whole forward-moving presentation can be seen as confrontational. Dogs, like most other mammals save primates, come together at respectful angles and sniff each other's fur and bottom to say hello. Try this routine the next time you meet a new dog:

- Turn sideways, facing away from the dog, and extend your hand.

- After the dog gives you a quick sniff, watch her face.

- If her ears drop, head lowers, and tail wags, the dog is friendly.

- If she holds her head up, turns, or backs away, she's blowing you off. Don't take it personally. Dogs are like people: Some like you, some don't.

ticed before. When dogs are happy, they move freely and rise up; when they're scared, they cringe and look for somewhere to hide. Sleepy dogs slump, alert dogs rise up, and sad dogs deflate. Flip to page 41 to see illustrations of dogs' emotions.

Mouth

For a quick check on your dog's mood, look at her mouth. An open mouth most often signals a smile (unless she's overheating), whereas closed lips convey concentration, nervousness, or frustration. Dogs also close their mouth when resting. Check in with your dog now—how is she feeling? Here's a list of mouth movements to watch for:

SLIGHTLY OPEN Happy dogs often express their mood with a relaxed, parted jaw.

SUBMISSIVE GRIN When dogs are nervous, they pull their lips back in this appeasement gesture. Though you might think they're laughing, they're not. Treats, toys, and happy talk can help them feel better.

REPETITIVE LICKING An anxious dog will lick her lips in social situations. If you're in charge, take the dog aside and calm her with pats and/or play.

PANTING Dogs pant for many reasons: when hot or thirsty, for sure, but also when stressed. This is an exception to the open-mouth-is-relaxed rule mentioned previously.

TEETH BARED Dogs bare their teeth when frustrated or scared. Do not approach! You'll likely get bitten.

PUCKERED When a dog feels threatened, she may pucker, puff out her lips, and blow air as a warning. This is not a happy face. It says, "Give me space." Respect the warning, or you may get bitten.

Ears

A dog's ears are very expressive. They can move independently or together, and can rotate up, down, backward, and forward. You can learn a lot about how your dog's feeling by watching her ears. Since dogs have different types of ears, from floppy to upright, there is no universal standard for interpreting ear position, but some general rules apply:

NEUTRAL Use a dog's relaxed ear pose as a starting point.

UPRIGHT, TOGETHER A dog's ears will lift purposefully when she's focused on something.

ONE UPRIGHT, ONE TILTED BACK Multitasking, canine style. Dogs can focus on two things at once.

BOTH TILTED BACK TOGETHER, NATURAL POSE This dog is either listening to a noise behind her or zoning. Check in with her eyes and posture to tell the difference.

BOTH PINNED BACK Scared, fearful dog.

BOTH UPRIGHT AND FORWARD This dog is defensive and/or frustrated. Combined with a forward-leaning posture and a threatening stare, this dog is saying "Back off!"

SEAL-LIKE SWIVEL With muscles on all sides of the ear, some immensely happy dogs swivel their ears to the side in a baby seal–like greeting that is simply irresistible!

Eyes

Your dog's eyes are nearly as expressive as her ears, but can be harder to read or get a clear fix on as you're not on the same level. Take a quick look at your dog's pupil—that dark circle in the center—when she's resting. The pupil will change shape in shifting light and in response to strong emotions.

NATURAL EYE Get a read on your dog's natural eye when she's relaxed.

WIDE EYE Pupils get larger at dusk to let more light in, but also widen if a dog is fearful or startled. (Ours do the same.)

LOOKING EYE Dogs—like people—look at stuff that interests them. If you're wondering what has your dog's attention, notice what she's looking at: a squirrel, a garbage can, the cupcake on the countertop.

SQUINTY EYE This is a scientific term. Seriously. Squinty eyes crinkle at the corners as the mouth pulls back into a submissive grin or open-mouth curve.

AVERTED GLANCE A dog won't stare at people or other dogs unless she's angry, terrified, or comfortable enough to play. Dogs signal submission by avoiding eye contact.

WHALE EYE When stressed, a dog's eye muscles strain, leaving a small white arc on one or both sides of the eye. Known as whale eye, this is not a happy glance. Do not touch or interfere. If your dog is whaling, change her focus by offering a toy or treat. (Don't worry or disturb your dog if you notice whale eye while she's sleeping. Dogs' eyes often roll back while resting.)

HARD EYE Hard eyes are glassy, unemotional, and still. They're paired with a still body, raised tail, and bad feeling. Back away immediately and slowly, whether this is your dog or someone else's.

Tail Talk

A dog's tail is always talking; watch how it moves and the tempo of each wag. Before you tune in, get a visual on your dog's relaxed tail. Some breeds like greyhounds naturally hold their tail low; others are stuck in a curl. The same guidelines apply for stumpy-tailed dogs.

RELAXED Use a dog's relaxed tail as a reference for the other positions.

TUCKED A tucked tail conveys anxiousness. This dog's not happy.

PLASTERED If a dog's tail is plastered to her belly, she's panicked.

ON ALERT A dog will lift her tail when she's happy, excited, or curious.

DEFENSIVE If the tail arches up and above her rump, she's frustrated or defensive. Watch out.

Tails also have wag speeds, which, when paired with position, signal emotion. Table 2.1 gives you a handy visual.

A WAGGING TAIL MEANS A HAPPY DOG

No, no, no. This myth can get you into trouble. Dogs use their tail to express everything from panic to happiness to aggression. Focus on the position and tempo. Middle position, full-body wags are generally confident and friendly, high wags signal excitement or agitation, and low wags communicate fear, insecurity, or surrender. A recent study out of the University of Bari Aldo Moro in Italy proved that dogs value symmetry, too, wagging right to convey pleasure and happiness, and left when anxious or defensive.

SIDE-TO-SIDE SWING Pair a full tail swing with an open mouth and full-body wiggle, and what do you get? A new friend! It's the canine equivalent of a happy smile.

ARCHING SWAY Short arching sways can mean different things depending on the tail's position. Tail-up, short sways signal excitement or curiosity; rump level sways indicate submission; a tail any lower conveys worry.

TIP TWITCH When the tip of a tail twitches furiously, a dog is experiencing an emotional tornado. If the tail is arched over her back, it signals agitation; tucked under the belly, it conveys panic.

TABLE 2.1 Tail Talk

ON ALERT	RELAXED	TUCKED	PLAYFUL	DEFENSIVE
This dog is trying to get a read on what's going on.	This tail rests comfortably below a dog's rump, signaling she's at ease.	If nervous or anxious, a dog will drop her tail.	Happy dogs wag more than their tail—they wag their rump, too!	This dog is preparing to defend herself.

Vocalizations

While dogs can't talk, they do use a variety of sounds to communicate their feelings. Dogs bark for a lot of reasons. There is a difference between a dog who barks from boredom, one who barks as an alert, and one who barks for attention. Can you identify your dog's different barks?

ALERT/TERRITORIAL BARKING

Most dogs develop territorial aggression between the ages of eight months and one year when their hormones begin to rise. Although some breeds, such as Doberman pinschers, mastiffs, and rottweilers, are more prone to territorial behavior, most dogs develop a sense of home and will first use elimination to mark their zone—hopefully outside or on papers! As dogs mature, many bark as an alert any time they sense something approaching. You'll know it's an alert bark if it's high pitched and repetitive.

BORED BARKING

Dogs get bored when left alone. They generally don't like quiet and will bark to fill the sound void. Boredom barks can also happen when dogs are left in a crate or isolated area and they hear someone in the home. Low and spaced, a bored bark is less frantic than an anxious bark.

ANXIOUS BARKING

Many dogs whine and bark when left alone, especially when first brought into a home. If your dog's a worrier, however, her barking may escalate to anxious barking as a way to relieve stress. This frantic, single-toned, repetitive barking is hard to ignore. While it brings people running, both the barking and the anxiety that prompted it get quickly reinforced!

ATTENTION BARKING

Dogs, like people, hate being ignored. Attention barking is more spaced than anxious barking and often occurs when you're present but busy with dishes, on the phone, or with the kids. If you give your dog any type of attention when she barks, guess what? She'll make a habit of it! I teach my furry students alternative ways to prompt some loving, like fetching a toy or sitting patiently.

WHINING

When dogs are frustrated or sad—caught up in what they crave but can't have—they whine. Anything goes here, from wanting your attention or the ball under the couch to being trapped inside when the kids are out playing. Whining never signals joy. It's annoying for anyone within earshot, including the dog.

GROWLING

Dogs growl when they feel overwhelming fear or frustration. A word bubble would read "BACK OFF." Belly growls are more serious than sounds that start in the throat or mouth, but all growls require immediate consideration. If your dog is growling at you, flip to chapter 7 to learn why and what you can do about it. If you're scared, get professional help.

HOWLING

The mournful howl echoes in response to a high-pitched noise like a siren or loneliness and stress. My husky, Kyia, would wail

---

DID YOU KNOW?

THERE'S SUCH A THING AS A HAPPY GROWL

Some dogs grumble when they're relaxed or excited. While their teeth may show, the lips of a happy grumbler are pulled up, not back, and their tail is relaxed and wagging. Before you call for help, check in with the rest of the body.

long, melodious howls whenever I left on vacation—even though she was with a close friend—until I came back.

WHIMPERING

Puppies whimper for their dog mama until they're weaned. It's a distress signal that only happens when mother and puppy are separated. Later in life, whimpers communicate loneliness or distress. Injured dogs whimper when they're in pain—handle with care.

BAYING

Hound dogs bay. It's an alerting sound that lets everyone know they're on a scent or announcing a visitor. Mixed breeds can bay, too: If your dog bays, they've clearly got some hound dog in their family tree.

Fur Facts

A dog's coat does a lot more than keep her warm. It also blocks dangerous sunrays and can be another indicator of her mood. Hair on the back may rise up when your dog is feeling any number of intense emotions, from defensiveness to fear to anxiety.

Dogs can also shed fur like rain when scared or frazzled. This happens frequently after routine trips to the veterinarian and with shelter dogs. Visit a shelter, and you'll notice that the majority of the dogs have thin, dull coats; it's surprising and heartwarming to see them fill out after being adopted.

MYTH BUSTER
CUTTING A DOG'S HAIR HELPS THEM STAY COOL

No. A dog's coat insulates it from heat and cold. Counterintuitive, perhaps, but the American Veterinary Medical Association (AVMA) agrees: Even for long-haired breeds it's kinder to leave your dog's hair its natural length year-round.

Strike a Pose

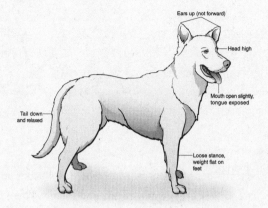

Ears up (not forward)

Head high

Mouth open slightly, tongue exposed

Tail down and relaxed

Loose stance, weight flat on feet

CALM DOG Relaxed dogs—like people—are calm. Notice your dog's shoulder muscles, face, tail, and the shape of her resting ears. Notice the open-mouth expression—it's the canine equivalent of a smile. Some dogs can relax anywhere, others only at home.

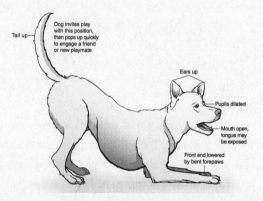

Dog invites play with this position, then pops up quickly to engage a friend or new playmate

Tail up

Ears up

Pupils dilated

Mouth open, tongue may be exposed

Front end lowered by bent forepaws

PLAYFUL DOG Dogs play when they're comfortable with where they are and who they're with. Tails arch up and wag back and forth; the body may wiggle or bow. They use balls, squeak toys, and sticks to engage with others.

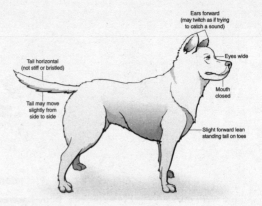

CURIOUS DOG Dogs love adventures. They'll perk up their tail and ears as they explore new scents and sounds. When they catch a whiff, they'll either lift their head (to catch a scent in the air) or drop it to follow a trail. Their head will bob to locate noises, too!

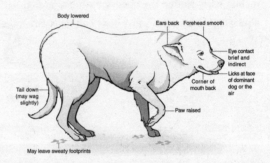

FEARFUL DOG, SUBMISSIVE Dogs lower their posture when they're afraid or confused. The tail drops as the ears flatten. Lips pull back into a tense smile, eyes squint, and the body curves into a "c" as they appear to beg for mercy.

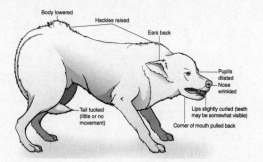

Body lowered
Hackles raised
Ears back
Pupils dilated
Nose wrinkled
Lips slightly curled (teeth may be somewhat visible)
Corner of mouth pulled back
Tail tucked (little or no movement)

FEARFUL DOG, DEFENSIVE Here's a pose your veterinarian knows all too well: ears and tail pulled back, body lowered, and hackles generally raised. Be on guard: This dog will bite to defend herself.

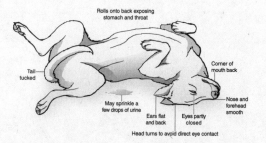

Rolls onto back exposing stomach and throat
Corner of mouth back
Tail tucked
Nose and forehead smooth
May sprinkle a few drops of urine
Ears flat and back
Eyes partly closed
Head turns to avoid direct eye contact

PANICKED DOG Panicked dogs cringe and drop to the floor in submission. Notice how the ears and tail flatten, the body pulls in tightly, the eyes squint, and the lips pull back into what looks to many like a smile.

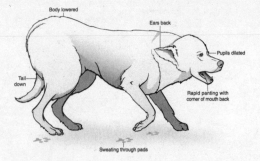

CONFUSED DOG Tail down, ears back, lips parted—confused dogs often look like they're pleading guilty. The mouth tightens in what looks like a smile—professionally called a submissive grin—while the eyes dart back and forth. This dog is scared and not sure what to do next.

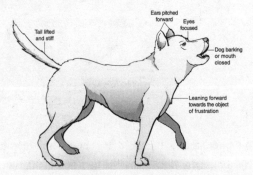

FRUSTRATED DOG The frustrated dog leans forward, ears and eyes focused on whatever has got her attention, such as a ball, deliveryman, or another dog. If prevented from exploring she may bark, pull, or jump in frustration.

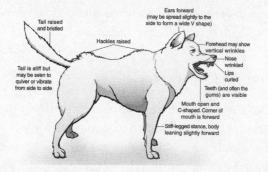

Tail raised and bristled

Hackles raised

Ears forward (may be spread slightly to the side to form a wide V shape)

Forehead may show vertical wrinkles

Nose wrinkled

Lips curled

Teeth (and often the gums) are visible

Tail is stiff but may be seen to quiver or vibrate from side to side

Mouth open and C-shaped. Corner of mouth is forward

Stiff-legged stance, body leaning slightly forward

DEFENSIVE DOG A steady gaze, rigid body, flattened ears. No matter what this dog is protecting—food, bones, a chewing gum wrapper, or a resting place—you should back off. This dog means business.

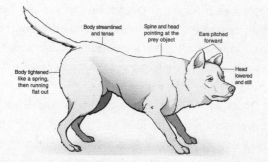

Body streamlined and tense

Spine and head pointing at the prey object

Ears pitched forward

Body tightened like a spring, then running flat out

Head lowered and still

PREDATORY DOG With tail and ears focused on the object of their obsession, the predatory dog crouches slightly, streamlining its body for the chase. Eyes focus on the object being targeted, and the body pauses before the chase begins!

See, dogs aren't so mysterious after all! If you watch closely, you'll see that your dog is communicating with you all the time. And once you learn to listen when she speaks, she'll be more motivated and excited to learn the meaning of words. Then watch the conversations flow!

Both you and your dog want the same things, really: someone

who understands you, someone who'll listen when you communicate, and, best of all, someone to love!

Sensory Rainbows

Dogs, it turns out, are even more remarkable than we once believed. Not only can they communicate without words, but they can identify smells diluted in gallons of water and recognize you with their eyes closed. While I may not be able to teach your dog to balance a checkbook or fix a light bulb, people are equally unable to imitate their sensory genius. To fully appreciate your dog's biological magnificence, take a look at the world through her eyes.

DOES YOUR DOG NEED GLASSES?

People love to explore. We hop in the car and head out to the beach, mountains, or amusement park where we size up our new surroundings with a quick glance. Whether we're staring at the ocean, assessing a trail, or gaping at a double-loop dragon coaster, we take it all in with our eyes.

Dogs, on the other hand, are utterly nearsighted. While their eyes can distinguish outlines and postures, their visual precision stops there. What dogs lose in detail, though, they make up for in other areas. For example, dogs detect motion better than we do. With their heads close to the ground, bigger lenses, and a wider panorama—they see a 240-degree field to our 180 degrees—there isn't much that goes unnoticed by a dog. Dogs can see in low light, too. They have a tapetum lucidum, a mirror-like lens that reflects incoming light so dogs can see even when it's dark outside. Ever wonder why your dog's eyes light up in photographs and yours don't? Now you know—it's the tapetum's glow.

Not long ago, a dog's visual talents were in high demand. Dogs were called on to guard livestock and family, track prey, and herd sheep. These days, overshadowed by the invention of high-tech locks and video cameras, the dog's employment is at an all-time low. What's a dog to do? Ever resourceful, most dogs accommodate. They chase other things, like cars or kids or the neighbor's cat. They stare out windows and survey the landscape, alerting you to everything that passes by or approaches the front door. Too often, these habits lead to trouble, and dogs get hassled for doing what comes naturally. If your dog's a persistent chaser or protective barker, flip ahead to chapter 7 for tips on refocusing her impulses.

Smell is your dog's go-to sense; it's how she sees the world and recognizes people, places, and things. With millions of scent receptors in the nose and mouth, dogs are able to sniff in three dimensions—identifying past, present, and even some future events with a single inhale.

Dogs' superior tracking ability is what brought our species together some fifteen thousand years ago. Before we had trash cans, dogs eagerly ingested our garbage and waste. Sure, it's gross to think about now, but back then, we depended on dogs for much more than companionship.

Of course, these sensory impulses get dogs into trouble these days. While rifling through day-old garbage, chewing discarded tissues, and nosing through Aunt Millie's purse might seem like poor form to you, it comes naturally to your dog.

Try comparing your nose to your dog's. If size wasn't a dead giveaway, look at the numbers. We have 5 million scent receptors in our nose, which sounds like a lot until you compare the number to a bloodhound's nose—they have 300 million! By all accounts, the

MYTH BUSTER
"DRY NOSE, SICK DOG"

Not always, although together with hot skin and fatigue these symptoms may indicate a fever. Noses also dry out when a dog is hot or dehydrated. Notice how your dog's nostrils change throughout the day, especially if you live in a warm climate or if your dog likes to hang out by the fire or heater.

Have you ever wondered why the tip of a dog's nose is moist? Her nostrils serve as magnets that attract and transport scent molecules to the brain for quick interpretation. Molecules stick better to moist surfaces.

average dog has thirty times more olfactory receptor cells than the average person.

People, ever the opportunists, are cashing in on dogs' olfactory abilities. Dogs are being taught to detect cancer, epilepsy, and endocrine conditions like diabetes. They're used to uncover concealed drugs, explosives, weaponry, and computer chips, too. Dogs can even sense parasites like bed bugs. We haven't invented a machine that can beat that!

So while good manners, on the trail and in the kitchen, can be taught, it's unlikely they'll come naturally. Dogs live in a world of sensory rainbows. Have compassion, go on an adventure, and let her have a good, long sniff around.

Do Dogs Bark at Nothing?

Have you ever accused your dog of barking at nothing? You may owe her an apology. Dogs hear better than we do. They can hear sounds at four times the distance and at frequencies we can't

---

DID YOU KNOW?
CHASER PERFORMS MATH!

Dogs are smart. They can judge your mood by how you sound and will be on the alert for the words you use most often. While sentences are confusing, your dog can learn a lot of words if you take the time to teach her. Chaser, a border collie who learned 1,022 words, could perform simple arithmetic skills and identify objects based on shapes and texture. If you haven't seen Chaser in action, check him out online. He's as eager and excited as a playful child. I call it the Helen Keller phenomenon: All dogs are capable of learning, but it takes a person with the patience of Helen's teacher, Anne, to break through. Check him out at ChaserTheBorderCollie.com.

imagine. The next time you think your dog's full of hot air, think again. She's barking at something—you just don't know what.

Long ago, dogs earned their keep by alerting their owners to intruders and listening for the sound of wandering livestock or rats in the barn. These days, most people want their dogs to hush up. Lifestyles have changed, too—we live stacked together or in close-knit neighborhoods. A barking dog is considered a nuisance. What's a dog to do?

Dogs need jobs, and if a sound-sensitive dog doesn't have an outlet, she might volunteer for the Border Patrol. Few sounds will go unnoticed. Flip ahead to chapter 7 for tips on quieting the incessant barker.

The Soothing Effects of a Mother's Tongue

When puppies are born, touch is their first experience: The puppies whimper, Mommy responds, and they nurse. Touch is good.

Loving touches have calming effects. The best way to settle or relax your dog or pup is to mimic the effect of a mother's tongue with long soothing strokes. Get a visual of this on ModernDog Parenting.com/Puppies101.

Aggressive touches—hitting, pinning, shocking, and poking your dog—are utterly confusing. Young puppies are too inexperienced and inhibited to understand our sometimes erratic moods and emotions. They often cringe in fear—which can get misinterpreted as an apology. As they mature, however, many of these dogs begin to use aggression to defend themselves. Touch should always soothe your dog; if it doesn't, she'll grow wary of hands reaching toward her.

Your dog will have two or more touch-sensitive spots located on the bottom of her feet and on the whiskers at the end of her nose. The pads of her feet and her nose deliver all sorts of information about the world around her, while her whiskers help her navigate around obstacles she can't see close up. Ever wonder why

While people use all sorts of hugs to show affection—quick hello/good-bye hugs, reassuring embraces, powerful bear hugs—dogs feel trapped when held against their will. If you adore hugging or you have kids (who hug dogs even when asked not to), increase your dog's hug tolerance with the following exercise:

- Take some treats and sit next to your dog—side by side, not face-to-face.

- Pet her calmly, as you offer yummy food rewards.

- Put one arm around her shoulder. Reward that. How did it go?

- Keep the rewards coming, giving one-armed hugs until your dog leans into you.

- Now try a light two-armed hug, keeping the food rewards flowing.

- Once you get a tail wag, say "Hugs!" to initiate the fun.

To see this in action, visit ModernDogParenting.com/ExtraHelp.

If your dog growls at you, stop. She may not be the hugging type. If she continues to growl over other things, get professional help. Respect a dog who stiffens or growls, or she may bite to make her point. Never hug another person's dog.

dogs don't kiss like we do or relish a nail clipping? Well, now you know. Sensation overload!

What the Tongue Can Tell

Until commercially prepared dog food became widely available almost a century ago, dogs roamed around the countryside chewing on sticks, rolling in poop, and eating whatever we tossed out.

Today, we helicopter over our dogs' every move and get alarmed when they explore nature, chew on pinecones, or sniff poop. While balanced meals in sanitized dishes and store-bought bones are perfectly fine, don't be surprised when your dog shows up with a decaying frog or a mouthful of cat litter once in a while. Just be glad you're not a dog.

Let's Go Shopping

Think back to your childhood—what did you like to play with? Were you sporty, or did you surround yourself with LEGOs? Maybe you were a wild thing, a bookworm eager to please the grown-ups, or the wandering type. Whatever your deal was, your parents couldn't change you if they tried. My point? Consider your dog when buying her toys, play puzzles, and chews. You want to keep your dog or puppy engaged, safely occupied, and happy.

Off we go! Each shopping spree is a blast (until you get to the checkout). Here are some of the essentials to focus on:

DOG BOWLS
Your dog will need a food bowl and at least a couple of water dishes. If you don't want your dog drinking from the toilets, get a water dish to put in each bathroom and one for outside.

WHAT'S MICROCHIPPING ALL ABOUT?

Microchips are small identification tags that, when inserted under a pet's skin near her shoulder, can be read by a scanner. It sounds like sci-fi, but microchips have been around for decades and are mandatory by law in some countries.

COLLAR AND IDENTIFICATION TAG

Dogs should wear a collar with an identification tag. If you're concerned about dog snatchers, get one that says "Needs Meds" on one side (even if they don't) and has your phone number on the other.

LEASHES

Puppies get curious and start wandering at about four months. Unless you're in an enclosed area, keep your dog on a leash or long line. Short four- to six-foot leashes are best around roadways or in heavily trafficked areas. Use a long line in an open area to give your dog more freedom to sniff and play.

Hands-Free Long Line

Twenty-five- to fifty-foot light lines secured to a dog's collar or harness give her a sense of freedom while still giving you control. I design lines, sold on Amazon, that are light, flexible, and bright blue so they stand out. Let your dog drag the line while you watch it, or secure the very end of the line to a leash. See these lines in action on ModernDogParenting.com/EverydayEssentials.

Retractable Leash

These leashes extend out sixteen to twenty-six feet to give your dog more freedom to explore. While they sound dreamy, they are dangerous near roadways, get wrapped around obstacles, and can cause painful rope burns. I like this choice for solitary strolls across a field or beach. I often attach a retractable leash to the end of my long line to give my dogs extra freedom.

Indoor Hands-Free Drag Lead

This light four-foot line (no handle) drags behind your dog inside, enabling you to calmly redirect your dog when she jumps up or sticks her nose where it doesn't belong. I sell them on my Amazon store; check out ModernDogParenting.com/EverdayEssentials.

Hand Lead or Finger Lead

Hook a short hand lead or finger loop to your dog's tag collar to give you quick and easy access when you need it most. Whereas a shove or push is confrontational, quick holds can steady your dog and remind her to stay calmly on all four paws.

Car Stations

Use a hand lead through the seatbelt or an adjustable leash to secure your dog to a harness of seatbelt-grade material while you drive. A 2013 study by the Center for Pet Safety ranks the Sleepy-Pod Clickit Utility harness as a top choice for car safety. Make sure your dog can easily turn around, stand up, and (if you'd like) rest on either the seat or the floor. Create a comforting resting spot with blankets and favorite toys.

Station Lead

This leash can be secured to immovable objects to help teach your dog to Stay in different rooms or situations.

MATS

A flat mat or dog bed will help your dog learn her place in the rooms you share. Dogs feel better when they know where to go to rest and find their things. Find a bed with a removable cover and strong fabric that will hold up to wash after wash.

ENCLOSURES

Enclose your dog in an area when she's first adjusting to being left alone and resting through the night. Offer her a comfortable resting spot and bones or interactive puzzles to keep her busy and

WIPE YOUR PAWS!

Teach your dog to wipe her paws when you come in from a walk:

- Leave a fluffy towel or bathmat in the entranceway.
- With treats or a toy, lure your dog in a circle on the mat.
- Once she gets the hang of it, say "Wipe your paws."

Check out the spinning trick outlined in chapter 6. See it in action at ModernDogParenting.com/Tricks&Games.

distracted. Being left alone is confusing—your dog won't be sure what to do. The most popular enclosures are crates. I like crates, although a few of my rescues did not. They'd spent enough time being locked in one to last a lifetime. If you have a crate-intolerant dog, read through the other choices.

Crates

A comfortable crate will feel like a bedroom—a safe place where your dog can relax. Teach your dog or puppy to love her crate by placing her water in or near the opening; feed her there, too. If you're feeding by hand, as I suggest on page 118, teach your dog to go in and out of the crate while you feed her one handful at a time.

When you leave your puppy, encourage her to stay calm by following a comforting routine. Play calming tunes (my dogs love their pet acoustics) and toss some treats in the crate as you escort your dog or puppy in with her favorite chew and/or puzzle toy. Dim the lights, tell her you love her, and off you go.

Gates

Gates are another way to create a safe area for your new dog. I close off a bathroom for my crate-phobic shelter dogs or section off rooms so I can keep my eye on them. Gates can be multipurpose or screwed into the wall.

Ex-pen

Envision a foldout playpen here. Wire or heavy plastic, these collapsible zones can be set up inside or out and are helpful in the early puppy stages or when introducing a new dog to other pets. As puppies get older, they want to explore and may bark if left alone in an enclosure. If you have a wide doorway, ex-pens can be extended into a wide gate.

COMFORT WEAR

Walking your dog should be fun for the both of you. Arm straining, leash tugging, cough inducing marathons don't add up to a good time in anyone's book. Instead, try one of these options, collectively called Comfort Wear, as they'll neither hurt nor strangle your dog. You don't have to be strong or coordinated to have an enjoyable walk; find a solution that works for you!

Head collars and front-clipping harnesses may take a few days to get used to—like braces or a training bra. Let your dog adjust to wearing it for a few days before attaching a leash.

Martingale Collar

Martingale collars slip over your dog's neck and wear much like a tag collar. The top third slips to provide momentary resistance if your dog pulls. If your dog responds to this, look no further.

Mesh Harness

A soft mesh harness can work well for young puppies and small breeds who have more fragile necks. Slipped over the head, they fit snugly over your dog's throat and clip from behind.

Head Collar

Head collars fit over your dog's face like a horse halter. Slide the noseband over your dog's muzzle, and gently lead her around like a show pony. Voilà! Where the head leads, the body will follow. These little gems don't require any strength and have a calm-

MY DOG HATES HER HEAD COLLAR

Dogs that are sensitive to body wear may react mightily to the head collar, like pain-sensitive kids getting used to braces. While it's normal for a dog to flail about for a day or two or rub her nose, if your dog's threatening to claw her eyes out or growls the moment the head collar comes near, look for a different option.

If you're still game but your dog's on the fence, add felt to the nose band for comfort. Condition her to wearing it by offering favorite treats for letting you put it on, and leave it on for thirty-minute intervals a couple of times a day. Distract her with treats and fun. After she's adapted, attach her leash and follow her around, rewarding her as you do.

ing effect, too. Popular brand names include Gentle Leader and Halti Head Collar. I use these collars for my dogs. Pocket some treats and reward your dog when she looks up to you.

No-Pull Harness

Most harnesses encourage a sled dog mentality: With the leash clipped across the shoulder, dogs forge ahead when they feel a tug. A few new harness designs—no-pull harnesses—however, restrain dogs across pressure points, which prevents pulling. It's magical. A few harnesses clip in front of a dog's chest, while others loop under the front legs. When you test these out, be generous with treats and compliments. Before you can say "Good dog," your walks will have a whole new look and feel. Cruise control!

LEARNING AIDS AND DISPLACEMENT ACTIVITIES

If your dog is awake, she's learning. Like a kid, she doesn't have much else to do. Try brushing her aside, and she'll develop an amazing repertoire of "tricks" to get your attention, like digging up

WHAT HAPPENED TO THE GOOD OLD-FASHIONED CHOKE CHAIN?

Choke chains cut off a dog's breathing—the theory being that a momentary loss of air will teach your dog not to pull. Strangulation, as it turns out, is not the best teacher. Anyone can forcefully hold a dog to their side, but strangulation teaches dogs to lunge or bolt when there's slack. Encourage good walking skills with a compassionate collar.

the yard and trashing the wastebaskets. Ignoring your dog can get very costly!

On the other hand, there are plenty of things you can make and buy to keep your dog busy throughout the day. These learning aids focus your dog on better habits like Retrieve, Chew This, and Come.

Clicker

A clicker is a small handheld object that makes a sharp sound when pressed. Think of it as a way to capture a moment—like you do with a camera. With a camera you get a photo; with the clicker you get a behavior or a chain of behaviors. It's cool and very addictive. We'll use clickers—or unique sounds like a clicker makes—to help your dog learn good behavior in part two.

Targets

You can easily teach your dog to point to things with her paw or nose. Known as targeting, it's a wonderful way to communicate and help your dog learn new words and routines. We'll discuss when and what to use your targets for in chapters 5 and 6.

Target Wand

Target wands can be used to guide your dog over obstacles or to places that would otherwise make her nervous, such as down stairs, into a car, or to a person. They're also great for teaching good walking skills and behaviors like Come and Go to Your Mat. Stores sell fancy target wands with clickers built in, but you can easily make one at home or use your pointed finger or an open palm.

Target Disc

A target disc can be bought or made from a container lid, cardboard, or heavy, slide-resistant fabric. Teach your dog to target the disc with her nose and/or her foot. Choose a direction for each: I say "On it" to mean her paw and "Touch" for the nose. Once your dog will target her disc on cue, use it in a variety of situations:

ON IT **Move the disc into her crate or the car or tape it to an object like her dog bed to teach her to go there. It's helpful to teach a "Go" direction, such as "Go to Daddy," or "Go get me water from the fridge" and other more advanced moves.**

TOUCH **Discs are also great for trick training: Once your dog will target the disc, it can be taped to a ball to teach her how to Roll or to a cabinet to teach her to Close It. Betcha never thought you could teach your dog that! You can teach her to open the cabinets, too, but we won't go there . . .**

BONES

Without hands to manipulate or play, dogs use their mouths. They enjoy chewing things. If you don't provide a suitable something, your dog might settle for your furnishings. Buy bones made in America, and supervise your dog with new bones to make sure she's okay with them. If she tears at a bone too intensely, chokes, or gets ill, take it away and search for another option. My dogs' favorites are bully sticks, pressed rawhide, Nylabones, and hard rubber toys stuffed with pasty, tasty goop. Some dogs eat bones too quickly, chip hard bones, or have sensitive stomachs. If so, try something else.

TOYS

Oh, the selection! The variety of dog toys is enough to confuse anyone. Pink flamingo squeakers, knotted rope toys, balls with holes, fluorescent balls that squeak, bouncy rubber balls that stimulate the dog's prey drive . . . What will your dog or puppy like? Before you fill your car with dozens of toys, get one from each of a couple of categories—such as a rope, a ball, a bouncer, and a stuffy—and see what your dog enjoys. Which one gets the biggest tail rise? Mine love squeaky balls and squeaky stuffed animals. My neighbor's dog is obsessed with rope toys, and my cousin's dogs like hard plastic bouncers. Go figure.

INTERACTIVE PUZZLES

If you've been to a well-run zoo, you'll notice that many of the predatory animals—like lions, bears, and tigers—have lots of interactive toys. They'd go crazy without them, developing obsessive-compulsive habits like pacing, destructiveness, or self-mutilation.

Your dog can get also bored and develop similar patterns, as well as chronic barking, licking, or chewing habits. But recently, someone got smart and developed lots of interactive puzzle toys that dogs love. They bring the thrill of the hunt right into your

FIND AN OBSESSION TOY

Does your dog have a favorite toy? Buy a bunch and help her identify them with a word like "Ball" or "Toy." Strategically place them around your home in baskets, and direct your dog to get one when she seems restless or bored. Keep some by the doors and a few by her crate. Each time you come home, your puppy gets excited, or someone visits, say, "Toy!" and encourage her to grab it. Teach her to grab her toy instead of jumping or nipping at you when she's happy. See this in action at ModernDogParenting.com/EverydayEssentials.

living room, where on the safety of your carpet your dog can paw, knock, and roll her meal straight out in front of her. If your dog is spending time alone or you're just too tired some days to take her for a long walk, consider getting some interactive puzzles to keep both boredom and destructive habits at bay.

OUTDOOR PLAYSCAPES AND CONTAINMENT

Dogs love to explore. If you have a yard, you're lucky. If not, scope out your neighborhood and find a park or field nearby. Use a long line to give your dog freedom in open spaces. A six-foot leash is too confining. If possible, find some playground equipment or a building or store that permits dogs. Build your dog's confidence by luring her over ramps, up stairs, and through passageways or tunnels that are unfamiliar to her.

FENCE OPTIONS

Back when I was a kid, there were no leash laws. Imagine the life: My dog would accompany me to the bus stop at 8:45 A.M., spend her day exploring with dog friends or following Joe the postman on his daily route, then circle back to meet up with me at 3:30 P.M. By dinnertime, she was ready for cartoons, ice cream, and finally sleep, curled up at the end of my bed.

Nowadays, that would lead to trouble on every front. Cars drive too fast, homes are stacked close together, people are more territorial. Fences, like the dog leash, have become a necessary evil— necessary because the world is full of dangers, and evil because they limit freedom. The world's not perfect. Here are your choices:

Underground-Wire Electric Fencing

An underground wire is installed, which loops around a section of your property and connects to a unit in your home. Your dog wears a receiver collar that pokes two pointed metal prongs into her neck and delivers a shock if she gets too close to the outdoor wire. Little flags are planted near the wire to teach your dog the boundary.

Shocking a dog for any reason can be frightening for some dogs and terrifying for others. Some dogs learn this system quickly; others respect the zoned area for a while, then run through when temptations are too strong. Some dogs simply freak out, cower at the door, and/or start peeing indoors. Of course, electric fences won't keep other dogs or wildlife from wandering into your yard, which can be an added distraction. Let your dog get used to you and your home before training her to this system.

When staking out your electric fence enclosure, consider these three things:

Exclude your driveway. It's too risky.

If your yard faces a road, keep the fence back as far as possible. Dogs who can see the road often become territorial. Pull your enclosure off the road by twenty feet, or better yet, put it in the backyard.

Include your home in the layout. Dogs love their "den," and it's been shown that dogs are calmer when they can wait by the door.

MYTH BUSTER

PUPPIES UNDER SIX MONTHS CAN BE TRAINED TO RESPECT ELECTRIC FENCES

No! Back when there was only one underground fence company, training a dog to the fence didn't begin until six to eight months. There was a good reason—starting training any earlier was not only ineffective, it was cruel. When more companies began to make and advertise this product, saying they could train puppies to the fence as early as eight weeks, all the companies joined in. Please stop and think. A young puppy is like a baby—they are learning to trust that the world is a safe place. If you're using this type of enclosure, do not, under any circumstance, introduce your dog to a fence system until she is six to eight months old.

Full-Yard Fence

Dogs love the freedom a fenced area provides. It becomes their territory. We fenced our new yard before we moved in, and my dogs were thrilled! They staked out the backyard for pottying and the front for playing. Putting in a fence can be expensive, but if possible, do it.

People often ask me how high a fence should be and what type of material is best. The answer depends a lot on your dog's personality, her athletic abilities, and perhaps your town's or city's zoning laws. If the fence is too wide, your dog will thrill to squeeze through it; if it's too low, she may jump straight over it! While a six-foot chain link fence is strong and secure, a picket fence, solid wood or even a strong wire fence might do—it all depends on your dog!

Think with Your Heart

About now you might be thinking, "Wow, dogs are a lot more complicated than I ever imagined!" And it's true. Once you know how your dog really thinks, living with her makes a lot more sense. It's a give and take. Provide for her needs so she feels secure instead of rambunctious, defensive, scared, or unsettled.

Take a look at your world through her eyes, and think with your heart. Try to laugh at the setbacks, like when your dog ignores you or darts through the kitchen with your underwear. Conditioning good habits doesn't start with punishments; it starts with learning and understanding. Together, you can create a lifetime of happy memories.

In the next chapters we'll focus on your dog's personality as well as her emotional IQ. It's nothing heavy; I make it fun. If you want to boost your dog's rating, make sure you're following her needs chart (see page 25) and enjoying life. Happy dogs not only behave better, they score higher, too!

3

Love the One
You're With

The greatness of a nation can be judged by
the way its animals are treated.
—GANDHI

The build-up before getting a dog can be more exciting than actually raising one. Of course there's the honeymoon period—perhaps you're there now. With the love hormones surging, everything seems so cute and adorable, and you happily stumble out of bed for that four A.M. potty run.

Cling to that feeling. Take lots of photos—your joy won't last forever. No one's does. When it ends, you and your dog will have some differing opinions. Your dog might jump when you'd rather he sit, run when you say "Come," or hightail it through your home with someone's dirty underwear dangling from his mouth. What you think is cute now won't be endearing forever.

Maybe you've read this far and are worried that you completely screwed up. You might even think it'd be easier to just start over. Stop and take a deep breath. What if you traded your dog for a newer model—a different breed, a new rescue or that cute face you saw on Craigslist the other night? I'm not saying you can't, but unless you change your approach, your frustrations will likely follow you. Your next dog might not soil the rug, but he'll do something equally obnoxious like chew the molding or bark at the postman.

Instead of starting from scratch, here's an idea: Try loving the one you're with. Get to know him. Let me play the role of both therapist and teacher—I'll help you make sense of your differences. Don't be embarrassed if you need more help. Raising a dog takes skill. No one would take up the piano or learn a new language without a good teacher.

Just remember that whatever you've got going on—teeth marks on the coffee table, uprooted rose bushes, stubborn carpet stains—you are not alone. I've rescued dogs with tremendous separation issues and even one that growled at my kids. With time, treats, and a whole lot of patience, each one of my dogs grew up to be happy, loving, and well adjusted. I'll share my secrets in this chapter.

Step 1: Look at Life from Your Dog's Perspective

My daily roster is filled with people who are confused by their dog's behavior. I love being their lifeline! It doesn't take ten lessons to change your relationship with your dog; sometimes it requires only a change of heart.

I'm going to let you in on a little secret: Dogs aren't perfect. I've worked with thousands, and each one has its own quirks, just like you, just like me. Some are jumpy, loud, or nervous. Others get manic or defensive in their attempts to find a purpose. When dogs are isolated, ignored, or bullied, bad habits get worse.

The first step in helping your dog make better choices is to look at life from his perspective. Use this chapter to discover his

EMPATHY UNDER MY ROOF

I'm either the worst foster mother ever or the best. It depends on who you ask. Either way, my home is blessed with a splendid collection of dogs, cats, rodents, and even a lizard who were all once homeless and now live cheerfully under one roof. Each came with a unique personality and a need for empathy, love, and patience. I'll sprinkle their stories throughout. For now meet the boys, Balderdash and Bamboozle.

BALDERDASH

Born and bred in the Czech Republic, German shepherd #58225—named Ezopp by his breeders—spent his days enduring rigorous protection and agility training while waiting for a permanent home. Enter Peter, a Connecticut lawyer. Recovering from a near-fatal illness, Peter spent his days in front of his computer, looking at German shepherd dogs. Peter fell hard for Dog #58225. Ezopp was going to America.

Within days, Peter knew he had bitten off more than he could chew. His fragile health and busy schedule left him little time for a full-grown, unreliably housebroken, travel-stressed dog. Peter called me, distraught. I volunteered to rehome Ezopp.

I brought this majestic dog home and set to work finding a suitable permanent home for him. Ezopp appeared resigned and a little lost. He was undeniably regal and possessed a gentle, yielding disposition, but there was no joy there. He sat on the kitchen floor, detached. He refused food, ignored treats, and seemed mystified by squeak toys.

All my life, I've been able to talk—and listen—to dogs. I pricked up my ears and turned to Ezopp. In no time, this sad, lonely dog told me everything I needed to know. Here is a little of what he said:

Language is hard. Staring at the long list of tongue-challenging Czech commands that accompanied Ezopp, I opted for hand signals to direct him. Almost overnight, his detachment began to subside, and he became attentive to my gestures.

Socialization is important. Raised in an isolated environment, Ezopp lacked some social graces. He had a tendency to stare at dogs and people—a habit that is both rude and frightening. A few quick admonishments, and the behavior subsided.

Children are good. It was my children who first ignited a spark of joy in Ezopp's eyes. Crated for the first two nights, he escaped on the third and headed directly for my daughter's room. He laid down beside her bed, where we found him in the morning, sleepy eyed and content. My then two-year-old son followed Ezopp from room to room: "My dog. Big dog. Mine," he prophesized.

Ezopp and I sat in the kitchen, browsing my contact list. I'd consider a family, then look over at Ezopp. Back and forth. Back and forth. No one seemed right. What was I missing? Finally, I turned to Ezopp. "Who?" I asked. "You," he said. "Ah," I said. And Ezopp—now known as Balderdash—had found his home.

BAMBOOZLE

I first met Boozle when a woman named Karen called to tell me of a recent puppy mill bust. Her niece had shown up at the door with one of the younger puppies—a skinny, scruffy-coated dog that could fit inside a handbag. She wanted to keep the puppy and hoped I could help him. Was Karen in the market for a dog? Well, no. Did she want or need a dog? No and no. Was this puppy the cutest thing she'd seen? Yes, in fact, he was.

It didn't take twenty-four hours for reality to hit. Milo, as she'd named him, barked when left alone. He peed and pooped in his crate. He snarled at dogs on the street. Karen, who had never owned a pet, was unsure how to manage the situation. She begged me to board and teach this puppy. I don't offer this service, so how the word "okay" came out of my mouth is still a mystery to me.

A little background helped to make sense of Milo's behavior. He was the sole survivor of a litter of Maltese-mix puppies. Motherless and without littermates, he was left alone in a bathroom for long stretches and fed cow's milk and macaroni. In this completely alien and unsuitable environment, Milo began to unravel, barking and nipping at anyone who came near.

Before we were a mile from Karen's home, Milo began to whine and spin. Then he peed. I pulled over and peered into his crate. This frail, odd-looking little dog had the emotional force of Yoda and the neediness of an abused child. "Settle, baby," I murmured. He was not so inclined. And we were still a long way from home.

After a forty-minute drive, we pulled into the driveway, and Milo's new life began. The first few days were a blur of reactive barking, fearful growling, and general lashing out. He panicked if we crated him. He flipped out if we left him alone. Milo was testing me professionally and emotionally.

A few days into The Milo Project, he grabbed a dog bone and took it back to his bed. As I approached with a treat cup—the first step in teaching a puppy to Drop on cue—I saw the dreaded flip in his face. His eyes hardened, his lips curled, the whale eye revealed itself. He growled deeply. At four months, Milo was resource guarding with the determination of a starved predator.

Little Milo was an emotional train wreck. The facts that his mother had died giving birth to his litter and that he had basically raised himself with no one to serve as his emotional reference or guide flashed in front of my eyes. If he'd had a mother and growled at her, she would have reacted swiftly—a response that teaches puppies social inhibition and respect.

Though it's not a technique I use often or recommend that anyone try without professional supervision, I quickly braced Milo, holding his head with my index and middle fingers so he could not twist around and bite me. When released, he leaped at my torso like Cujo on steroids. Defensively, I repeated the sequence and soothed him with my voice.

Although this technique would not work on a larger dog, it had an immediate effect on Milo. In that moment, I felt something release from the little dog, something writhing and ugly and isolating that had been holding him hostage. His body relaxed, yielding. I lifted Milo and held him to my heart. There he stayed, as though he'd finally found a mama, an interpreter, someone he could trust.

In a literal heartbeat, I came to see this needy, desperate little dog as mine.

Within twelve hours of the bone incident, Hurricane Sandy hit, confining us to the house. Unable to gab on the phone, watch TV, or spend time on the Internet, we had some serious family time, and Milo thrived on it. He switched from reactive to yielding, from snapping at the other dogs to extending gestures of play. "Could this be?" I thought. "He's like a different puppy altogether."

So why? And how? Am I that good of a teacher?

Truthfully, I think it had everything to do with Milo's capacity for love. Before I was able to break through his guard, Milo couldn't see himself as a loving creature. Interaction had been scarce in his developmental stages, so when it was offered, he was frantic to sustain it. As I watched him those first few days, I thought that he was a little too far gone—that his desperation and fears were insatiable.

But life proved me wrong again. For a solid week I held this now exhausted puppy to my heart, stopped crating him, and, thanks to the superstorm, basically kept him with us 24/7. Mind you, it's not a course of action I'd recommend or use with any normal puppy, but Milo was no normal case.

And then came the fateful call: Karen couldn't wait to see her puppy. It was time for Milo to go home. My son, who'd played hide-and-seek with Milo for hours was beside himself. As if he understood my son's anguish, Milo lay still under the couch for an hour before we could find him. His time with us was a success, so why did we feel so sad?

Karen met us in the driveway where she scooped Milo out of his crate and asked about his routine. I handed her his schedule, which included extensive family participation as well as daily socialization. Suddenly her eyes widened; she did not want to be interrupted while she worked in her home office. Milo would need to be calm for at least six to eight hours a day. Did I think he could do it? No. Could she tie him up in the backyard? Not unless she wanted him to be carried off by a hawk. As I explained the level of care, Karen grew less and less excited about taking him back. In the end, she asked if I would rehome Milo. *That's an easy one*, I thought. At the bus stop, I watched my son climb off the bus, head downcast until the moment I pressed the little white dog to his chest. "Can we keep him, Mommy?" he asked. I smiled and gave both of them a hug.

We renamed him Bamboozle, because we had to bamboozle my husband into a fourth dog. Boozle can get unsettled, especially when there is too much going on, but I know that jerky strips and squeak toys will cheer him up. After what he's overcome, I think I love him more for his quirks and imperfections.

personality type and find out what lifts his spirits. All dogs have unique talents and love to be acknowledged. Try looking at your dog's behavior from the eyes of a nurturing parent rather than an insistent trainer. Empathy isn't just for people—it's the first step in having a good relationship with your dog, too.

So now it's your turn. What's your dog's story, and which of his personality quirks might be leading to bad habits? Perhaps they're not so bad after all. With a little insight you can shift your dog's focus and condition good manners almost overnight.

Step 2: Discover Dogality

The second step to being a happy dog lover is to get a handle on your dog's personality—what I call his Dogality. It influences everything from your morning snuggles to how he reacts when left alone. Knowing his disposition will help you shape a world where your dog feels accepted and adored.

Like people, dogs are a blend of nature and nurture. Your dog's personality is the nature part—you can't change that. But you're the nurture part, and there is a lot you can do to bring out the best in your dog.

TAKE THE DOGALITY TEST

Dogs are born with their own unique worldview. Some face new situations enthusiastically, while others would rather hide under the

---

DID YOU KNOW?

SURVIVAL OF THE FRIENDLIEST

Scientists routinely connect personality with natural selection, what Darwin called "survival of the fittest." Brian Hare, coauthor of *The Genius of Dogs*, questions the phrase as it relates to dogs. He points out that dogs evolved some fifteen thousand years ago from their wild relatives due to their friendly genes, not because they were the fittest to survive on their own. He calls it "survival of the friendliest." Pointing to the population decline in dog ancestors canny enough to go it alone—the wolf, coyote, and dingo—he shows how even the fittest cannot survive human overpopulation.

PERSONALITY TESTS

Respected researchers and facilities like the ASPCA and the Humane Society of the United States offer personality tests. People like Benjamin Hart, DVM; Stanley Coren, Ph.D.; and Ian Dunbar, DVM, have greatly influenced me and include extensive personality tests for dogs and puppies in their books. Refer to the bibliography for their titles.

Many breeders, shelters, and rescue groups temperament test their dogs or puppies: Listen to their opinions. They often have people like myself on staff to match each puppy to the right home and to offer support once you take your baby home.

couch. This Dogality test is meant to be both fun and informative. There are no right or wrong answers. Some of the questions might be hypothetical, like what does your dog do when the doorbell rings (even if you don't have a doorbell)? Others ask you to work with a helper. Take as long as you need to complete the test.

Although your dog's breed could predict many of the responses—for example, most German shepherds will bark when the doorbell rings—each dog has a unique temperament. Responses will vary from dog to dog, even within a breed or litter.

If you've already started lessons, answer the questions based on what your dog's responses would have been before you began. Of course, this leads us to the most important point of the Dogality test: Nothing is set in stone. With patience and positive encouragement, you can help your dog learn self-control and better coping skills. Use his score as a guide to shape a life you both will enjoy!

I've divided the Dogality test into three parts based on where you perform the exercises. Most will take place in your home—what your dog considers his den. You'll also study his reaction in your yard or neighborhood—his territory. Like you, your dog's

KEEP THESE THINGS IN MIND BEFORE YOU TAKE THE TEST.

AGE FACTOR   Puppies under thirteen weeks are in an important phase called the critical socialization period when their senses are underdeveloped and their brains are still growing. Until four to six months of age, puppies need lots of sleep, loving interactions, and positive social experiences. Dogs become more predictable as they age, but still enjoy fun times and adoring people. Wait to perform this test until your dog's more than six months old. If he's scared by the balloon pop or umbrella in the first section, make note of it. Expose him to unfamiliar objects and unpredictable situations as described in the socialization section of chapter 5.

SOCIALIZATION   Dogs who had a variety of experiences early in life will test more confidently than those who aren't well socialized. If there's a puppy nibbling on your shoelace, prioritize social outings over lessons. You'll have a lifetime to teach your dog new things, but if your puppy isn't socialized well, he won't be able to focus outside of your living room.

HISTORY   A dog's history can have a tremendous effect on his score. Dogs generally play games and explore what interests them. Certain dogs love water, while others prefer to chase squirrels or follow a good scent. If you've rescued a dog who has been neglected or abused, he might have missed out on exciting life experiences, and his test score might show it. Use the score as an opportunity to learn more about your dog's past and what you can do to make him happy.

more confident in predictable and familiar surroundings. How does his reaction change in different locations? Circle the answer that best applies, and tally the number of times you chose each letter at the end.

1. Ask a friend to make an abrupt, loud noise, like popping a balloon or dropping a pot, in another room. Does your dog . . .
   a. Bark or growl, lift ears and tail, and investigate
   b. Bark and look toward the noise, then get excited
   c. Do nothing
   d. Look to you
   e. Lower ears, tail, and posture and/or retreat

2. When the doorbell rings unexpectedly, does your dog . . .
   a. Position himself between you and the door
   b. Bark and run to the door, jumping up enthusiastically
   c. Lift head and stay quiet
   d. Walk to the door with you
   e. Bark, freeze, or retreat

3. When greeting you or a family member, does your dog . . .
   a. Stand in front of you and sniff intensely, or jump up and lean into you
   b. Run around, jump, or bark in happy greeting
   c. Calmly say hello and accept petting
   d. Greet with a full body wag and stay with you
   e. Approach you with tail and head lowered, pee in submission

4. If you live in a multi-dog household, does your dog . . .
   a. Rest and explore on his own
   b. Play, rest, and wrestle with the other dogs
   c. Do his own thing
   d. Only play if you're around
   e. Interact when your home is quiet and predictable

5. Place a toy in a cardboard box. Shake the box and toss it six feet away. Point to the box. Does your dog . . .
   a. Act defensive, lifting tail and ears and/or barking at it before approaching
   b. Pounce on and/or tear open the box

    c. Explore calmly

    d. Follow your point

    e. Jump back, nervously approach the box, or avoid it altogether

6. When a delivery person comes to your home, does your dog . . .

    a. Run to the door and either jump or bark aggressively, ignoring your direction

    b. Bark and run to the door to greet them

    c. Turn to you momentarily before returning to another activity

    d. Look from you to the new person

    e. Cower, approach then avoid, or hide in another room

7. In your home, does your dog focus on . . .

    a. Himself, reacts assertively

    b. Anyone—including new people

    c. Everyone

    d. One person (owner)

    e. Himself, reacts anxiously

8. Ask a friend to hold your dog as you walk fifteen feet away. Call your dog, but have your friend wait five seconds before letting go. Does your dog . . .

    a. Pull to get away from your friend

    b. Strain, jump, and/or bark in anticipation

    c. Sit calmly

    d. Strain to come as soon as called

    e. Seem worried, not sure what's going on

9. Take your dog's favorite toy/treat and show him you have it. Have a friend hold your dog as you hide the toy or tasty treat on a low shelf in the next room. Call your dog in and point to help him locate the toy. Does your dog . . .

    a. Sniff around, seeming to ignore your directions, but find it anyway

    b. Run around excitedly

    c. Play along but act nonchalant

d. Follow your point eagerly

e. Seem confused, cling to you

10. Call your dog when he is resting comfortably. Does your dog . . .

a. Look up momentarily, walk away, or ignore you

b. Jump up and hop around excitedly or race to the door

c. Stay where he is

d. Look up and come over

e. Look to you with concern/confusion

11. Shout at the wall like you're mad. Does your dog . . .

a. Act defensively, look around, or vocalize

b. Bark and run to the wall to explore what you're staring at

c. Ignore you

d. Nudge you or lean against your leg

e. Run away or tuck his tail and ears

12. If someone other than you shouts in your home, does your dog . . .

a. Bark or act aggressive

b. Run back and forth between you and the shouter

c. Ignore the whole situation

d. Go to your side, lean against you or lick you

e. Retreat or watch nervously

13. When you're getting ready to leave, does your dog . . .

a. Take a position at a post or block the door

b. Wag his tail excitedly and run back and forth to the door

c. Watch, but doesn't get up unless invited

d. Hop around, hoping to be included

e. Act stressed and nervous about being left alone

14. Place a treat under one of three cups on the floor. Move the cups around so the treat isn't in the same place. Point your dog to the wrong cup. Does your dog . . .

a. Sniff all the cups for the treat

b. Bash into the cups

c. Knock the cups over in no particular order

d. Sniff the cup you point to

e. Look at all the cups but do nothing

15. If you're home with your dog, does he . . .

    a. Take a position by a door or window and alert you to sounds or motions

    b. Pace around, lie in a central place, or nudge you constantly for more attention

    c. Have his own favorite spot

    d. Lay at your feet, licking and leaning on you

    e. Rest in a crate, in a corner, or under a piece of furniture

16. Place an unfamiliar object (like a large umbrella or kids' toy) in the middle of a familiar room. Does your dog . . .

    a. Walk up to the object, sniffing it inquisitively

    b. Pounce on the object excitedly

    c. Politely sniff the object or ignore it

    d. Look to you before investigating

    e. Nervously look to the object and back away

IN YOUR YARD OR NEIGHBORHOOD

17. When your dog hears a noise outside, does he . . .

    a. Bark and run to the window or door, seeking the noise

    b. Bark and run around

    c. Lift his head but seem uninterested

    d. Perk up but keep quiet

    e. Lower his ears, move away from noise

18. If an unfamiliar person appears on a walk, does your dog . . .

    a. Bark, lean forward, and either growl defensively or jump excitedly

    b. Clearly view the new person as an opportunity for friendship

    c. Look casually and take it in stride

    d. Alert you, look back, or return to you

e. Act startled, lower his tail, ears, and posture, and freeze or run backward

19. When meeting a new dog, does your dog . . .
    a. Rise up, stiffen, and attempt to stand over the other dog or growl defensively
    b. Jump around playfully
    c. Sniff the dog in a relaxed fashion
    d. Turn to you
    e. Freeze, lower his tail, ears, and posture

20. When a stranger bends over your dog, does he . . .
    a. Stiffen and close his mouth
    b. Jump up or throw his body against this new friend
    c. Act noncommittal
    d. Lower his ears, roll on his belly, or lean against the stranger
    e. Lower his ears, tail, and posture, or retreat behind you

IN THE WORLD BEYOND

21. When seeing moving objects (children running, a person on a scooter, etc.), does your dog . . .
    a. Show great interest
    b. Chase happily to join the fun
    c. Watch with his eyes
    d. Seem interested but look to you
    e. Freeze, watch, or back away, ears and tail down

22. In an unpopulated area, does your dog . . .
    a. Walk around, ignoring you as he alerts you to or barks at every unfamiliar distraction
    b. Run around happily
    c. Sniff around
    d. Explore but look back every few seconds
    e. Stay close with tail and ears down and react nervously to sudden changes

23. When encountering a small animal, does your dog . . .
    a. Chase aggressively
    b. Chase with joy as a potential playmate
    c. Focus but ignore the animal unless off-leash
    d. Get excited but still listen to you
    e. Stay focused on the animal and get manic
24. When socialized with other dogs, does your dog . . .
    a. Sniff the other dog stiffly, stand on their shoulder, or fight
    b. Play with other dogs and ignore you when it's time to go
    c. Greet, then ignore or play calmly
    d. Look to you even as he approaches and plays
    e. Stay by your side cautiously or snap at dogs who approach
       excitedly

TALLY YOUR RESULTS

Tally your score to see where your dog fits in. Don't be surprised if you get mixed results—dogs are complex! Many rescue dogs give a varied score; it's hard to pin down their natural reactions until they feel safe in their new home.

___ a
___ b
___ c
___ d
___ e

FIVE DOGALITY TYPES

Each letter corresponds with one of the five different character types described below.
    a. Type A
    b. Party Animal
    c. Laid-Back

d. Head-of-the-Class

e. Over-Thinker

Regardless of your score, your dog's behavior is not set in stone. Using a more positive and structured approach, you can calm impulsive dogs, soothe anxieties, and center defensive reactions. Who wouldn't want to spend time with a dog who loves life and knows how to behave?

Type A

Type A's are independent, clearheaded dogs with quick reflexes and active minds. Intelligent and confident, they focus on whatever they're engaged in, whether following directions, tracking a scent, or defending your threshold from the pizza guy. Task oriented and serious, these dogs prefer work to play.

To live happily with a Type A dog, discover his passion, assign a word to the activity, and include this routine in your everyday life. Does your dog love hunting—chasing squirrels or following a scent? That's an easy one—use a simple "Go get 'em!" If he's athletic, dog sports like Agility or Flyball could be a good outlet. If he's protective, teach him one cue for barking and another to stop barking as described in chapter 7.

When left alone, Type A's need to assume some role. They usually enjoy destructive rampages (provide bones and you'll be safe), homeland security (barking when anything gets too close to the home or yard), or predatory excitement (window watching). Look up "Energy Busters" under the Displacement Activity section of chapter 8.

Shift your dog's attention from annoying habits to useful routines, and you'll have a dog most people will envy. Get a handle on this spirited bunch so you can embrace their never-say-die attitude!

TYPE A'S COME IN TWO VARIETIES: DEFENSIVE AND MANIC

Defensive A's are protective, take-charge dogs who are physically bossy and use their weight to show strength versus affection. Once mature (around two years old), they may remain on high alert and grow more territorial and/or food-possessive, unless directed with consistent lessons. Defensive A's will approach unfamiliar objects and people without hesitation, tails held high, body and facial features pressed forward.

Manic A's are assertive and fast moving but less aggressive. They often come across as playful and friendly, but they don't settle down with petting and are always on the go. Sometimes these dogs are labeled with ADHD, but with routine exercise and lessons, they can learn how to calm themselves with a toy or bone.

Party Animal

Party Animals have quite the life. They love everybody, attract attention wherever they go, and love to make a splash. More playful and friendly than task oriented, this group lives to have fun and can suffer terribly if not taught how to manage alone time. If socialized with other dogs, they can be nearly as happy in their company, but nothing beats hanging out with the people they love.

How do you recognize a Party Animal? It's easy—they're actively underfoot, knocking into you and gazing up at you hopefully. Clever and eager to be part of the action, they often choose misbehavior to get attention. A Party Animal will grab the shoe you just kicked off, steal your sandwich when you turn your back, and dig up the garden after you're through planting. Walks may turn into a chaotic pulling-fest, and while facial licks and crotch sniffing will guarantee new dog friends, few people will be enthused. The good news? Party Animals are smart, loving, and eager to learn!

Please don't confuse their restless neediness for dominance.

HOW MUCH CLOSENESS IS ENOUGH?

Dogs love varying levels of physical closeness, just like people. Party Animals crave physical connection, as do the Head-of-the-Class bunch. Velcro fabric comes to mind—why just sit near you when they can lean up against you? Don't confuse this attachment with dominance. These social dogs do best with lots of displacement activities like bones and interactive toys, positive interactions, and a consistent schedule.

A Laid-Back dog likes to be in the thick of things, although he'll rarely seek out more than a pat on the head. Approach this dog with a chew toy or treats to help him connect loving interactions with good things. Type A's are busy—they prefer chores to rest when people are around. Teach a good Down Stay and use interactive toys as described in Chapter 5 to work out their excessive energy. The Over-Thinkers may also be too caught up in their own thoughts to relax and enjoy soothing interactions, although with positive, calm touches, these dogs can learn to associate safety with loving contact.

They don't want to rule the world; they just get bored easily. Instead of sitting in a corner, they'll act out. Simple tricks can be really useful: Teach your Party Animal to Carry objects (chapter 6) and suddenly you'll have someone to help bring in the groceries, pick up the kids' laundry, and fetch a new diaper!

Laid-Back

This group is even tempered and unconcerned with life's interruptions. Living in the moment, they channel whoever's around and can cope with routine separations. A great choice for busy families, they make loyal and easygoing friends when socialized with children and other pets.

These dogs are not dumb, but they have a hard time understanding the concept of discipline. Their motto? "Don't worry, be happy." Lessons might seem an unnecessary burden, but having a common language with your Laid-Back dog is important. All dogs should know directions like Sit, Stay, and Come. Although long, repetitive lessons may induce temporary narcolepsy, short, rewarding interactions are fun. Offer savory treats, play a game or two that excites your unflappable companion, and schedule outings and lessons before meals.

Head-of-the-Class

This devoted bunch is genuine and eager to learn. Their needy, people-pleasing nature makes lessons breezy and fun. When isolated or ignored, however, these dogs will end up on the naughty list. Without routines and directions to follow, they agonize over what to do with themselves, leading them to act out and draw any attention they can.

Have you ever wondered, as you're correcting your dog over and over for the same thing, if your dog's slow? The reality might be that you have the smartest dog in the class. Your dog might be so desperate for interaction that he'll settle for your frustration over being ignored.

If your dog delights in your homecomings, trails you when you're home, and wags his tail the moment you speak, you're in good shape. With little effort, your annoyance will melt into pride—it's kind of nice to have someone so completely committed to you. Be kind, consistent, and positive during lessons, and your relationship will bloom.

Overthinker

Sharing your life with an overthinker—a dog who thinks twice before reacting—has its pluses. These thoughtful dogs resist chaos, keep to themselves, and don't get caught up in confrontations. Self-preservation is a priority. While these dogs do bond with their family, they don't actively seek relationships outside their group and may not remember occasional guests. If untrained, these dogs may agonize over every new interaction, either freezing up or hiding from new people or situations.

There is an important catch to remember with this group. These dogs can develop paralyzing phobias if undersocialized. If your dog scored high in this category, socialize him and play confidence games with him. Introduce your Thinker to every new person, place, and thing, using savory treats and toys to link new activities to exciting rewards.

Make a list of all your dog's triggers—street grates, manholes, loud equipment, screaming children, raised arms, other dogs, bicycles—and spend days or weeks around those distractions until your dog feels more comfortable with them. If your Thinker ducks behind you on a walk or outing, let him. Do not force him to approach anything he's uncomfortable with. In fact, make a habit of standing between your dog and the distraction and, when possible, model confidence: Step on the grate, pat the neighbor's dog, shake hands with the postman. Help your dog make the association that the world is a safe place. Flip to chapter 8 to gather more tips about working with anxious dogs.

Step 3: Whatever Lifts Your Dog's Tail

Can you list five things that get your dog's tail wagging? Most dogs love food, which makes socialization and early teaching super easy and fun. But what else? How about a special toy, or the sound of your happy voice? My dogs love to play Tug and go for walks or ride in the car. They love to hear me say "Daddy's home!" or "Time to go get the kids!" I have one who loves freedom, and my childhood dog used to love to pull on the leash (she was a husky mix).

Here's a list of other rewards people sometimes don't think of. Each can be used to reward your puppy or dog for a job well done!

FREEDOM **Most dogs love to run free! This reward can be offered with a direction like "Go free!" Just make sure your dog is enclosed or on a long line or retractable leash.**

SCENTS Dogs love to follow scented pathways. This is a great reward after a lesson or leash-walking excursion. I use "Explore!" to let Mojo, our bully breed, know she's free to follow her nose.

PULLING Dogs bred to pull sleds or carts love to pull. If your dog's a draft dog or sled dog wannabe, find a special harness for this purpose and use it after lessons. Hold on tight!

TUG Dogs who love to tug *really* love to tug. It's a great way to play, redirect, and reward your dog, but first, flip to page 124 and teach your dog to release things immediately when directed.

CHASING/RETRIEVE If your dog loves to chase, learn the retrieving game in chapter 5 and use it to reward your dog after a lesson. Indicate your toy with a word like "Ball," "Disc," or "Squeak." You might find, as I did, that for some dogs, nothing gives them more pleasure!

TRICKS I can sense a trick dog a mile away. They bow, they dance, they turn. Most are very paw expressive or like to bark. You can shoot for the moon with these dogs. Teach tricks like Dance, High-Five, and Roll Over, and get yourself an agent. Use trick time to reward your dog for lessons and self-control. You'll find some lessons on tricks at the end of chapter 6.

Each dog has unique likes and dislikes; knowing them gives you a roadmap to a happy life. While you may be disappointed that your retriever doesn't like fetching or your running buddy gets tired after the second mile, look for his hidden talents. You'll find plenty to celebrate.

RATE HIS PRIORITIES

Read over the following questions, circling or numbering priorities. If something doesn't apply to your dog, just write "DA."

WHAT EXCITES YOUR DOG?

Dogs focus on three things with varying enthusiasm: eating, playing, and social interactions. What's most important to your dog?

__Food

__Toys/Play

__Attention

DISCOVER YOUR DOG'S OBSESSION TOY

Most dogs love toys, but not equally. Rate his favorite ones.

__Ball

__Bone

__Rope

__Stuffed Animal

__Anything that squeaks

__ _____ (fill in the blank)

WHEN MEETING A NEW DOG

If your dog is comfortable with other dogs, he probably likes to make new friends. When meeting a new dog, does he:

__Start playing

__Grovel

__Stand still

__Climb onto the other dog's back

__Mount the dog

WHERE IS HIS HAPPY PLACE?

Dogs need a happy place—somewhere that makes them feel safe and free. If your dog could go anywhere, where would he go?

__Home

__Dog park

__Familiar streets or pathways

__Lake, stream, or ocean

__Somewhere brand-new

__The car

WHAT HAPPENS WHEN TWO URGES CONFLICT?

When visiting a new place or taking your dog to the park, offer him a savory treat or favorite toy a few minutes after you arrive. What does he do?

__Snatch the reward quickly

__Ignore the offering and remain with you

__Take it calmly and continue exploring

__Ignore the reward and strain to meet other dogs/people

WHO WOULD YOUR DOG SURROUND HIMSELF WITH?

__Only you

__You and your family

__Family and close friends

__Familiar dogs

__All friendly dogs

__Everyone

__Jumping

__Following a scent

__Alerting you to noises

__Digging

__Chewing

__Retrieving

__Tugging

USE THE RESULTS TO SHAPE YOUR FUTURE

Since your dog can't speak, it's up to you to voice his opinion! Know your dog, separate him from stressful situations, and celebrate his superpowers. No, you don't have to let a jumper lounge on your bed or wipe his muddy paws on your favorite blouse, but all superpowers can be redirected to people-approved activities— because they won't be snuffed out!

Don't fall into the trap of believing that your dog should be good at everything and friendly to everyone. Like kids, they make their own magic and have no issues with their own quirkiness. Reward your dog with his favorite toys, treats, and games, and brighten his week with a visit to his special place.

Now that you've got a handle on your dog's personality, it's time to take a selfie. In chapter 4, we'll look at the different lifestyles and human personality types that affect our furry friends.

4

You Be You

*To be yourself in a world that is constantly trying to make
you something else is the greatest accomplishment.*
—RALPH WALDO EMERSON

When raising a dog, learning what wags her tail is only half
the battle. Knowing who you are and what you want in
your relationship is equally important, too. Whether
you're permissive, detail-oriented, obsessive, or kind, you're okay
just the way you are. Parenting a dog is like parenting a child: You
have to find a style that works for you. Sure, it'd be nice if there
was a one-size-fits-all teaching approach, but there isn't.

If you start out your Happy Dog Adventure Story by comparing yourself to celebrity trainers or your neighbor with a three-
time Agility champion border collie who competes around the
globe and has been on TV, you're going to get disillusioned fast.
Communicating with your dog can feel like you're talking to an

alien at first—just remember that professional dog experts, like superstar athletes, take years to master their art. Your dog doesn't need to learn two hundred words or secure a talent agent or be a therapy dog to be happy. I'll teach you what you need to know in the chapters ahead. You can do this, and I will help.

In this chapter we're going to focus on you. Using quizzes similar to the ones that revealed your dog's personality in chapter 3, we'll learn about you. Sound daunting? I'll make it fun! After getting a handle on your life now and in the future, you'll discover your breed spirit, what I call your Breedology, and learn how your personality will affect your parenting style.

Step 1: Life from Your Perspective

Use this section to get a handle on your life now and in the future. What's going on in your world now, and how will it change one, five, or ten years from now?

PERSONALIZE YOUR WISH LIST

Set some goals for life with your dog. Forget what you "should" do. This is your dog. Talk to everyone in your household and decide on some basic ground rules and habits. Circle your choices in the list below:

DAILY FREEDOM   Inside unless walked   Fenced yard   Free range

SLEEPING   Outdoors   Enclosed away from bedroom   Enclosed in bedroom   On bed   Other_____

POTTY   Inside   Outside   Both

EXERCISE   Yard only   Indoors   Running/hiking   Swimming   Mix/other

TRAINING   Minimal   Basic obedience   Off-leash   Tricks
Pet therapy   Agility/other dog sports   Class/private help

GROOMING   Do it myself   Hire a groomer
Find someone to clip nails

CHILLAXING   Doggie on the floor   Doggie on the couch
Doggie outside

Of course, every choice has its consequences. If you let your dog on the couch, she'll climb right up there with Grandma Ruth. If your kids love feeding your dog from the table, you'll likely be living with a beggar. Don't mind your dog chewing on an old shoe, riding shotgun, or barking when the mailman comes to the door? Including these rituals in your everyday routine communicates that they're okay with you anytime, anywhere. Which is totally fine, unless of course, it's not. You decide.

Lifestyle, Now and in the Future

Consider your life now and ten years down the road. I've listed possible lifestyles below—what'll your next decade bring? Sure, you might be single now, but are you considering family life when you find that special someone? Are kids on the horizon? Maybe you're working now but looking forward to retirement a few years down the line: What will that look like? Socialize your dog or puppy to all the things she'll experience in her lifetime.

SINGLE

You're not getting a dog to simplify your life, right? While a dog can improve your social standing, once you get one you're not really single anymore. In fact, you're now a dog parent, and your dog will depend on you 24/7, every single day of the year, in sickness and in health, whether you're rich or poor. Find backup just in case you're sick, caught in traffic, or traveling. Your dog can't take care of herself. She'll need routine outings, feeding, and exercise.

Now, consider the next decade: Are you engaged, or do you hope to start a family? Socialize your dog with all types of people so she'll embrace the changes as they come.

WORKING PARENTS

Working parents get a bad rap. True, if a dog is left home for hours and hours, day after day, it will go bonkers—that's not good. But most working parents are obsessively aware of their dog-baby's needs, enlisting dog walkers, doggie day care centers, and family members to help out when they're not there.

Whether you work nine to five or from home, organize your dog's schedule and find people to fill in for you when you're not home or are too busy. When possible, bookend your day with two free-play runabouts—either at the dog park, in an enclosure, or on a long line—versus restrictive leash walks.

FAMILY LIFE

Kids are the ultimate game changers. Before motherhood I would spend hours, *hours*, with my dogs. Now, although the dogs are always underfoot and rarely left alone, I'm lucky if I can sneak away for ten minutes with them. Whether you've raised your dog before the kids or are raising them together, each age group has its quirks that dogs need to accept.

Children under two years old

Babies are time vacuums! Before you're forced to choose between rescuing your toddler and walking the dog, set up a schedule ahead of time, and enlist helpers when you need them.

Children two to seven

With this age group, the words "chaos," "perpetual motion," and "demanding an audience" spring to mind. "Mom, look at me climbing up the stairs backward," "Dad, look how fast I can run/

ride my bike/pour tea/fold a napkin." But these kids can take part in feeding and care rituals with supervision. By age seven, children can learn the values of empathy and kindness, too.

Children seven to thirteen

Ahhh, the age of enlightenment. These kids can respect a dog's feelings. This is a huge turning point. Create your Daily Needs Charts (see page 25) together and share responsibilities. Some children may even discover a passion for it!

Children thirteen and up

Teenagers lose sight of everything. Forgive them—their brains are still growing, and life beyond your four walls is more interesting than life within them. While they may still show love and affection for their dog, they just aren't home as much. This inconsistency can be confusing for everyone, but don't press it. Most dogs learn to go with the flow.

RETIRED

The only downside to this phase is that it comes during the second half of life, when the body has trouble keeping up with the spirit. Map out the next ten years, and decide what new things—if any—might come your way. Hoping for grandkids? Planning to downsize? Moving to the city? Get your dog or puppy used to everything so new situations won't add stress.

With a loose and often random schedule, your biggest dilemma might be separation stress. Sound familiar? Although leaving might be optional, your dog will need to cope. Flip to chapter 7 for tips and solutions.

HOME SWEET HOME

It used to be that responsible dog breeders and shelters would only sign off on adoptions if someone was home 24/7. Nowadays, home or not, you can hire dog walkers and day care services to step in for you anytime day or night. Although you might feel guilty that

DID YOU KNOW?

Have you considered who will care for your dog if you're suddenly unable to? In most states you can include your dog in your will. But what if you're only temporarily incapacitated or held up overnight? Search the web or download an app on your smartphone (I use the Pet Home Alone app by Hamilton Law & Mediation) to notify your chosen caregiver if you're in a bind.

HOME LIFE, THEN AND NOW

Back when dogs appeared around our campfires, there were few niches they didn't fill. As our protectors, hunting partners, and waste management centers, it's questionable whether we could have evolved without them. Back then, there were no houses or beds to speak of, no industry or businesses to support, no breed standards to maintain. It was just them and us against the world. And we did good.

Fast-forward to now, and a lot has changed . . . at least in our minds. Here in the twenty-first century, we're hyperconscious, refined, and enlightened (or so we think). Dogs are selectively bred into easily identifiable shapes, sizes, and temperaments. Instead of running free, dogs are locked down, kept inside or behind fences where they're fed balanced diets and offered sterilized toys. It works for us, but less so for dogs. Most dogs still want to go adventuring and defend their home. Stressed by hours of isolation, they long for the freedom to sniff, explore, and scavenge.

you don't have an ideal lifestyle for your dog, the truth is, there isn't one. Sure, farm life sounds dreamy. But I've done the farm thing and spent many nights scrubbing skunk spray out of my dog's fur. City life sounds smoggy and congested, but all those aromas electrify a dog's senses. Every place has its ups and downs. Dogs are very adaptable. Here's a quick look at different living situations. Where do you fit in?

City

City dog lovers can be the most organized, dog-conscientious group and have a built-in socialization system right outside their front door. If you live in a city, start a social group for dog lovers in your neighborhood. Scope out dog-friendly parks, cafés, and restaurants.

Suburbia

The suburbs are a mixed bag for dogs. Yards are fabulous, but unless you fence yours in, supervision is a must. Streets are dangerous—be careful out there. Home alone or left outside, even sweet dogs can become defensive of their space. To offset boredom, socialize your suburban dogs with everyone and everything—from repair people to bikes and other dogs.

Country

Open spaces, cool breezes, shady trees. Heaven. Heaven, that is, until your dog gets into a fight with another dog or tangles with an angry raccoon, snake, skunk, cougar, bear, or porcupine. Country life can be a dog's dream lifestyle if you're aware and mindful of the dangers that surround you. Work hard on directing your dog's prey drive, and keep chipping away at your off-lead Come.

Multihome or Vacation Rental

Your dog can adjust to different homes—just socialize her to the demands of each location. Create a comparison chart that lists the peculiarities of each place.

Step 2: Discover Your Inner Breed

In the last chapter, you learned to accept your dog as she is. Every dog—like every child—is an original, a work of art. Is yours loud, demonstrative, affectionate, unsure, demanding . . . ? What three adjectives best describe your dog?

Now let's take a selfie. Consider how your personality fits into your Happy Dog Adventure Story. What three adjectives best describe *you*? What makes you laugh, feel sad, or want to scream in frustration? How do you soothe yourself or redirect your impulses? Raising a dog isn't easy, but learning to nurture and accept yourself will free up your mind and bring you closer to your dog.

BREEDOLOGY

Let's have fun with this. You can discover a lot about yourself and others by playing a game I call Breedology. Are you feisty or mellow, cheerful or sour, extroverted or introverted? Learning about your dog type will leave you with greater self-awareness and compassion for others, no matter how many legs they walk on.

To start, think through these everyday situations and write down your initial impulses chosen from the list below. After you finish the quiz, tally your score and discover your breed. I've listed six breed types in the Breedology chart on page 100. You can share it with your friends, partner, and kids. What about that barista in the coffee shop—is she an easygoing beagle or a fiery Jack Russell terrier? How about that guy who argued with you over that parking space?

Remember—there are no right or wrong answers. Parenting, no matter what species, is open to everyone.

DISCOVER THE BREED IN YOU

1. Your doorbell rings. You . . .
   a. Stop what you're doing, break all conversations midsentence, and dart to the door to see who's behind it
   b. Finish putting the dishes away, end conversations, then go to the door
   c. Check your look, tidy the area, alert the family

    d. Look out the window to see whose car it is, then gauge your response by who is outside

    e. Do several completely unnecessary chores before going to the door, like watering the plants or rearranging the spice cabinet

    f. Pretend you're not home

2. You just got a new iPad, so you . . .

    a. Show and share with everyone—from friends to curious strangers at the coffee shop. Everybody loves a new toy!

    b. Study the manual until you've mastered it

    c. Take up residence at the nearest Genius Bar until you learn exactly how to use each function, "Oh, so that's how you sync the address book with the calendar with the iMovie with the YouTube channel . . ."

    d. Attack it freestyle

    e. Download a bunch of apps

    f. Hide it where no one can find it

3. You're watching your kid—or a friend's child—and she/he wants to play a make-believe game with farm animals. You . . .

    a. Go along with it, inventing clever voices and names (Sir Oinks-A-Lot and Moosey McGoo)

    b. Engage momentarily, then stop to clean your refrigerator or file your nails or brush the dog

    c. Line the animals up, reorganize the farm's layout, and put the farm feeding on a schedule, taking charge to such a level that the child stops playing, but you continue

    d. Create your own story line involving competition, combat, and challenge

    e. Help decorate each animal enclosure with interactive activities and music

    f. Say no

4. A friend invites you to a party. You . . .

    a. Socialize with everyone and enjoy meeting new friends

    b. Stick with your friend and wait for proper introductions

    c. Start a conversation that attracts a crowd (*Grey's Anatomy*, anyone?)

    d. Talk politics and religion, always taking the opposite opinion just for the fun of it. You like a good argument

    e. Take in the décor, sample the edibles, observe the fashions.

    f. Take a nap on the couch

5. You've gotten into an argument with a friend. You . . .

    a. Text, call, and e-mail, apologizing profusely whether or not it's your fault

    b. Keep trying different approaches until you come to an agreement

    c. Beat the argument to death, then, suddenly, move on

    d. Wait for an apology

    e. Try to understand their point of view and get them to understand yours

    f. Feel indifferent

6. You're in town and want a cup of coffee. You prefer to . . .

    a. Go the nearest coffee shop, look around, and strike up a conversation with the person nearest you

    b. Go to the coffee shop, keeping your gaze in check, sit down with your coffee and paper, and pray you don't see anyone you know

    c. Get your coffee and leave

    d. Go to the McDonald's drive-through to avoid any potential small talk or conversation

    e. Go to the coffee shop, peruse the center kiosk, buy some chocolate for later . . .

    f. Go home and make your own coffee—$3.50 for a latte?

7. You're approached by a stranger's child wandering alone. You . . .

    a. Drop what you're doing, lower your eyes, and talk reassuringly. Poor kid!

    b. Grab the kid and look for the parent

    c. Admonish the stranger for letting his or her child wander

    d. Ignore the kid altogether

    e. Look at the how the child is dressed—is her hair brushed, is her face clean? If she looks hungry, you buy her a snack

    f. Scare the kid to teach her and the parent a lesson about "stranger danger"

8. You're riding on a subway during rush hour. There's only one seat and it's crowded on either side. You . . .

    a. Squish between the two people and start a conversation

    b. Sit down and pull out your iPad

    c. Move into the next car to find a space

    d. Remain standing, get out ASAP, and walk the rest of the way

    e. Sit on the very edge, people watch, and take in the sights and smells around you

    f. Sneeze loudly, without covering your mouth, so people move

9. You're in the grocery store, and you see a stranger drop a carton of blueberries. You . . .

    a. Stop to help him and strike up a conversation

    b. Call for a sales clerk

    c. Roll the berries into a pile and move on

    d. Walk away quickly

    e. Help pick them up and check to see if the berries are ripe, overripe, or a mixed batch. If they're in good shape, you buy your own carton when the clean-up job's done

    f. Stare at the person and quietly judge them

10. You've decorated a cake for your friend's birthday party. You . . .

    a. Lick the icing off the knife and sample the different toppings (strawberry flowers!)

    b. Put it in the fridge. It's for the party!

    c. Leave it out and welcome the compliments. After all, you spent three hours on it!

    d. Reprimand anyone who so much as looks at the cake

e. Stand back, gather some crumbs on the icing knife for a full sample, and take a photo

f. Why would you waste your time decorating a cake?

CATEGORY KEY

a. A sociable, sunny golden retriever

b. A steady Schnauzer

c. A focused border collie

d. A plucky, spirited Jack Russell terrier

e. A sensual beagle

f. An indifferent chow chow

So how do you measure? Were your results consistent, or did you get a varied review? A lot of people are mixed breeds—I am. That's known as hybrid vigor. It's a good thing!

TABLE 4.1 Breedology Chart

GOLDEN RETRIEVER

DISPOSITION: Sunny and cheerful, you're straightforward and fun lovin'! Preferring adventure to thinking and socializing to solitude, you're a sporty golden retriever type.

WITH FAMILY: You can relax with family, enjoying meals and cheerful interactions. You tend to zone out of disputes and prefer laughter and love to confrontation.

SOCIABILITY: Nothing lifts your metaphoric tail faster than making new friends, no matter how many paws they walk on!

UNLEASHED: Free to go where you please, you'd beeline it to the beach, preferring to make new friends rather than explore on your own.

SIMILAR BREEDS: Other retrievers, Cavalier King Charles spaniel, Newfoundland, well-socialized bully breeds

SCHNAUZER

DISPOSITION: Diligent and serious when focused, you can enjoy a little downtime as long as a good day's work is done.

WITH FAMILY: After a day's work, you can slip into relax mode but generally prefer activities that disengage your brain (TV, computer) over ones that require interaction.

SOCIABILITY: Like the herder, you have little time for sociability but can tolerate meeting and engaging others if the purpose of doing so is well defined.

UNLEASHED: Though interested in the world around you, you rarely stray far from home. You are loyal and committed to those you love and don't often roam unless something captures your full attention.

SIMILAR BREEDS: Boxer, Doberman pinscher, Siberian husky, Saint Bernard, Portuguese water dog, mastiff breeds

BORDER COLLIE

DISPOSITION: You have a strong, intelligent mind-set. Focused on your life's ambition, you set to one task and can be obsessive, unyielding, and a little snappy if prevented from pursuing your vision.

WITH FAMILY: You prefer predictable interactions and see little need for socializing outside of work. You thrive at home, preferring familiar surroundings to new adventures. You do best one-on-one or in structured groups.

SOCIABILITY: You see little need for seeking new friendships. Your life's purpose is your work. Vacations are stressful, excursions are pointless, new adventures are boring.

UNLEASHED: You'd go back home or gather your group around and fret over when you could go home.

SIMILAR BREEDS: German shepherd, Shetland sheepdog, Bouvier des Flandres, Belgian Malinois

JACK RUSSELL TERRIER

DISPOSITION: Spirited, determined, and feisty, you take a bite out of life and hold on tight. Independent and alert, you can ignore the pain when you're set on a task.

WITH FAMILY: Downtime? What downtime? You have two speeds: active and overactive. Thrill seeking and physical endurance excite you whether at home or on family adventures.

SOCIABILITY: You could live without stuffy social encounters and group activities. High-risk adventure—pushing yourself—is life's greatest thrill.

UNLEASHED: See you later! Off-leash, wild, and free is the only way to live, although you find your way home when you get hungry or need a good snooze.

SIMILAR BREEDS: Soft-coated Wheaten terrier, Airedale terrier, West Highland white terrier, Border terrier

BEAGLE

DISPOSITION: Spiritual and happy, you live to follow your sensual desires. You are creative and outgoing and enjoy everyone's company but can let life and all its sensual pleasures lead you away.

WITH FAMILY: Activities are more fun if they engage your senses. Cooking, music, and lovely visions leave you in your happy place.

SOCIABILITY: Life is far more fun in a group.

UNLEASHED: As an adventure seeker, you'll scan high and low for a thrill. Your never-say-quit attitude may lead you down the wrong path more than once!

SIMILAR BREEDS: Basset hound, Irish wolfhound, dachshund, whippet, Afghan hound

CHOW CHOW

DISPOSITION: You're aloof and have no issue with what other people think of you. Proud and confident, you're surprised that people find your lack of empathy uncaring. You care—you're just too busy to get touchy-feely. Seriously, all that emotional gush is a little embarrassing.

WITH FAMILY: Your family is about all you can tolerate. And you often get tired of having to cope with them. Love, yes, but you still need your personal space.

WHO AM I?

I'm a self-proclaimed mutt—a border collie/golden retriever mix: a Golly! At times, my eagerness overwhelms people, and then suddenly, I can set to a task with unshakable focus. My husband would swear I have some terrier in my bloodlines, especially when I'm overtired!

SOCIABILITY: Socializing is just not your thing. When forced to, you're perceived as snobbish, but it's more because you feel awkward than superior. Chatting with strangers . . . really, what's the point?

UNLEASHED: Off-leash you'd choose the solitude of the mountains or a snow-capped ledge, finding a nice private spot to survey the valley or take a snooze in the sun.

SIMILAR BREEDS: Lhasa apso, Tibetan mastiff, shar-pei, Pekingese

BEYOND BREEDOLOGY

Within each breed, there's always the question of personality types. In chapter 3, we categorized dogs as being Type A's, Party Animals, Laid-Back, Head-of-the-Class, or Over-Thinkers. Now the question begs—who are you?

THE DOG PARENT PERSONALITY QUIZ

Use this quiz to get a handle on your personality type and parenting style. You might find that you react differently with your dog than with your family and friends. It's not uncommon; raising a dog can feel really awkward at first.

As you're reading through the questions below, imagine experiencing the situation firsthand.

1. When you come home, you'd like a dog who . . .
    a. Sits still until you pet her
    b. Grabs a toy and runs around

    c. Rolls over for a belly rub

    d. Jumps up for attention

    e. Not sure what to expect

2. When walking a dog, you envision . . .

    a. Training her to walk behind you

    b. Letting her greet people and other dogs

    c. Walking at her pace, stopping to let her sniff around

    d. Letting her pull you, comforting her when she is upset or angry

    e. Not sure what to expect

3. When you sit down to dinner, you'd like your dog to . . .

    a. Sit on a mat or go into a crate

    b. Hang out under the table

    c. Go wherever she wants

    d. Chew a bone, eat her own meal, or play with a toy

    e. Not sure what to expect

4. For fun with your dog, you would . . .

    a. Explore Agility or other organized group activities

    b. Play games like Chase, Retrieve, or Tug-of-War

    c. Go for a walk or play

    d. Play with toys or get a small swimming pool for your dog

    e. Not sure what to do

5. When company comes over and your dog jumps on them for attention, you would . . .

    a. Physically try to get your dog to stop

    b. Laugh, pull your dog away, and give her a toy

    c. Try to ignore the situation

    d. Give your dog a toy

    e. Not sure what to do

6. If you arrive home late from an outing and find your dog has pooped on the carpet, you would . . .

    a. Be furious

    b. Find something funny about it to tell other people

c. Clean it up

d. Feel bad for your dog

e. Not sure what to do

7. In the early days of having your dog or puppy, you . . .

   a. Created a detailed schedule and hired dog helpers to keep you on track

   b. Did the best you could to follow a schedule

   c. Didn't really have a schedule

   d. Had a hard time putting your dog in the crate or leaving her alone

   e. Felt daily stress

8. You're sitting quietly reading or watching TV, and suddenly your dog jumps up and barks frantically at the window. You . . .

   a. Scream at her or put her in her crate

   b. Laugh and call her over

   c. Wait until she stops

   d. Pet her lovingly as you tell her nothing's out there

   e. Not sure what to do

9. When you weren't paying attention, your dog sat in a puddle and is now covered in mud. You . . .

   a. Curse, yell at, and/or haul the dog in for a shower or hosing-down

   b. Laugh and clean off the dog

   c. Leave the dog outside and wait until someone can help you clean off the dog

   d. Admire your dog for cooling herself off and having fun before cleaning her

   e. Not sure what to do

10. Your dog keeps escaping upstairs and chewing the kids' toys or your favorite pillows. You . . .

    a. Get a shock collar or call a trainer to help teach your dog to stop

b. Find humor in it, teach the kids to pick up their toys, and look for help online or with a trainer

c. Clean it up and move on

d. Buy more chew toys and clean up the kids' rooms

e. Not sure what to do

TALLY YOUR RESULTS

___ a

___ b

___ c

___ d

___ e

Where do you fit? Although you might lean toward one type of reaction, most people get a mixed score. Mixed is good—it shows insight. A one-size-fits-all approach rarely works well when dealing with dogs or people.

FIVE PERSONALITY TYPES

Each letter corresponds with five common dog-parenting styles described below.

a. Detail-oriented

b. Comic

c. Relaxed

d. Comforting

e. Unsure

Detail-oriented

Detail-oriented people—aka perfectionists—have strong opinions and get a lot done. Great at organizing everyone's schedules, they keep things running smoothly if allowed to make all the decisions. However, they are easily frustrated, especially when ignored. Detail-oriented people have a low tolerance for chaos, disrespect, and inactivity.

On the plus side

Dogs benefit from an organized schedule. Consistent expectations help dogs know how to behave, how to earn praise and goodies, and where they fit in.

Of course

Life is not all about details. The Detailed person's challenge is to learn when to steer and when to let their dog relax and have fun.

Comic

Comic people see humor in everything and are happiest when people (and dogs) get along. Generally uncomfortable in the control seat, they recognize good habits but don't always reinforce them. Even when their dog's behavior demonstrates emotional stress—like chronic barking or destructive chewing—they have a greater tendency to laugh it off than to look at the deeper issues.

On the plus side

Comic personalities can find humor in just about anything, from toilet training to counter cruising, and rarely lose their temper unless an issue becomes a glaring behavior problem.

Of course

Someone needs to play the grown-up! Dogs, like kids, like to know where to go and what to do, and if the Comic doesn't create rituals, her dog will feel lost.

Relaxed

Relaxed people have a calming effect on everyone around them. As self-appointed peacemakers, they are happier watching life unfold and responding to other people's needs than making waves.

On the plus side

Relaxed people are easy to get along with and mindful of everyone's needs.

Of course

Dogs—especially as puppies—need a lot of direction. If no one takes action, a dog's curiosity can lead to trouble. What might seem like bad behavior might just be a curious dog poking around.

Comforting

Comforting people are nurturing, soft-spoken, and persistent. They enjoy taking care of other people, often at a cost to themselves.

On the plus side

Comforting people make wonderful parents, no matter what the species. They can soothe upset feelings with a touch. Their gentle hands, warm tone, and do-whatever-it-takes approach make everyone feel better—dogs included!

Of course

Prolonged eye contact, high-pitched tones, and deflated body postures, while reassuring to a person or child, read less confidently to the dog who isn't listening to what a Comforting person is saying so much as watching their body language.

Unsure

Life with a dog can get very confusing, especially if you've never had one before or if your first dog was easy and this one isn't. Either way, if you're Unsure, you are definitely not alone.

On the plus side

If you feel uncertain, don't be discouraged. Unsure dog owners are some of my favorite clients: They are steady, responsive, and follow directions well.

Of course

Beware the blank stare! It's okay to have those deer-in-the-headlights, I-have-no-idea-what-to-do-next feelings, but fake it until you make it with your dog. A blank stare is hard to read and a little scary.

Remember, there's no perfect personality for raising a dog. Sure, Detail-oriented people are super organized. You might think they'd be the best dog owners—and they would be for the right dog—but a shy dog needs more empathy and could buckle under the demands of a Detail-oriented parent. A Relaxed type is a good match for a Laid-Back dog, but what if they fall for a dog who is an Over-Thinker? These dogs need direction and reassurance, which are not a Relaxed type's strong suits.

Step 3: Borrow from the Best

If you've discovered that your personality type doesn't quite match your dog's personality, don't despair. Two of my four rescues, Hootenanny and Boozle, aren't a perfect match—Boozle's an Over-Thinker, while Hoots is a Party Animal. Both personalities irk my Detail-oriented personality type. I felt guilty when we first adopted them, thinking they would do better with a Relaxed mommy. But then I sat myself down and talked to myself like a client. "Sarah,"

I said, "you need to make a few minor adjustments." And I did. I coached myself to turn away when Hootenanny baited me, tail held high, with a dead frog or sock dangling from her mouth. I use my happy jolly voice with Boozle when he freezes with some imaginary concern. Nurturing these two—taking time to experience life from their paws—helped me understand how neglectful beginnings can stick with dogs long after they're rehomed. I'm a better person for meeting them at their level and practicing patience instead of losing my temper. You will be, too.

If you're concerned about how you'll cope, try the Borrow-from-the-Best Challenge. Check out table 4.2 and pair up your personality with your dog's to discover what you can do to reconnect with your loving feelings. For example, you have a Type A dog who is smart, eager, and hyperresponsive. But you're a Comforter—more into reassurance than organizing activities. Read through how other people deal with Type A dogs and borrow a strategy they use to help you out. You might use a schedule from a Detail-oriented person's calendar. On the other hand, maybe you're the super-organized one with a Laid-Back dog. Print out the body cues in chapter 2 (obvious to Comforters, but not to you) and be mindful of your dog's mood and reactions. Modify your demands to help your dog understand how to fit in with your family.

QUICK TIPS FOR EACH PERSONALITY

Here are some quick tips for each personality type.

Detail-oriented

If you're a Detail-oriented person, learn your dog's postures and tail talk (chapter 2), and borrow some of the Comforter's nurturing impulses.

Comic

Comics often wait until their dog is totally out of control to step in and fix the situation. If you've got a funny bone, don't let

TABLE 4.2

PERSON/ DOG	TYPE A	PARTY ANIMAL	LAID-BACK	HEAD-OF-THE CLASS	OVER-THINKER
Detail-oriented	This can be a match made in heaven or a personality clash. Channel your dog's interests and motivations, and work together on exercises and games you'll both enjoy.	Detail-oriented people depend on rules; Party Animals like to bend them. Find humor in their antics, and channel their enthusiasm to an activity you both can enjoy!	These dogs move to their own rhythm and can provide good emotional therapy for detailed-oriented people, if those people can let go of the need to control.	Smart and eager to please, Heads-of-the-Class can get stressed if demands are too high or corrections are harsh. Focus on positive efforts and reward accomplishments.	Over-Thinkers are pleasing and sweet. But overwhelmed by demands, they will become anxious. These dogs need a kind and gentle approach to feel safe and happy.
Comic	Type A dogs need lots of direction. Comic people prefer laughter to structure, but humor aside, they need to provide a plan. Without it, their dogs may develop annoying habits like barking, chewing, and jumping.	Here is an entertaining union! When this fun-loving pair bonds, they can have a lot of fun or self-destruct. Party Animals still need to learn basic directions like Sit, Stay, and Come.	Funny people are quick thinking and responsive; Laid-Back dogs are the opposite. This can be a great match if the dog's tempo is appreciated, or disappoint-ing if they are viewed as slow or stupid.	Heads-of-the-Class like clear direction and may be confused by a Comic's slant. If humor rewards good behavior and lessons teach the dog where to go and what to do, then all is well. If not, the dog will end up misbehaving to get attention.	Over-Thinkers need reassurance and guidance more than comedy. Anxiety is no laughing matter. Use rewards to encourage self-esteem, and save the comedy for your own species.
Relaxed	Here's a funny mismatch. Type A dogs are eager, intelligent, and driven. Relaxed people are the opposite. In this situation,	Party Animals may run circles around Relaxed parents. What begins as a hilarious antic, e.g., stealing the toilet paper, gets old fast.	Here's a happy pair: low stress on either end of the leash. A little basic training will provide a common language and a daily routine. If	Heads-of-the-Class constantly wonder what's expected from them and need direction. Relaxed people prefer others take	Over-Thinkers need direction to feel safe. Relaxed people can be carefree and unstructured, often dropping the ball with this

TABLE 4.2 (continued)

PERSON/ DOG	TYPE A	PARTY ANIMAL	LAID-BACK	HEAD-OF-THE CLASS	OVER-THINKER
	Borrow-from-the-Best to become the parent your dog needs you to be.	Be sure to teach your dog good manners.	frustrations arise, a few changes in the routine should solve the issue.	charge. If no one takes the lead, the Head-of-the-Class will stress and develop bad habits in their demand for recognition.	group. Over-Thinkers become overanxious when their feelings are ignored.
Comforting	Type A's may see too much comforting as a sign of insecurity, leading to reactivity (think barking and leash lunging) and resource guarding with food, objects, and resting spots.	Party Animals tend to run circles around their do-no-wrong parents. Adoring yet mischievous, the Party Animal may jump, tug, and grab-'n'-go to get more attention. Comforters, take note: This group needs direction!	Laid-Back dogs revel in Comforting parents. Comforters have low expectations and love nurturing their dogs. Laid-Back dogs ask for little more. Training is important, as it provides a common language.	Heads-of-the-Class can get confused by too much comfort. Addicted to learning, they need direction, lessons, and positive reinforce-ment. Teach first, then comfort for a job well done!	Over-Thinkers can confuse comforting with timidity. Comforters need to pay special attention to posture and tone to give an air of authority when Over-Thinkers are overwhelmed.
Unsure	Type A's need a plan; Unsure parents haven't got one—at least initially. With professional help, however, Unsure parents can learn to take charge.	Party Animals take advantage of Unsure parents who are charmed by their dog's sense of humor. Professional help may be necessary to take control of this situation.	Laid-Back dogs are forgiving and self-directed. They are often the easiest match for first-time dog people or those who feel unsure about their responsi-bilities.	Heads-of-the-Class are both eager and watchful. Unsure people often give mixed signals or none at all, leaving their dog in a state of total confusion. Professional help might be necessary.	Unsure parents can unnerve Over-Thinkers. They need confident direction and become nervous in unfamiliar situations. Unsure parents may need help to prevent anxiety and reactivity.

bad routines become habits! Borrow a schedule from the Detail-oriented type's handbook, and stick to a plan.

Relaxed

Relaxed people are easy to be around, but they can overlook important signals from their dog and their surroundings. Check out the Detail-oriented person's day schedule, and look for some tips from the Comforters. Memorizing postures and ear positions from chapter 2 will help you tune into your dog when she's reactive.

Comforting

While there is a time and a place for loving interaction, strong reactions, e.g., meeting new dogs or people or visiting someplace new, require someone to take charge. When dogs are stressed, they need direction. Borrow a page from the Detail-oriented hand-book, and you'll have the perfect blend of structure and kindness!

Unsure

Unsure dog owners aren't necessarily hesitant all the time. They're often compassionate with family or detail-oriented at work. If that sounds like you, learn about dogs' social skills, and borrow from a little of each category until you find a rhythm that works.

So there you have it. You are as important a player in your Happy Dog Adventure Story as your dog. And while you don't have to change who you are, loving your dog might mean you'll need to make some small adjustments to what you're doing. That is, after all, what all good parents do—set aside their differences and de-sires to take care of those they love.

PART TWO

Don't Dominate, Communicate!

Now that you've finished touring Doglandia, you're ready to teach your puppy or dog words and household etiquette—however you define it! First, we'll focus on your vision: Do you want your dog to live free in your home, outside, or just downstairs; on or off the furniture; tagging along with you or content to stay at home? If loved, nurtured, and taught a common language, your dog can adjust to any lifestyle and schedule. Although there are a few musts, like teaching Drop to release objects and Come when encouraged, you get to decide how to plan your life together. Gather your family and friends and talk it through—what's most important to you?

Although there will be times when you and your dog don't see eye to eye, learning shouldn't be a struggle. I've made a passion and an art of creating a learning platform that both dogs and people enjoy. Follow my Five-Step Learning Strategy to bring love and laughter to your teaching protocol. It's an accelerated approach that works on dogs of all ages, breeds, and personality types. You'll love it, too! Lessons are presented in short three- to five-minute bursts buffered by encouragement that will leave your dog wanting more. You might notice that your dog starts to prompt you with her new manners. Learning is fun, fast-tracked, and addictive!

I also take a fresh and fun approach in the problem-solving chapters, with science once again backing me up. Let me help you tackle everything from proper greeting manners to housetraining, chewing habits, separation stress, and much more. Dogs, like kids, like routines. It's easy to find solutions once you establish good habits and consistency with everyone involved!

With my encouragement as your copilot, you'll learn how to use your words as a road map to develop a a future where the certainties of love guide you and your dog happily down the road of life together.

Love doesn't stop when lessons start!

5

Three Secrets
for a Happy Life

Believe You Can and You're Halfway There.
—THEODORE ROOSEVELT

There are three secrets to leading a happy life. We'll cover them all here and then thread them into the learning and problem-solving chapters. But first, see if you can you guess what they are. They're as universal to people as they are to dogs—to every species, really.

The three secrets for a happy life are good eats, good fun, and good company. A well-balanced life that includes all three is blessed indeed. You might notice that I left out lessons. Your dog doesn't need a lengthy vocabulary list or competitive prizes to be happy. Celebrating over good food, fun times, and positive social experiences, on the other hand, is a must.

Secret #1: Food

Your dog's first meal came right on the heels of life itself, when Mama's sweet elixir filled his belly until it dripped from his chin. Achieving that full-belly feeling is a primal urge. If you want your dog to love and trust you, to race to your outstretched hands, feed him good, nutritious food, and—initially, anyway—feed him by hand. It's not enough to say we love them; dogs like proof!

If you've got a new puppy, feeding him by hand will help with many things. First and foremost, he'll bond to you instantaneously. Let your puppy snuggle into you as you deliver each piece of kibble. Second, use food to condition the habits you choose right from the start. Don't want a jumping dog? Then don't feed your puppy until he's on all four paws. Don't want a barker? Walk away when he barks for second helpings.

Feed your puppy while he's chewing his own toys, laying on his bed, and licking you or the kids, and you'll inspire him to do it again. You won't need to hand-feed him forever, but do so as often as you can initially. Of course, if your dog growls or snaps over his rations, you've got a problem. Stop and reach out to a lifeline—a friend or professional—who knows how to help.

If you've rescued a dog or are turning a fresh page with one you already love, remove the bowls for a week or two. There's no rule saying you must feed a dog from a dish. Inspire your dog to earn his food by offering you a variety of behaviors. Initially you might get some you don't like—like barking, whining, or pawing. That's all fine: You can extinguish those habits quickly. Just ignore your dog or walk away. If you catch your dog sitting, resting on his dog bed, or playing with his toys, however, feed him quickly. Then watch—he'll do it again. Now, let's say he's playing with a ball or horsing around with a squeak toy. Ask him to Drop It as you whip out a handful of breakfast. Praise him and toss the toy again. It's learning the fun way.

Hand-feeding adult dogs helps them form new associations

THE DOG DISH MYTH

The dog dish is a relatively new accessory on our timeline. While I'm the first to spot a clever dish design, my dogs would be just as happy if I still fed them kibble by kibble or portioned out each meal in their puzzle toys. Their favorite winter game is Toss-'n'-Go, when I open the door, fling a scoopful of food into the snow, and then release them to go find their meal.

to hands and the people who operate them. Dogs that have been grabbed, slapped, or poked grow wary of hands and study our faces to predict what we're planning to do when we reach out. This high-alert state isn't good for dogs or people. You want your dog to feel happy when he sees hands reaching out to touch him.

Once your puppy or dog welcomes your gifts and responds with self-control, invite everyone—friends, family, and strangers—to participate in mealtimes. Hand-feeding will also help you shape a gentle mouth, good manners, and impulse control (more on these in Chapter 6), but for now, just bond. Bond, baby, bond.

Secret #2: Play

The second secret to a happy life is play. Laughter and fun are marvelous spirit boosters for both dogs and people. Don't have time to play? The joke might be on you: Dogs are addicted to playing and can make up games you never saw coming. Ever get suckered into chasing your dog around the coffee table or playing can't-catch-me tag, even when you're twenty minutes late for work? You might think your dog's having a good time, but it'd be more enjoyable if you chose a game you both liked to play. Pick some of the games described on page 122 and teach your dog the rules. I'll show you how!

Just about anything goes for play, but do check your competitive

DO DOGS LAUGH?

Yes, in fact, they do. And like kids, dogs learn better when they're having a good time. My friend and colleague Stanley Coren taught me how, standing inside the Pennsylvania Hotel in New York City one February evening just before the Westminster Kennel Club Dog Show. He informed me that "Patricia Simonet at Sierra Nevada College in Lake Tahoe did a study where she recorded sounds made during play at a dog park. She noticed the sounds—which sounded like normal panting—were actually faster and more patterned breaths, as though the dogs were laughing."

"Here, do this," Stanley directed me, parting his mouth slightly and pursing his lips. "Now breathe quickly and make a *huhh, huhh, huhh* sound." Reaching over to lay an index finger on my larynx, he corrected me: "It's all in your mouth—don't bring the air into your throat." I swear, twenty of the world's top show dogs stopped in their tracks, looked up at us, and wagged their tails.

impulses at the door and have some fun. You don't need to win at everything or correct every infraction. Dogs who jump during play or hang onto toys can be encouraged to learn better self-control without the use of force (see tug-of-war), but don't quash your dog's enthusiasm for being with you by being too serious.

Dogs have unique playing styles that depend on their age, breed, and life experience. There are three categories of play behavior:

PARALLEL PLAY is when you play alongside your dog using multiple objects rather than interact with him more directly. Ideal for eight- to twelve-week-old babies, children under the age of ten, or anxious dogs who aren't sure of themselves.

INTERACTIVE GAMES are fun toys and games you play together like Tug and Retrieve. These are great energy burners!

STRUCTURED GAMES like Find It and Name Games boost impulse control and self-restraint.

FIVE RULES OF PLAY

1. Play must be fun for both players.

2. Play involves give and take. Sometimes you win, other times you let your dog win.

3. Play is never about who's in charge. Check your competitive impulses.

4. Play stops if someone gets hurt.

5. End a good game with social bonding, a light snack, a drink, and/or a few moments of calm side-by-side affection.

Avoid staring directly at your dog while playing with him. Dogs only stare each other down when they're battling or involved in tough play. If you stare, your dog might zip frantically around the yard, snap when you approach, or look back at you with a confused gaze. Lots of people misinterpret this as spite: "He knows what I want, he just won't listen." But your dog doesn't know why you're staring, and you're freaking him out. Staring positions you as an oppressor. Your dog's not your enemy. If he looks scared or defensive, back off. Walk away and give yourself a time-out.

Instead, link your gazes with food, toys, and calm affection (see chapter 2 for tips on giving gentle hugs) to convey your love. It's better for your dog to sense that the safest place is at your side.

Play-Centric Learning

Dogs can learn a lot of habits and words through play—you decide what to encourage. Want to speed up word response or teach your dog better impulse control? Discover how games and learning go hand-in-hand to redirect frustrating habits in table 5.1.

Remember circling your dog's favorite activities and discovering his number one superpower at the end of chapter 2? Now it's

TABLE 5.1

FRUSTRATING HABITS	IMPULSE CONTROL
Your dog jumps up or grabs toys from your hand.	Before you toss a toy, have your dog Sit or Stand calmly.
Your puppy or dog runs away when you call him.	Say "Come" each time your dog runs over for a treat or toy.
Your dog won't let go of the toy when playing Tug.	Teach Give while playing Tug so your dog learns a release word, too.
Chase is an out-of-control-fun game that your dog learns to play by grabbing any object that will fit in his mouth.	Assign words to end and redirect a structured game of Chase.

time to use your results to find games that'll leave you both smiling. Here are a few of my favorites:

TWO-BALL TOSS

This one's a good choice for kids and people who are still a little unsure of how to play with a dog. Dog-wise, this game is great for socially challenged dogs, and puppies who are socially unaware (until fourteen to sixteen weeks) or are too nervous or assertive to play interactively yet. Newly rescued dogs often fall into this category. Here's how it goes:

ENERGY BUSTERS

I call games that involve tons and tons of action "energy busters." Long-distance ball throws, bike rides, and safe off-leash adventures are great energy busters. When his energy is used up outside, your dog is more relaxed at home.

Too many energy busters, though, and you run the risk of conditioning a professional athlete—one who need lots of stimulation to be satisfied. Limit your energy busting to two or three days a week and before major holidays or parties so your dog will stay calm when his home is anything but!

Take two objects that excite your dog, identical ones, if possible. We'll use two identical balls in the example here.

Get your dog or puppy excited by waving the ball around and saying "Ball!"

If your dog jumps, freeze, lift the ball up and away, and look at the ceiling. Wait until his excitement passes.

Introduce the toy again. If your dog knows Sit or Wait (see chapter 6), ask him to do so before the first toss.

As you throw the ball, say something like "Go get your ball!"

Praise your dog as he runs toward the ball.

Some dogs will bring objects back to you; others won't. For now it doesn't matter—retrieving is not the point.

The moment your dog or puppy turns around, pull out the second toy. Now look and toss that one up in the air. Ignore your dog completely. Don't stare, wave, or holler at him. Pretend that the second ball is made of gold!

If your dog comes running back, ball in mouth, great. Teaching him to retrieve (described on page 125) will be a snap. For now, it's your dog that has a problem, not you. He has a ball, but you have a better one. Hmmm. What to do? Your dog or puppy may either jump or try to snatch it. Turn slightly, ignore him, and keep playing with your ball. Or maybe he'll race by or run away, pretending to ignore you. That's okay, too. Just toss the ball in the opposite direction and play on your own. Two can play at this game.

If he drops the first ball and looks at you, he wants your ball. Yours is better; that much is clear. Now's your chance!

The moment your dog stands calmly in front of you, toss the second ball. Then pick up the first toy and start over!

See this game in action at ModernDogParenting.com /Tricks&Games.

TUG

Dogs love to tug. If you don't like the idea of tugging together, hang a toy from a tree branch or secure one to a banister (although nothing beats playing your favorite game with the one you love—just saying). Here are tips to make it fun for both of you:

> Pocket some tasty treats, like freeze-dried meat or jerky rather than dry dog biscuits.

> Take out a toy with good tug potential—a long rope or fabric toy, a cloth Frisbee, or a lengthy squeak toy. It should be long enough that your fingers won't get chomped accidentally. Wave the toy in front of your dog or puppy.

> Your dog may pause or even back away. Perhaps you've discouraged tugging. It won't take much to tempt him, though. Gently wiggle the toy in his mouth to encourage a tug. Praise the slightest pull.

Once your dog gets the point, teach him two prompts: "Give" and "You Win!"

GIVE

To teach him to let go, pull a treat out, say "Give," and wave the treat in front of his nostrils until he drops whatever is in his mouth. Do this religiously for several days, then gradually replace snacking with praise. Another technique to teach Give is to play with a so-so tug toy, then wave a more treasured toy in front of your dog, saying "Give" as he spits out the first one.

YOU WIN!

I like to let my dogs win. I'm happy to play the sucker for my kids, too. I know lots of people say you should never let dogs win,

TUG-OF-WAR AND CHILDREN

Before letting the kids play tug-of-war, be sure to teach your dog self-restraint and a release cue like Give. If you're concerned your dog is a little too possessive or assertive, and is still nipping you or your family, skip to chapter 7 and refer to the section on mouthing. Wait until you've got a handle on it or skip this game altogether. All children should be able to end the game by saying "Give" or "You win!"

but what fun is that? Try not to overthink it. Dogs, like people, like to win sometimes. This one's easy—just say "You Win!" and let go!

RETRIEVE

I always break this game into three parts and teach each part separately. Professionals call it chaining. Let's give it a whirl!

Give

The first step is to teach the release. Look above under Tug for directions on Give. I like "Give" to mean "in my hand" and another word like "Drop" to mean "wherever I tell you." This is important if your dog is around kids or socializing with other people. For a visualization of each, visit ModernDogParenting .com/Tricks&Games. To teach Give:

Find a secluded room or quiet hallway, just you and your dog. Bring a couple of his favorite things and some treats.

Encourage him to take the toy by tossing it up in the air or bouncing it in place.

If he grabs it, praise him, and let him keep the toy as you congratulate him on what a nice dog he is.

After five to ten seconds, whip out a snack, say "Give" as you present your open palm beneath his mouth, and wave the snack under his nose. If he's a food snob, use a second toy instead.

Do it again but without the hand under his chin, say "Give," and reward him for doing that.

Vary the Give/Drop sequence.

Bring

There's a little aerobic activity involved in teaching this part of Retrieve. Since running straight at people is scary for dogs, the best way to teach Bring is for you to run away from him. First practice in a small room or hallway. Put some yummy goodies or a favorite toy in your pocket and go find your dog.

Show him you've got the goods, then run away calling his name. Make silly sounds or clap to amp his enthusiasm as you hightail it in the opposite direction.

Extend your treat as you turn to stop, but withhold it until he's standing or sitting calmly.

Take one of your dog's favorite toys into a hallway or larger room. Show him the toy to excite him.

Give the toy a toss, then once he's got a good hold on it, say "Bring" as you run away from your dog.

When he comes to you, treat, and request either Give—drop it in my hand—or Drop—drop it on the floor.

Gradually extend the toss, running away from your dog as you tell him to Bring.

Go Get It

If retrieving seems inconceivable or pointless to your dog, see if he'll mimic you. Throw the toy and chase it yourself, or play with a family member, friend, or other dog. Say "Go get it," toss the toy, and send your new partner out. Reward them with a treat so your dog will see good things come to those who play!

KICKBALL

When I was a kid in the 1970s, all the neighborhood kids would gather after school to play kickball. Dogs would come around, too, but only one would play—my dog Shawbee. I taught her how to block second base.

Your dog can learn certain ball games, too. Soccer and lacrosse are all the rage these days, and football and Frisbee are also great choices. Just teach him the rules, and I guarantee he'll love participating!

When playing ball games with your dog, use Get the Ball to mean just that, Wait to tell him to freeze, and Away to back him away from the ball or the players. If grabbing the ball is important, then teach a quick Give, too (see page 125).

Start your lesson with two identical toys:

Since dogs can get overexcited in play, teach your dog to Wait before rushing in. Ask a friend to kick the ball around while you hold your dog on the sidelines and give him treats. Say "Wait," then treat, "Wait," then treat, and continue until Wait ensures pause and focus.

Teach your dog Back by playing one-on-one. Hold the ball or step on it. Say "Back" and toss some treats behind his tail. If he runs back, kick the ball! Do this until it's routine. Now say "Back" and toss a treat a little farther. If your dog's not interested in treats, use a second ball. When your dog turns to face you, throw/kick your ball. Don't worry if he doesn't bend it like Beckham just yet—just help him learn to run back when you say "Back."

Now pair a word with the most exciting move of all—playing! You won't need any treats for Get the Ball!

TAG

Dogs love Tag, and you can play it with just a few dog-savvy modifications. When you're "it," hold a toy or treat to focus your dog so he doesn't jump and grab you in all the excitement. Then say "Can't catch me" as you dart away. Always chase at an angle, and never stare. Sound complicated? It's not—it's just plain fun!

Dogs like when games go back and forth. Tag should start with a stooped, quasi-play bow posture and laughing noises described in the box on page 120. If your dog looks dazed, scared, or confused (see chapter 2), don't continue. If he gets excited and runs from you, tail in the air and mouth relaxed, chase him around for a bit. End whenever you like—you don't need to tag to win. To signal Game Over, fish a few treats out of your pocket and slow down to a stop. Request Sit, say "Game over," and reward and praise your dog calmly. Play is fun, but it can be a little tiring, too!

The beauty of this game is that the reward also teaches impulse control. When it's Game Over, your dog will stop because you've got what he wants. Don't give him the reward until he's standing or sitting still.

Stop the game if your dog tries to catch you with his mouth; get help for mouthing and other predatory-like behaviors in chapter 7.

HIDE-AND-SEEK

Here's one kids love! Although it sounds straightforward, teaching your dog to scout around for you or other family members is a little perplexing in the beginning. If you're playing one-on-one, hide just out of sight and shake a treat cup to provide a clue to your location.

If you're playing with a friend or family member, use Hide-and-Seek to teach your dog to identify people by name. Tell the person hiding to call out to your dog when they hear you say their name. Say "Go find Mark!" or "Go find Daddy!," prompting the identified person to call out and shake a treat cup to give your dog hints!

It's fun to teach dogs to find things. This game caters to your dog's superior sense of smell, so he'll love it, too. Once your dog learns how to play, he'll be real asset around your home. You can teach him to find things like your keys, cell phone, or your toddler's favorite binky. We had a bat problem, so I taught my little guy Boozle to Find Bat Guano, aka bat poop. As far as I know, he's the only Bat Detection Dog on the East Coast. Teaching this game is easy and fun!

> **Take a smelly food treat and ask your dog to sniff it.**
>
> **If your dog knows how to Sit and Stay, great—do that. If not, ask a helper to hold him as you hide the treat around a corner. Create a scent trail by waving the morsel in the air or dragging it along the floor as you hide it.**
>
> **Go back to your dog and pause until his wave of excitement subsides. Tell him to Go Find!**
>
> **Initially, some dogs are clueless. If yours looks dumbfounded, bend over or get on the floor and sniff around. He will catch on!**
>
> **Once your dog gets better at this game, hide the reward in different spots and teach him the words "You're Hot" by saying it excitedly when he's close and "You're Cold" in a flat tone to call him off that direction. After giving the You're Cold clue, point him in the right direction.**

Start hiding more than one reward at a time. Teach your dog More as you urge him to keep looking. Want to parlay this game into something more useful like finding your keys? Visit ModernDogParenting.com/Tricks&Games to see this one in action!

LIFE'S A PLAYGROUND

This is less of a game than a statement. Most dogs love climbing, jumping, and exploring. They love to race into and around bushes, dig holes, and splash in puddles. Modern landscapes offer few opportunities. Take advantage of every chance you can to go out with your dog. Follow his bliss, labeling each activity he's drawn to. Does he love to feel the earth under his paws? Slap on some garden gloves, grab a hand shovel, and bury some treats, then say "Go Dig" and help your dog unearth them. Got a climber? Say "Up, Up" as your dog leaps onto a rock or log. Exclaim "Under," "Over," "Through," or "Track Back" as your dog navigates through nature.

INSIDE GAMES

Once you've used these cues outdoors, bring them inside on a rainy day. Make an obstacle course out of stuff you have buried in the closet.

Broomstick Hurdles

This one is easy—find two objects of the same height: cereal boxes, toilet paper rolls, soup cans, etc. Set the items three feet apart and lay a broomstick on top (the height should be equal to or lower than your dog's front leg at the elbow; shorter if your dog's younger than six months). Say "Over" then run with him or toss a treat over the hurdle. If your dog dodges the jump, position it in a hallway or narrow passageway.

Hoops

Place a hoop in a doorway, the bottom initially touching the floor. Toss a treat through it and say "Through." Raise the hoop to no higher than your dog's front leg at the elbow. Once your dog learns Through, he can learn to jump through your arms using the same steps.

Climb Under

Say Under, then lure your dog under a chair, coffee table, or your bent legs with a toy or treat. Your kids will also love to make a tunnel by kneeling down.

Climb Over

Say Over, then lure your dog to jump over your legs, a pillow pile, or another obstacle.

Weave Through

Grab a treat or your target wand as described in chapter 2. Encourage your dog to weave through your legs as you take slow, giant steps!

To see these moves in action visit ModernDogParenting.com /Tricks&Games.

Secret #3: Socialization

Socializing your puppy or dog is the best way to guarantee that he'll feel relaxed wherever you go in his life. Sounds easy enough, but have you ever wondered what socialization is and how you go about "doing" it? Socialization for children involves acquainting them with social norms; for dogs, it's a little different—they need to be introduced to all the peculiarities of human life. From train whistles and baby carriages to computers, television, and walkie-talkies, our world is full of things your dog would never before have experienced in the natural world.

Not only does your dog need to get used to these distractions, but he ideally should experience them during his critical socialization period, between six and sixteen weeks of age. Why so young? It's a brain thing: Before sixteen weeks, his brain is most open to coding new experiences. Once something registers, it becomes part of your puppy's mental landscape. After four to six months, however, the open funnel flips, making it much harder—but not impossible—for a dog to trust unfamiliar sensory experiences.

Sights, sounds, touches, and even smells can startle a dog who has no recall of a similar experience.

Imagine a young puppy with an open funnel positioned above his head. Experiences of all types pour into his brain. When he's standing near his person, he knows everything will be all right.

Now imagine an older, poorly socialized dog that had few outings when he was little because no one understood the importance of early puppyhood socialization. As he grew older, his funnel inverted: New experiences were unfamiliar and suspicious. He snapped at other dogs and neighborhood children because he was scared. His first family gave up on him. After six months at a shelter, he was adopted into a loving home, but now he's having a hard time opening up. Some new experiences are unfamiliar, while others remind him of the past—like the voices of children and men wearing boots. It will take him longer to trust his new, happy life.

Rescued or undersocialized dogs may be scared of anything beyond their front gate. Many people feel discouraged and wonder if there's any point in helping their dog overcome his fears. Sure, toddlers can be avoided—as can trucks, men in boots, sewer grates, people in sunglasses, leaf bags, black dogs, skateboarders (the list really could go on and on)—but your dog will be happier if he can learn to cope. If not, small worries may morph into bigger ones when the new blender sounds like a truck, your plumber arrives sporting a new pair of shades, or the new tenant moves in with a friendly—but very large—retriever. Life can't be avoided! Help your dog learn to cope. He may never be Lassie, but feeling more comfortable in the world is a worthy goal.

Remember, brains are elastic; they get stiffer with age, but the funnel never fully closes. Socializing an older dog just takes a bit longer.

Meanwhile, if you have a puppy, start socializing him. You might have a good excuse: Life's busy, you're not feeling well, the weather is crummy, yada, yada, yada. Make the time. Living with

REMEMBER YOUR FIRST-TIME FEARS?

Once, we fostered a dog (who we named Gadzooks) from China who was afraid of puppets. Puppets! We gladly hid the kids' collection, but he almost knocked a kiosk over at a local toy store when startled by a wall of them. I did not see that coming. It took months to refocus Gadzooks's fear onto feeding or fun, using extra delicious treats and toys. My kids helped by laying a line of treats all around the toy store, gradually inching closer to the puppets. We played ball and Tug games across the aisles, and I let him watch my kids play with the puppets, too. It took time! Be patient. "There's a first time for everything," the old saying goes.

Remember your first-time fears? First times can really make your palms sweat, whether you're jumping off a high-dive platform, eating sushi, or switching cellular carriers. During those nerve-jangling moments, it can help to have an experienced guide, someone who has already "been there, done that."

a poorly socialized dog is sad for him and way too restrictive for you. Twelve years (the average life-span of a dog) will seem like forever when you can't take him out of your home.

I'll end this section with two socialization formulas: one for young puppies, another for older dogs. Not sure where your dog/pup fits? Read both. The more you know, the more you grow.

THE OPEN FUNNEL

The only real obstacle to socializing your puppy is his inoculation schedule. Some veterinarians worry that since puppies are susceptible to infections, they should be quarantined until they've had all their vaccinations. I get this. If your doctor told you to socialize your puppy from day one and he contracted parvovirus, you'd be devastated. Heck, if I knew what veterinarians know, I'd probably tell you to lock your dog in a closet for the first six months.

But I'm not a veterinarian, and I've seen too many sequestered dogs become emotionally crippled by social anxiety while thousands of other carefully socialized puppies grew up to be delightful dogs. It's a decision you'll have to make.

If you take your dog out socializing, carry him into clean homes or buildings and only allow him to interact with other well-cared-for dogs. If you're worried about where your puppy will potty when you're out, bring papers and place them down by a window or door—that's almost outside, and good enough for now.

Make an effort to bring the world to your doorstep, too. Have a party, get quotes for a home improvement project, host Thanksgiving in July. Do what you can to introduce your puppy to new people, noises, and other animals.

The best time to expose your puppy to new and unfamiliar experiences is between six and sixteen weeks, so try to find a breeder or shelter that takes advantage of this important time. A steady flow of happy voices and sweet caresses will ensure that your puppy feels safe with you long before you even meet. Once you've taken over, though, the responsibility is on you.

Think of everything your puppy might see or hear in his lifetime. Obviously, if you live in Florida you won't be going skiing every day, but improbabilities aside, detail your puppy's socialization calendar with everything life may throw at him and you. Think well beyond your doorstep to all the sights and sounds within a hundred-mile radius. Dogs need to experience life beyond your home. Changes can sneak up on all of us. Get your puppy used to the world at large.

SIGHTS AND SOUNDS

Think through the certainties of your everyday life: smoothies, vacuuming, school buses, a neighbor's dogs barking . . . Get your puppy used to it all ASAP. Consider your hobbies, your neighbor's hobbies, and the sports your kids like to play. Wheels can excite predatory impulses—balls can, too. Make an effort to get your puppy habituated to these distractions while he's still young and impressionable.

What if you love snowmobiling and it's July? Uncover your machine, prop your laptop on the fender, and pull up some snowmobiling videos on YouTube. The same goes for other objects, off-season or not: leaf bags, rakes, snow shovels, skis and snowmobiles, garden tools, pool equipment . . .

Now let's cast your socialization net out even farther. What might your dog see in town, at the park, or on a trip to his veterinarian? Buses, trains, delivery trucks? Imagine you're a puppy with supremely superior sensory powers. What do you see, hear, and smell?

PEOPLE

Most puppies socialize with visitors and random admirers without a hitch. But dress a nice person up in a big hat or hand them a garden hoe, and they'll look plenty scary to a young puppy. Children are another category: They look, move, and smell like a

100 SILLY FACES

One of my heroes is veterinarian Ian Dunbar, author, speaker, and founder of American Pet Dog Trainers (APDT). He has tirelessly preached his humane message of positive reinforcement and has significantly changed how the world sees dogs. Ian Dunbar is also a numbers man—he enjoys quantifying experiences. He suggests that each puppy meet a minimum of one hundred new people before the age of twelve weeks. See that group of helmeted roadsters stopping for a water break? Pull over and pass out the treats. Got a doughnut shop nearby? Go hang out until a police officer comes by. At train and subway stations, you'll meet more than a hundred people during rush hour alone. Bus stops, community parks, and many outdoor cafés and delis also draw crowds. Hand everyone a treat and ask them to greet your puppy.

different species to dogs, especially if the dog/puppy doesn't have any kids in their home. How you handle these early meet-and-greets will shape your future. Want a visual? Visit ModernDog Parenting.com/Lessons&Learning.

Home Helpers

People who help keep life running—from housekeepers, gardeners, and pool people to exterminators, plumbers, and electricians—are as integral to everyday life as delivery people and babysitters. Socialize your dog not only with these people but also with the stuff they carry and manipulate. Ask everyone to stop when they arrive, lay down their tools, and if your puppy's willing, to play and feed him as they walk in the door. Overall take-home message? "When my family is happy, I'm happy."

Kids

Kids are quirky. They are their own kind of wonderful and are different at every age and stage, too. That the majority of dog bites happen to kids under the age of twelve is no surprise to parents—kids can be annoying. Mine are no exception, in case you were wondering, so it's unlikely that yours are or will be. Kids yell, throw things, and run around like frenzied rodents. For this reason alone, they can bring out the prey drive in even the most docile dogs. Kids also stare, even though you tell them not to, and hug—another thing dogs aren't fond of. Kids don't do these things to be cruel or bratty; they do them because they love their dog, and they just can't separate their feelings yet. It's a kid thing.

Don't let your dog become another bite statistic: The law won't look favorably on him or you, and a dog-bite case could re-

Got kids? Sometimes it's hard to get through to them—they think they know it all. Check out the videos on FamilyDog.com! Kid stars with a kid-centric message play acted in a musical message that's sure to make a big impression, guaranteed.

sult in legal fees reaching into six to seven figures. You do not want to go there. Socialize your puppy with children even if you don't have any. Target every size, age, race, and gender. Then sit back and watch how kids interact with one another and with dogs. Mimic their mannerisms while feeding your dog filet mignon. I am dead serious. Get your dog used to some hugs and some staring while—at the same time—feeding him steak.

Uniforms, Boots, and Hats

The outfit your dog will be most comfortable seeing you in is your pajamas. Purses and ties get linked to social isolation before your puppy cuts his first baby tooth, but cope he must.

Take special care to socialize your dog to people in all sorts of get-ups. Start by dressing up yourself: One day, dress up like a clown with ginormous sneakers and a big red nose; another day, surprise your clan by serving dinner dressed as your favorite super-hero. Make Fridays silly hat day. Can anyone fool your puppy? As you play different characters, feed your puppy by hand, and have visitors dole out treats. Now go into town. Bring plenty of yummy treats and encourage everyone to hand-feed your dog.

Other Animals

If your dog tolerates small children, other domestic animals like cats, hamsters, and lizards should be a snap. That said, keep all potential prey animals safely away from a new dog or puppy, and separate him from any animal large enough to do him harm. Like a cow.

When your new rescue or puppy is loose in your home, make sure he's separated from other animals by a gate. Each time your puppy seems curious, call to him using his name as you shake a treat cup, clap, and run in the other direction. Practice targeting or use sound markers and rewards to teach your puppy to stay

Conditioning a new puppy or dog to a multipet household is an adjustment. Few of your older residents will be overjoyed. In fact, they'll be more than a little put out. To ease their pain, arrange a new floor plan so as not to disturb their feeding and resting spots, and reward them with the first and most treats so they learn that the new pet means they get more, not less. Separate the new dog if he's being annoying, and soothe your pets if they get snappy or defensive. Promise they'll always be first in your heart, and isolate the new puppy before you shun the old pets from your side. No matter what you think, if you start yelling at your pet, he's never going to like the newbie.

focused on you instead of thinking about the creatures sitting out of reach.

Surfaces

Dogs have a big collection of sensory neurons in their paws. They learn a lot about the world by just stepping on it. Condition your dog to various surfaces including the obvious—pavement, dirt, and sand—and the maybe-less-obvious—footbridges, metal docks, and grates.

How to Handle Each Situation

Before you go out, pack a Socialization Party Bag that includes a familiar mat or blanket, favorite chews, yummy rewards, and/or your puppy's meal. Review the posture chart on page 41 so you can gauge your puppy's reactions to new experiences, as well as the moods of other dogs you may encounter. Until seven months, your puppy won't be a good judge of character—he won't respond to social cues well. While some dogs can infer his puppy-ness from his mannerisms, a poorly socialized dog might take offense. Avoid this if you can.

Master the following techniques to ensure each social experience goes smoothly:

BRACING

To encourage your puppy to stay down while meeting new people, offer treats or toys under his chin to keep his focus down. If he's still bouncy, gently secure your thumb through his collar under his chin. Your fingertips should be pointing down. If your dog still wiggles around, pat his back with your open hand and try to angle him so he's standing next to each admirer, not facing front. Excitement's like a wave: It builds, peaks, then passes. Ride the wave.

Between Dogs and Distractions

Whether your puppy is overexcited or nervous about unfamiliar what-have-yous, position yourself between the dog and the distraction. This may sound easy, but sometimes it isn't, especially if you have a wildly enthusiastic adolescent. If your puppy is big, strong, and friendly, consider using a harness or head collar when socializing him. Flip to chapter 2 and read about Comfort Wear.

When possible, engage the distraction. Talk to the person, watch the train go by, touch the statue—all while keeping your dog at your side until he's confident enough to sniff, approach, or explore it himself. When this happens, speak softly and offer your puppy treats and attention. It's okay to let him cling to your legs; just don't turn your attention away from the distraction.

CALM CONFIDENCE

If you want your puppy to be calm while socializing, show him what that looks like. Adopt a "been there, done that" attitude so he will feel confident looking to you when he's unsure. What do dogs think when their people get high-strung and jittery? I don't know, exactly, but it doesn't inspire a sense of calm confidence. Just keep him next to or behind you, stay focused on what's going on around you, and reward him for settling down if he does.

The Inverted Funnel

Most people don't intentionally mess up their dog. Life gets busy; people have other priorities and demands. But the calendar won't pardon excuses. Puppies need a rich and dedicated social schedule.

If you missed the boat or have adopted a dog who clearly didn't get it, all is not lost. Socialization and learning never end, although you've got a bigger job on your hands. As kids who've had tough childhoods know, when bad memories block good ones, it's hard to feel the sun. How your older dog will condition to new experiences depends on:

His age—young is usually better, but that's not always the case.

Past memories—any frightening or abusive memories that trigger strong reactions can, and often do, cloud your dog's trust in the here and now. This can improve over time.

Resilience and hope—some dogs are so immensely forgiving, it's like they've waited their whole lifetime for that one special human connection.

If you've adopted an older dog or are otherwise late to the socialization game, relax. Many dogs are adopted from shelters and even more deplorable conditions, but, with some extra effort, turn out fine.

Perhaps your dog is great at home. He's the King of the Castle; she's the Belle of the Ball. He's comfortable with you, okay with visitors, pleasant to live with. But then you drive to the veterinarian or take him to the park, and *bam*—he loses it. His reactive state can take many forms, from barking at the door to pacing or trying to jump out the window, but the point is, he is not the same dog he is at home.

If your dog's personality does a one-eighty the minute you step beyond your humble oasis, step back, reconsider, and organize a plan.

Find a harness or head collar so you can handle your dog calmly instead of jerking him around.

Reward using entire meals, even upgrading to canned food. Feed by hand or with a spoon on your adventure days. If he's agitated in the car, stop a few times on the way to give him some food (no more than one-quarter of his meal ration).

Gauge your dog's tolerance. Is he okay at the coffee shop? If not, start in a back parking lot and gradually move into the center of business.

Once you find a happy-enough spot, hang out. Don't start drilling vocabulary words—your goal is to fill his brain with happy thoughts. What makes your dog happy? Eating, sniffing, chewing, or playing with puzzle toys while sitting on his favorite dog mat? Great, fish it out. Sit down and play with him as you feed him. Don't think about the world around you or who might be looking on, thinking you're strange.

Now the question might be, how long should you stay? If your dog's nervous, three to five minutes will be enough. If he's wearing a happy face—mouth slightly open, head and tail held at rump level or higher—wander around a bit, stopping often to feed and check in. Leave while his tail's still in the air; five to ten minutes should do it. In chapter 6, we'll start using a vocabulary list, but for now, just work on happy.

If your dog is a basket case or won't look at a toy or treat, you have some work ahead of you. Overwhelmed dogs come in three varieties: scared, hyper, and defensive. We'll go over these strong reactions more in chapters 7 and 8, but in each case, you'll need to work on your dog's impulse control.

Don't stare or look at your dog very much. Staring takes your focus off the world he's unsure about. Good dog parents keep their eyes peeled for danger, remain calm, and don't hesitate to put themselves in the line of fire.

Don't greet anyone. Some dogs are too reactive. If someone approaches to pet your dog tell them, "Sorry, not today," or "I have my hands full," or "No, my dog is not friendly." If people still won't listen, just use my line: "My dog's got the mange."

If your dog is getting worse, more hyper, nervous, or aggressive, call a professional to help you. It's cheaper than a lawyer.

Ghosts in Your Closet?

Sometimes a dog can be afraid of things in and around your home. This is common with rescue dogs who may never have been conditioned to living inside. These dogs may be afraid of wood floors, stairs, vacuums, a vegetable chopper—you name it. Rescuing a dog is a loving gesture—I've rescued nearly every one of mine—but it's not without certain complications for both you and your new dog.

Your home should be your dog's safe place: his den where you come together to eat, rest, and enjoy each other's company. If your dog has a worry, address it. I find targeting, mimicry, and counter-conditioning work best.

TARGETING

Grab a spatula or buy a target wand at a pet store or online. Your goal is to teach your dog to touch the wand with his nose or paw and reward him with food when he does. Once he learns to target, play this game to help him overcome his concerns. If he growls nervously when he sees a man in a hat, ask your behatted neighbor to come by while you whip out a target wand and reward your dog. Host a hat party and ask everyone to treat your dog, and even ask some of them to target and treat, to help your dog see that behatted people carry spatulas, not shotguns, and have the world's best treats! Hats are awesome!

Here's how you get started:

Go to a special, safe room at set times.

Present the target wand—use a spatula if nothing else is around—wait until he touches it, and reward him.

This is a great time to use a clicker or sound marker (what the pros call a secondary reinforcer) like "Yes!"

To see targeting in action, visit ModernDogParenting.com /ExtraHelp.

MIMICRY

Mimicry shows your dog that you feel confident interacting with the very thing that frightens him. Another dog, a staircase, an unfamiliar surface or sight—he learns by example that whatever it is can't be all that bad. Instead of forcing your dog to approach the frightening object, let him lag behind while you go check it out. Involve friends and family with this one, too. Ask your kids to do their homework sprawled out on the wood floor, sit on the middle step and shoot off a few texts, handle (but don't start) the vacuum.

COUNTERCONDITIONING

Socialization is a tricky subject. Some people might tell you to socialize your dog regardless of age, believing that treats will help your dog overcome all his fears. This is not so. Some dogs are so afraid of a situation—a storm or loud noise, for example—that they won't eat. They can barely move. Socialization only works if your dog feels comfortable enough to be in the general proximity of whatever triggers his fear. Then and only then can you use treats and toys to shift his emotions from fear to seeking and play.

Using a visual prompt like a target wand and a sound marker like a clicker or a word (as described in chapters 2 and 6), counter condition your dog to objects or places he has feared in the past. Since each touch of the target is rewarded with food, use it to gradually move your dog onto the wood floor, into the elevator, or closer to the young child. If your dog won't respond to the food game, use his favorite toy to associate the once-traumatic trigger with the excitement of play. If your dog becomes overwhelmed, increase the distance between your dog and the distraction.

The three secrets to a happy life really aren't that secret at all, and they work for everyone. Nobody wants to live a lonely, isolated, emotionally depleted life—least of all your dog! Celebrate food, play games together so that the words "Ball" or "Tug" offer joy no matter where you are, and socialize your dog to the world around you. A common language really does open so many doors. Adventures are more fun with a dog at your side!

6

Lesson Time

Whether you think you can, or you think
you can't—you're right.
—HENRY FORD

At long last, behaviorists and scientists have proven what dog lovers have known all along: The most effective and reliable ways to teach a dog are through encouragement, play, and positive reinforcement. Which is good news, because if you're like most people, you'd rather your dog feel happy than scared. Turns out, joy inspires understanding better than any other system out there.

Of course, being like most people, you also want your dog to listen. You want her to prioritize your voice above all other sounds, pick her head up the instant you speak, and drop everything when you come into view. These lofty goals are not entirely far off, even if your dog is ignoring you now. The only hitch? Your dog needs to learn how to listen, and you need to be the one encouraging her to do so.

In chapter 2, you discovered that listening to words isn't second nature for your dog. Her first language is body talk—a subtle but very recognizable interplay of eyes, ears, tails, and posture (recognizable, that is, once you teach yourself to "listen" with your eyes instead of your ears).

Before we start our learning journey, consider the reality. You're asking your dog, a completely different species, to prioritize you and your voice in a sea of distractions. It is the eighth wonder of the world.

First Words

If I asked eighty people the first and most important words their dog should know, most would say Come. Others might add Stay, No, or Drop It.

I'd say they were all incorrect. The first words to teach your dog or puppy are the ones that map out her everyday life. With repetitive sounds outlining her day, your dog will pair words with actions and begin to alert everytime you speak. Start using words to highlight the important stuff from potty runs and quiet time to eating and play, as you reward your dog for each completed action. She won't just have a spark of understanding, she'll be a firestorm of excitement! Suddenly, words have meaning.

What Your Dog Really Wants to Know

All dogs (and puppies) need to know two things in life: where they should go and what they should do when stuff happens. Consider your household: Where would you like your dog to go and what would you like her to do when someone arrives, when you're heating up dinner, or while you're watching TV? How should she handle herself when the kids are playing or at nighttime?

Imagine being plopped into a household where no one speaks your language. Day after day, the same people repeat the same words over and over as they look at you, eager for the correct response. You stare back at them, hopeful at first, but soon exasperated, clueless, and homesick. No matter how often or how loud they repeat a word, you have no idea what they mean.

Then, a visitor arrives who speaks good-enough English. You perk up as her friendly, reassuring manner gives you hope. The best parts are the coins and candies this newcomer gifts you for each new association. Everyone else is impressed and exhilarated—you're clearly much smarter than they'd ever imagined!

Now can you better understand your dog's confusion?

You don't teach your dog lots of words and good manners so you can win at the Westminster Kennel Club Dog Show. You teach your dog to listen so you can direct her throughout the day and help you both live better, happier, more engaging lives.

In chapter 7, you'll learn how to deal with daily frustrations like jumping, barking, and destruction, but before we can address your grievances, you need to teach your dog what you'd like her to do instead. Once she learns that certain words have special meaning for her, inspiring good behavior will be surprisingly straightforward and systematic.

Everyday Words and Routines

Your dog doesn't need a three hundred–word vocabulary to lead a fulfilling life. Once she learns that words direct routines, she'll excite to the sound of your voice and wait hopefully for the next word she knows.

Consider the list below: Which words can you use in your

THE NAME GAME

First things first—help your dog develop a positive association to her name. How? Pair it with food, attention, and toys. Say your dog's name when she is awake throughout the day, then shake a treat cup, clap, or toss a toy to get her attention. If she's more focused on the cup itself, bring the treat to your eyes and encourage eye contact before lowering the treat in a flattened palm. Good dog! To see this all-important word lesson, visit ModernDogParenting.com/Lessons&Learning.

everyday life? What you choose is a personal thing, but the more your dog knows, the closer to you she grows. Say each word just before you do each action, and reward your dog for following along.

As you teach your dog new words, speak clearly and use gestures to emphasize what you mean or where you're going. Say and show, don't say and stare. Staring confuses your dog; just say what you mean and do it. Check it out live online at ModernDogParenting.com/Lessons&Learning.

TABLE 6.1

WORD	MEANING	SIGNAL
Inside/Outside	Say as you lead your dog in or out the door.	Point to the door or passageway.
Upstairs/Downstairs	Say as you go up or down a flight of stairs.	Point to the stairs.
Mealtime/Water	Say as you prepare each meal, etc.	Point to the feeding or water station.
Car	Say as you head out to your car.	Point to the car door as you go there.

TABLE 6.1 (continued)

WORD	MEANING	SIGNAL
Ball/Toy/Bone	Say as you reach for or toss each object.	Point to your toy basket or the object.
In Your Room	Say as you lead your dog to her enclosure, crate, or sleeping zone.	Point and go.
Daddy's Home; Wake Up, Sissy	Help your puppy identify your family by name (see chapter 5).	Point to the person's location.

TREAT CUPS AND TOY BASKETS

If you reward your dog—with a loving pat, treats, toys, or happy talk—when she responds to your wordplay, she'll be more eager to listen to you. Fill up a few baskets with the toys and bones your dog likes best and strategically place them around your home. If you're worried your dog will chew the basket, use a pot. Make treat cups with old Tupperware, spillproof toddler cups, or washed-out candy or gum containers. Fill each container with your dog's food and/or a mix of tasty treats. Life is but a box of ~~chocolates~~ dog treats.

Play the Learning Game

The fastest way to teach your dog that words have meaning is to pair each one with a positive experience. The problem is, dogs often jump from one behavior to the next so quickly that it's hard for them to keep track of what they were doing that made us light up. Say "Good Dog" three times fast in your happiest voice, and during those 2.5 seconds, your dog may have actually been doing several behaviors: sitting, yes, but also leaping out of the Sit, standing on her hind legs, and planting a wet one straight across your kisser. Which behavior did you like? How's a dog to know?

Mark the Moment!

In a game I call Mark the Moment, you choose a marker—a sound or other sensory indicator, like a flash of light or a soft touch—to highlight one specific behavior that you'd like your dog to remember and repeat. By pairing the marker with a satisfying reward, your dog will—as if by magic—start repeating the behavior that prompted the marker.

Most people use a clicker or whistle. Laser lights are especially useful for deaf dogs or in loud environments like a kennel, but you can also use a word like "Yes" or "Good!" I use clickers when I can, but also rely on the one-word marker "Yes" to target the behaviors I want my dog(s) to remember and repeat.

Mark the Moment is a fun, fast-paced learning game that's proven to be the most exhilarating and effective way to teach your dog good listening skills and manners. Whether you choose a clicker, light burst, word marker, or the latest tools technology has to offer to help you encourage cooperative behavior, this approach will inspire a lifelong love of learning and deep trust. Dogs taught with encouragement show greater long-term memory and express creativity in their thinking and problem-solving skills—how cool is that! Best of all, it'll free you from all those traditional methods that rely on punishment and leave both of you feeling discouraged and resentful.

Fortunately for both dogs and people we live in an age of technology that used creatively will inspire fun on both ends of the leash. I'm not talking shock or spray collar here—far from it! Precision Bluetooth technology—aka Smart Animal Training Systems, LLC—are changing the way we interact and communicate with our dogs for the better! Want to engage your dog from your smart phone or computer when you're out? You can do it! Think you don't have the coordination or focus to reward behavior in the moment? Don't worry—you can purchase technology that can outperform even the most experienced trainers and even do it when you're not at home!

One of my favorite tools is the Pet Tutor—a silent, Bluetooth-operated, programmable feeding device used by shelters, animal hospitals, and dog parents alike. While I enjoy using it with my own dogs to inspire thinking games and fun indoor learning, the Pet Tutor has many other applications. I also use the device to help clients address their dog's separation anxiety, phobias, and aggression. Get a visual of technology in action at ModernDogParenting.com/Lessons&Learning and look to Smart Animal Training Systems for more devices and other applications.

Get Started Now

To play Mark the Moment, choose your marker and link it with food, toys, or attention. If you're using a clicker, make the click sound once, then offer food. Keep repeating sound-food-sound-food until your dog has linked the two together. One mark, one reward. If clickers don't appeal, use a word marker like "Yes" or "Good!" and pair it with the same rewards.

In professional dog speak, you'll hear words like "secondary reinforcer" tossed around to mean "marker." Same deal applies: Before a secondary reinforcer can be effective, it has to be linked to what is known as a primary reinforcer, something your dog

TABLE 6.2

TERM	DEFINITION	REAL TIME
Classical Conditioning	When a normal occurrence creates an involuntary response.	The sound of the food dish causes your dog to drool and jump around in excitement.
Operant Conditioning	Learning that's motivated through either positive or negative reinforcement or punishment.	To teach your dog to keep four paws on the floor during greetings, you give her a treat whenever she isn't jumping.
Positive Reinforcement	Encouraging a behavior by giving your dog something she likes.	When you arrive home, wait to pet and play with your dog until she either Sits or picks up a toy.
Negative Reinforcement	Encouraging a behavior by taking away something your dog doesn't like.	Some suggest pinning a dog's tongue down when she nips and only letting go when she withdraws her mouth as a way to prevent nipping in the future.
Positive Punishment	A behavior is discouraged when your dog receives something unpleasant.	A dog will stay in a yard if she is shocked anytime she leaves.
Negative Punishment	Discouraging your dog by taking away something she wants.	If you're trying to teach your dog to Sit and she jumps, you remove an offered treat.
Premack Principle	Allowing your dog to do something she'd consider more rewarding after she does something that's less rewarding.	After holding a Sit Stay, you release your dog to eat her dinner or play with another dog.

TABLE 6.2 (continued)

TERM	DEFINITION	REAL TIME
Counter-conditioning	Linking a threatening situation with a positive reward.	If your dog is afraid of men in hats, you offer treats or attention any time she sees a man in a hat.
Primary Reinforcement	Gratifying your dog's daily need for play, food, and interaction.	Rewarding your dog with food when she lies down on her mat.
Secondary Reinforcement	A sensory mark (sound, light, touch) that gets linked to a primary reinforcer to reward good behavior.	You make a clicking sound when your dog Comes to you, then treat her.
Generalization	Understanding a new direction in various settings.	Your dog responds to the word "Sit" whether you're in the kitchen, out on the trail, or wearing a costume.
Trigger	Something that provokes a strong reaction in your dog.	Doorbells, food dishes, and the leash are positive triggers; thunderstorms, loud noises, and sharp objects are negative examples.
Desensitization	Getting your dog used to a stimulus by introducing it at greater distances or lower intensities. Often used with counter conditioning.	To desensitize your dog to the sound of the vacuum, you first play a recording of vacuum noises at low volume or run the vacuum in a distant room. You gradually increase the volume of the recording and decrease the distance of the running machine.

(continued)

TABLE 6.2 (continued)

TERM	DEFINITION	REAL TIME
Red Zone	The area around a trigger where your dog's behavior is most unsettled and she has a hard time prioritizing your directions. When desensitized, the distance shrinks over time.	Your dog is terrified of skateboards. If she's within ten yards of one, she barks and lunges at the end of her leash. She is said to be in her Red Zone.
Discrimination	Your dog's ability to tell the difference between two stimuli or signals.	If you've paired a whistle with food but not a clap, your dog will expect a reward after she hears the whistle but not the clap when you ask her to Sit.
Extinction	When a behavior stops because it fails to get desired results.	If you ignore all barking for attention, eventually it will stop.
Learned Helplessness	When your dog gives up trying because she cannot adjust her behavior to avoid a negative response.	Your puppy keeps slipping and falling every time she tries to walk across your wood floor so she stops moving.
Luring	Using rewards to guide your dog into action. Although a stellar way to get started with language lessons, phasing off the lure quickly is important to avoid treat dependency.	Presenting your dog with a treat, then lowering it to the ground between her paws to teach her Down.

TABLE 6.2 (continued)

TERM	DEFINITION	REAL TIME
Capturing	Using a conditioned reinforcer—a clicker or word that's been linked to a primary reinforcer—to highlight a behavior that your dog does naturally.	Rewarding your dog with a click whenever you catch her lying down on her own.
Shaping	Reinforcing small steps or parts of your dog's actions to build a new behavior.	To encourage your dog to lie down, you'd first reward her for looking at the ground, then for lowering her head, then for moving her body toward the ground, and finally for lying completely down.
Chaining	Teaching each individual step of a complex routine then linking them together.	Teaching Retrieve in separate parts—running away from you, picking up an object, bringing the object back, and then Give/Drop.
Back Chaining	Teaching the last step in a routine first, then working backward.	Teaching Come starting with being together, then running toward you, then alerting at a distance when "Come" is called.
Modeling/ Molding	Moving your dog into a position after speaking a corresponding word.	Positioning your dog's body after you say "Sit" rather than waiting for her to process the request and respond to you on her own.

(*continued*)

TABLE 6.2 (continued)

TERM	DEFINITION	REAL TIME
Mimicry	Encouraging your dog to learn by watching you move through the motions or get into a position yourself.	Showing your dog what you mean by "Under" by climbing under a table and lying there yourself.

needs and wants, like food. It can get confusing, but it's good to know we've got science on our side.

CAPTURING

This is the one step of the Mark the Moment game that can take some time and patience. First, decide on the behavior you want to inspire—say you want your dog to Sit. Professionals would call the Sit your criteria. Criteria can and do change, but it's good to know what you want before you set out to capture it.

So, if Sit is the behavior you want, all you do is stand around and wait for your dog to Sit. When she does, mark that moment with your clicker or word, and reward your dog. Say what? If you think you're confused, watch your dog. There you are, standing around when suddenly she decides to plant her rear to the ground

FUN WITH FOOD!

The best time to play the Mark the Moment game is right before meals. You can use your dog's actual meal or choose a treat your dog loves, but don't get carried away—you'll only need a tiny bit of food to pair with each mark! Some dogs will do flips for a single Cheerio while others might need chopped liver. Keep the treats small so you don't fill your dog up or slow the game's momentum. Food is the best motivator when starting out, but eventually you'll phase off treats and mix in play, toys, and happy talk!

and you mark the moment and hand over a delightful tidbit. Bonus. That's what I call happy confusion!

It might take a few minutes—or it might not—before your dog Sits again. When she does, *pow*—mark off again and fish out another reward. Double bonus. Once your dog catches on to your little capturing game and connects the dots between Sitting, marking, and your treats, the behavior will start happening more and more frequently. See this in action at ModernDogParenting .com/Lessons&Learning.

Of course, Sit is a fairly naturally occurring behavior; teaching your dog to do more complex moves can get tricky. You might have to wait for days before your dog decides to chase her tail. For more complicated behaviors, another early learning skill known as shaping can come into play.

SHAPING

To help your dog's learning process—especially with complex moves and tricks—use shaping to encourage the behavior step-by-step. To shape Sit, for example, you'd break it into tiny steps. First, mark the moment and reward your dog when she stops moving, then mark and reward when she stops moving and starts to lower her rump to the ground. Next, mark and treat when her bottom touches the ground, then again when she shifts her weight back and settles into the Sit position. Then mark and treat for calmer and longer Sits, and associate the cue "Sit" with her behavior. Your dog will be as reliable as the dog that committed to the whole behavior all at once!

While Mark the Moment learning takes time in the beginning, your dog will catch on quickly and find great excitement in trying to read your mind. Dogs taught this way are the most creative, fun-loving, expressive dogs because they're always trying to figure out how to get their person to interact with them. As long as you only reward good behavior, good behavior's all she'll offer! To see a live demo, log on to ModernDogParenting.com/Lessons&Learning.

This learning system was first discovered by a scientist named B. F. Skinner. If you don't know his work, check it out; I reference him in my bibliography, but much more about his life and passions can be found online. His assistant, Keller Breland, first carried clicker training—what I call Mark the Moment learning—into the animal world when he applied Skinner's shaping techniques on marine animals. Ever seen a dolphin or whale leap out of a pool? Mark the Moment learning in action.

Operant conditioning was popularized in the pet industry through the tireless and ongoing efforts of Bob and Marion Breland Baily who used chickens to teach conditioning principles to trainers of all animals. Karen Pryor, Ph.D., author of *Don't Shoot the Dog*, took it a step further. She is heralded for introducing operant conditioning to the masses in a movement known as "clicker training." Now, Wes Anderson, inventor and trainer, is advancing positive reinforcement in the twenty-first century with his line of precision technology including the Smart Clicker™ and the Pet Tutor®. Flip to the bibliography for more information on these great, innovative thinkers!

Luring: Modified Mark the Moment Learning

If you love the thought of using secondary reinforcers like I do but don't have the luxury of time, consider a modified approach. Use a treat to lure your dog into position, then say your direction word and click or mark to reward her position. Timing is still important: Focus on the moment your dog does the exact behavior you want.

Mark the Moment Learning for Kids

While the Mark the Moment game is fun for kids, children under twelve should be supervised with clickers, as it's easy to overdo it. One click, one treat can become two clicks per treat, then three, then four. Too much clicking can easily confuse your dog. Choose one behavior and work together with your kids to follow the same one click, one treat shaping routine to encourage your dog's understanding. It's a great exercise in patience. Kids can use the clicker for lots of things, like Sit, and other basics like Jump, Over, and Spin. Flip to the end of this chapter for fun tricks the whole family can enjoy!

Direction Words

You started by pairing words to everyday routines, which helped your dog connect your voice to her actions! Then you learned how to play the Mark the Moment game to learn Sit. Using this same approach, we'll teach your dog the expected response to other directional words, like Drop, Stay, and Come.

Take a look at the Vocabulary List on the next page. Circle the directions you'd like your dog to know. She can learn them all, but she certainly doesn't have to. Would you like your dog to stay on her mat and chew a bone while you sit at the kitchen table? Circle "Bone" and "Go to Your Mat." Want a dog who greets visitors on four paws instead of two? Teach her "Toy" and "Say Hello." Eager to take your dog to the coffee shop on Saturday mornings? "Follow" and "Under" ensure that she'll relax at your side.

Cross off the directions you don't need, change the word if you'd like to use another, or add more to the list. Once your dog learns a new direction, share it with family and friends so they can help her feel included and appreciated, too!

You can print this list from ModernDogParenting.com/Free Downloads.

If you're not sure which directions to choose or in which order you should teach them, think through your day. Which directions might make it easier for your dog to understand what you expect from her?

TABLE 6.3

DIRECTION	WHAT IT MEANS TO YOUR DOG
Sit	Sit back on her hind legs.
Go Free	A release to do as she pleases.
Down	Lower her body to the floor.
Stand	Stand up and hold still.
Wait	Stop, look, and listen.
Stay	Be still in one position for a period of time.
Go to Your Mat	Relax in a designated spot or on a mat.
Come	Go to your side.
Follow, aka Heel	Walk on a loose leash at your side.
Let's Go	A looser invitation to follow you or change direction when off-leash.
No	Avoid something.
Leave It	Ignore something tempting like food, people, or other dogs.
Under	Go under your legs or a table for emotional security.
Back	Step back or stand behind, especially when distracted or excited.
Away	Back off when you or your visitors need personal space.
Toy/Ball*	Grab a toy when excited or wanting to play.
Bone/Chew*	Play with her bone or chew, especially when bored, overwhelmed, or anxious.
Give/Drop*	Spit out whatever object is in her mouth.
Tug*	Pull on something; game on!
Bring*	Hold something in her mouth and carry it to you.
Find It*	Search for treats, toys, or people.

* Review the Daily Needs Chart in chapter 1 for linking the words "Toy" and "Bone" to routines, and chapter 5 for teaching directions like Give and Tug.

Five-Step Learning Strategy

Since words are your dog's second language, it'll take a little time before she'll prioritize your voice—but we're talking weeks, not months. Some dogs learn new words in days.

To speed things up, use my Five-Step Learning Strategy to teach your dog the connection between words and actions. I'll ex-

LEARNING SPEED

How fast will your dog learn? Every dog is different, even from one word to the next. Your dog will learn the new meanings at her own rate—many dogs get Sit in a day or two, while other dogs take twice as long. Though a lot depends on your dog's puppyhood, life experiences, breed, and personality, it will generally take two to seven days to teach a new word. The more lesson bursts you do, the faster it will go. Just remember: Learning is not a race, it's an adventure.

Watch my favorite dog-training movie, *The Miracle Worker* (Penn, 1962), which doesn't even involve a dog! Here, Helen Keller, a girl struck deaf and blind, is coddled by parents who adore her but make no demands on her intellect or thirst for knowledge. What a metaphor for dog lovers! Who rescued Helen from her world of dark confusion and rage? Her teacher, Annie, whose patient insistence that Helen learn a new and unfamiliar language—signing—taught Helen to link words to objects, actions, and feelings. Once your dog learns to pair words to meaning, she won't want to stop!

When possible, do your lesson bursts around the same time, in the same place every day. Routines are really important as they fuel your dog's excitement for learning—just watch! Choose a distraction-free Learning Zone for steps 1 and 2—it can be your living room, bathroom, or a hallway, as long as it's relatively quiet. Pocket some of your dog's favorite goodies and/or toys, a flat mat, and your marker if you're using one, and lead your dog there off-leash. If she hasn't been to the area before, let her sniff around. Remember: Dogs see the world through their noses.

plain each step using Sit as an example. Practice from one to four times a day if you're able, for short three- to five-minute lesson bursts. Once your dog knows a direction, use it around your home and while you're out socializing.

STEP 1: MARK THE MOMENT

There are three ways to introduce new directions to your dog: capturing, shaping, and modified shaping, aka luring, as I described on page 154. Don't get caught up with people who claim their school of learning is superior. All these methods are kind; you love your dog, and she loves you. Choose a technique that feels most natural.

Capturing

Stand quietly and wait for the moment your dog Sits in front of you and looks up. Capture the moment with a mark and reward! She will know there is food to be had: She's got a nose.

Shaping

Shaping involves capturing small steps toward the full behavior or trick. Let's say you've got an active dog: Start by marking and rewarding when your dog stops the perpetual movement, then when she stops and looks to you, then when she stops, looks, and lowers her haunches either partway or all the way. Once your dog makes it to the full Sit, mark and reward for Sitting calmly and looking to you again. By rewarding each step of your dog's

---

THE SILENT STEP

During step 1, button your lips. See if your dog can guess what behavior you want without any clues. Mark and reward only the behavior (e.g., Sit) or steps that lead up to it (holding still and looking at you). You can use a word marker and praise once she nails it, but see if you can keep quiet until then.

behavior, her engagement and enthusiasm will become their own rewards!

Luring

Use food or toys to guide your dog into position and reward her when she assumes the posture:

Hold a treat six inches above your dog's nose. If she jumps, stand tall, lifting the treat out of reach. Look up and remain calm: no eye contact, rewards, or attention for jumping.

Still jumping? That's not uncommon—your dog may have learned that jumping gets attention. Stand up quickly and repeat above. You're teaching her that jumping doesn't pay.

When she looks up at the treat, bring the lure slowly back above her ears.

Say "Yes" or click the moment she shifts into Sit, and offer the reward when she is in position.

Practice at this level until your dog promptly Sits when she sees a treat.

STEP 2: SAY AND SIGNAL

Gather up your kibbles and learning mat and take your dog into her Learning Zone off-leash. Since Sitting ended in a positive reward last time, your dog will offer a Sit to see if it works again. Yup—still works! Walk around to get her up again, then turn, say "Sit," then signal by drawing a quick line with your finger from just above your dog's nose to your eyes. Mark the moment and reward with a treat, toy, or pat. Take a step to a new spot and wait for her to Sit again.

Depending on the time of day and your dog's energy level and personality, you might get some hyperanxious behavior like jumping, nipping, or barking. Ignore these by folding your arms

WHEN YOUR DOG IS NOT IN THE MOOD TO LISTEN

Sometimes, your dog's not going to be in the mood to listen. It happens to the best of us; like you, she could be tired, sick, or having a bad day. Maybe the dog walker was late or in a bad mood. You just can't know everything.

The great thing about the Mark the Moment game is that you don't have to get all mean and ugly if your dog doesn't listen every time. Sure, there are times when listening is a must, but around your home, cut her some slack. If she's clearly not listening, just blow her off and walk away. Pretend to eat the reward yourself or show some affection to another pet or person. If it's a game you were hoping for, play with yourself or someone else. Your dog won't like that, but continue to ignore her until she does what you've asked. She'll catch on fast—have faith. Positive attention for cooperation always wins out in the end. Dogs, like people, like to be noticed for what they can do!

and turning calmly toward the wall for five to ten seconds to show your dog that annoying behavior gets less—not more—attention.

Same deal: Lesson bursts, one to four times a day, three to five minutes each. Try to practice before a meal using choice food rewards to prompt her interest and cooperation.

If your dog seems confused, go back to step 1 or ask a dog-savvy friend or teacher to help you troubleshoot. Remember, it's not a race.

STEP 3: PROOF AND GENERALIZE

Practice your new direction around your home and when socializing with different people to make sure your dog generalizes "Sit." Continue to use your marker and treats/toys to reward her cooperation during step 3. Have her Sit on the elevator, in the barn, or on the sidewalk. Ask her to Sit while greeting the mailman, a cop, or a clown.

To make Sit a reinforcement in itself:

Stand by the door just before leaving for a walk, or stand with a treat or toy in hand as though you've forgotten what to do with it. Your dog will be enthusiastic for your next move, but stay standing and calm. Ignoring barking, jumping, nipping, etc. When she Sits, open the door, and out you go!

Play the Elevator Game: Call your dog over and hold out a favorite toy or bone. If she jumps up to snatch it, the elevator (your hand) goes up above your head. Ignore her until she's grounded, and present the object again. When she Sits, the elevator quickly drops to the ground floor with palm open to offer her the reward!

On the road, ask your dog or puppy to Sit before entering the animal hospital, while visiting a friend, or before going into the dog park. Sit unlocks a world of opportunities!

After a week or so of treat rewards, begin to let the release to do fun things be its own reward.

Don't be too discouraged if your dog initially ignores you around distractions. Most do, and I think it's a good sign. Your dog knows you love her and won't just abandon her if she blows you off. So what if she ignores you? Kids ignore their parents all the time; so do family and friends. Heck, when is the last time you ignored your GPS? Were you being spiteful, or were you just distracted? Sometimes, dogs just can't take it all in at once. Remember, words aren't their first language, so be patient. Your dog's trying to generalize words that are still pretty unfamiliar to her.

If your dog doesn't seem to register your direction or looks confused, repeat yourself slowly and more clearly. Overexaggerate the signal—a posture that is, after all, more familiar to her communication style.

"GO FREE"

Use one word that lets your dog know she's free to go. Make it short, snappy, and full of life, like "Go Free!" or "Okay!" Pair it with an outward sweeping gesture of the arm and a step forward to signal to your dog that she can do as she pleases.

If she's still clueless, let it go. Go back to steps 1 and 2 and practice later in the same spot using a food lure to give her a hint. She'll catch on, I promise.

STEP 4: VARYING REWARD PATTERN

Research has shown that dogs (like people) work harder and more passionately for variable reinforcements. So vary the rewards, both in timing and type.

Start offering treats of different types and mix in other rewards like toys and happy talk—praise for learning.

Vary how often you give a food or toy reward. Give a physical reward every third or fourth Sit; then really mix it up. Hold off for seven Sits, then give two rewards right in a row. Next, reward the third time your dog Sits when asked, then the second time, then after five Sits. In professional circles this is known as a variable reinforcement schedule—it works (metaphorically speaking) in casinos, too.

Make a list of other things your dog loves: greeting the kids, playing at the dog park, jumping in or out of the car, getting a fresh bowl of water . . . you name it. Now encourage your dog to listen to her new direction, Sit, before you let her do each of these favorite activities.

Within two weeks, drop food as the main motivator and only offer it as a surprise bonus. The direction, in this case "Sit," becomes the ultimate reward!

DO YOU EVER STOP TREATING DOGS?

Personally, I don't, but I'm a hopeless foodie. I love feeding everyone, no matter how many legs carry them into my kitchen. But I don't use food as motivation after my dogs have learned the meaning of a new direction. Variable rewards, as I described on page 166, are good for people like me because I don't have to keep score.

Phasing off the treats will keep your dog on her toes and excited to see which reward or adventure her new word will unlock. Sometimes, your dog will get a big smile, other times a ride in the car or a release into the dog park. You can still use food on occasion or to reward your dog's cooperation around a big distraction like the doorbell. Something as challenging as that deserves a gigantic reward and lots of goodies, especially in the beginning. In professional circles, that's known as a jackpot!

STEP 5: FREEDOM AND PRIORITIES

A lot of people ask me when they can let their dog go off-leash. I never know what to say. There aren't many beaches, fields, or sanctuaries left that are dog-friendly *and* far from a roadway. Even hiking trails can be dangerous. Letting your dog off-leash is never without risks—even well-schooled dogs get distracted. The only one who knows your dog well enough to judge her responsiveness around distractions is you.

That said, there is a lot you can do to teach your dog to prioritize your voice for "Sit" and other encouragements. Here are some hints to help you develop distance control and teach your dog to be alert to your voice above all other distractions.

Keep your tone consistent even when at a distance.

Practice your distance control indoors first.

Teach your dog that directions mean the same thing no matter what angle or position you're standing in. Say "Sit" from the front, back, left, and right while standing, sitting in a chair, or lying on the sofa.

Now introduce your direction outside. If your dog runs from you, check your tone. If any frustration creeps in, you might sound scary.

Gradually increase the distance you stand from your dog. She'll likely be confused at first. If she is, don't take it personally—she's not stupid, just distracted. Approach her calmly and repeat yourself every three seconds until she listens—you're letting her know that this is important and you won't let it go. Vary the rewards as described in step 4.

In chapter 5, you learned about targeting for tricks. Targets can also be used to encourage distance responses. For Sit, hold out a target wand or send your dog to stand on a target disc, then say "Sit."

When you start outside, use treats to encourage your dog's cooperation. If she runs from you, use a long line, but only step on it to prevent her from running or endangering herself. Call your dog back to you or play games like Tug and Retrieve to keep her within twenty to thirty feet of you at all times.

Don't overdo the wordplay: No one likes to be nagged. Use your new direction no more than three to five times an outing until it's well understood and pleasurable.

Gradually vary the location and distance so your dog learns to generalize that "Sit" means Sit, no matter where you go.

Word by Word

As you work through my Five-Step Learning Strategy, introduce your direction words one at a time. Start with the directions you'll use the most on a daily basis. While my dogs know all of the words listed in table 6.3, I started with Sit, Go to Your Mat,

Come, and Stay. Decide which directions are the most important to you and begin there. If your dog is handicapped (dogs with hip dysplasia have a hard time Sitting), avoid directions that would make her uncomfortable. If you have a deaf or blind dog, exaggerate your signals and words accordingly.

Your dog's interest in learning will also be affected by her personality, time of day, and the rewards you wave in front of her. Although you should phase out food treats before they become a bribe, using meals and treats to reward her is awesomely fun for your dog, as well as quick and easy for you. If you can't find a food your dog loves, use a toy or your happy voice to build her enthusiasm.

To see these in action, visit ModernDogParenting.com /Lessons&Learning.

DOWN

Down tells your dog to lower herself onto her belly. As you're teaching this one, look at the very spot you want her to go to. Don't stare at her—she'll want to jump at your face, roll around, or nip. Dogs, like people, feel uncomfortable when anyone stares at them for too long. Stay calm as your dog figures this out—too much excitement from you inspires play, not concentration.

Gather your marker, mat, and rewards, and take your dog into her Learning Zone off-leash.

Step 1: Mark the Moment
Wait for or encourage a Down position in one of three ways:

a. **Stand and look calmly at the floor as your dog tests out different behaviors to see which one brings you to life. Capture the moment by marking and rewarding the very instant she goes Down.**

b. **Shape the Down step-by-step by rewarding her for even tiny steps in the right direction. I did this with Mojo, our recent bully rescue. At first I'd reward her for lowering her head to the floor; a few days later I waited for her to stretch a paw** forward; and a few sessions after that, I held out for a full Down. And I got it!

c. Hold a lure in front of your dog's nose, then lower it to between her front paws. Another fun way to go at this is to drag the reward under your bent knee or a chair to encourage your dog to lower her shoulders as she follows it. My kids love playing this game throughout the day!

Step 2: Say and Signal

With treats, mat, and clicker, go into your dog's Learning Zone off-leash, say "Down" then point to the spot between her paws. If your dog doesn't respond in three seconds, repeat "Down" as you stare at the floor between her legs. Now wait. She may bark, jump, or lunge at your hand. Are your treats out of view? Did you practice step 1 long enough so she knows which behavior you're focused on? Look calmly at the floor and wait and wait and wait. Your dog or puppy may stand, stare, bark, and jump at you, or she may grab her mat and thrash around. Breathe in, breathe out. She may throw herself down in frustration or excitement—it doesn't matter. The second she does, come alive—mark the exact moment with a click or "Yes" and reward! Practice at this step until the direction Down excites your dog.

Step 3: Proof and Generalize

Practice Down in increasingly more distracting areas of your home. Ask friends or family to make noise or use appliances as you say, signal, and reward her cooperation. If she's confused, do what I call a Flash Round: Stop and use tasty treats to do three push-ups—Sit-Down-Sit-Down-Sit-Down—in a row. Repetition can work wonders on the brain.

Step 4: Varying Reward Pattern

Phase off your treat reliance by using other things your dog finds rewarding, like toys, freedom, and play. Encourage your dog to Down before offering a meal, opening the door or tossing a toy.

Step 5: Freedom and Priorities

As you and your dog grow more comfortable with Down, use it when you socialize and encourage her to listen when she's over-excited or plays or greets too roughly. Here are three ways to encourage her understanding:

a. With your dog standing a few feet away from you, say and then signal "Down." If she doesn't listen, approach her calmly and repeat yourself. Kneel down and point to the floor, repeating yourself a third time. If she still doesn't respond, walk out of the room and ignore her for a few minutes. Go back a step and practice more. When she does listen, praise her calmly, and offer varied reinforcements at random times. Let her know that she doesn't get to enjoy your company if she doesn't respond to your request, even when she's a little too distracted to prioritize it.

b. Anchor your dog's leash to a door or banister or ask a friend to hold her for you. Stand three feet away, look at the ceiling, and wait a minute or two. At first, your dog might strain or fuss. When she stops, praise her. If she was really upset, don't ask for more until she is calmer when you stand apart. Once she can handle you leaving her side, point and stare at her front paws, then say "Down." If she does, mark the moment and have your friend toss her a treat.

c. If you've practiced with a target disc, try some distance Downs and practice saying "Down" at various angles.

Gradually increase the distance you stand from your dog as you request her cooperation. Try not to use this direction too much—no more than three to five times a day. It can be a buzz kill if your dog relishes play and freedom.

STAND

This direction is great when you need to brush your dog or tend to her feet. I use it on rainy days to avoid the wet-tushy dilemma. If you're planning to show or do sports with your dog, knowing to Stand still is a must.

Gather your marker, mat, and rewards, and take your dog into her Learning Zone off-leash.

Step 1: Mark the Moment

Wait for or encourage the Stand position in one of three ways:

a. Stand calmly and capture the moment she happens to Stand still, even just for a second, with a mark and reward!

b. Shape your dog's Stand still step-by-step by rewarding your dog for increasingly still moments.

c. Hold the lure in front of your dog's nose, then very slowly bring it straight forward so your dog has to Stand to follow the reward.

Step 2: Say and Signal

In your dog's Learning Zone, say "Stand" then signal by drawing an imaginary line out from your dog's nose with your index finger. If your dog doesn't respond in three seconds, repeat "Stand" as you stand next to her and signal with your finger again, urging her to step forward. Now wait. Your dog may be totally baffled or just bounce around, clearly still confused. Keep your treats out of view and stay calm. The second she stands still, mark the moment and reward!

Step 3: Proof and Generalize

Practice Stand in increasingly more distracting areas of your home. Ask friends or family to make noise or use appliances as you say, signal, and reward her cooperation. If she's confused, do a Flash Round with tasty treats and mix it up: Sit-Stand-Down-Stand-Down-Sit-Stand . . .

Step 4: Varying Reward Pattern

Phase out the treats by using other things your dog finds rewarding, like toys, freedom, and play. Encourage your dog to Stand still before you offer a meal, open the door, or toss her a toy.

Step 5: Freedom and Priorities

As you and your dog grow more comfortable with Stand, use it when you socialize, and encourage your dog to respond to the word at gradually increasing distances.

WAIT

Wait encourages your dog to stop, look, and listen. After saying "Wait," you might just release her with a "Go Free" or encourage her to Sit, Down, or Come depending on the situation. Any direction can follow Wait.

Gather your marker and rewards, and take your dog into her Learning Zone off-leash. Go to a stairway or door, or prop a broom across two small objects of equal height, like two books or thick magazines, and stand on one side of it.

Step 1: Mark the Moment!

Wait for or encourage your dog to Wait in one of three ways:

a. Stand calmly and capture the moment your dog stands and looks up to you at the edge, then mark and reward that moment.

b. Shape her staying on your side of the threshold by rewarding her for standing anywhere on your side of the division. Progressively mark and reward moments of her standing closer to you.

c. Hold the lure in front of your dog's nose then bring it to your side as you approach the threshold. Mark and reward her!

Step 2: Say and Signal

Go into your dog's Learning Zone off-leash and walk up to the threshold. When your dog comes to your side, say "Wait" then signal with a quick arm swing in front of her face and an open palm. If your dog ignores you, that's okay. Just stand still or turn, walk around the space and start again. Mark the instant your dog pauses and looks up to you—even just for a second—and reward her before you leave the zone. Encourage increasingly longer pauses, coming alive the moment she looks to you.

Step 3: Proof and Generalize

Once your dog responds to the direction and signal, practice Wait around your home in increasingly distracting areas. Say "Wait" as you get to a door or threshold; "Wait" as you ask a friend or family member to walk up or down a staircase in front of you; "Wait" as your kids leave home to head to the bus. Use a happy voice and rewards to encourage eye contact, varying her focus from one to four seconds before offering the prize and releasing her! If she's confused, attach a light hands-free drag lead as you practice indoors and out. Use the line only if your dog's endangering herself or others.

Step 4: Varying Reward Pattern

Phase out the treats by using Wait before offering other things your dog finds rewarding, like toys, freedom, and play.

Step 5: Freedom and Priorities

Practice Wait when socializing and even at a distance. Place your dog on a hands-free long line if her response is delayed. Start at four feet and continue to practice at greater distances until you can call "Wait" from fifty feet and know your dog will stop and check in.

This is one of the directions I rely on most, especially when playing or hiking with my dogs off-leash. Wait stops my dogs in their tracks, at which point I can alert them to a new path, adventure, or bonus reward!

STAY

Stay tells your dog to hold still. It can be tough and boring, especially in the beginning and for young pups. I'll try to make it fun. Don't worry about position now: Sit, Stand, or Down is fine. Reward short Stays initially; it'll build her concentration like a muscle. Watch for times outside of lessons when your dog puts herself in a Stay and looks to you for confirmation. She's testing you to see what gets your attention! If you ignore her impulse control, don't blame her for acting out.

Gather your marker, mat, and rewards, and take your dog into her Learning Zone off-leash.

Step 1: Mark the Moment

Wait for what comes naturally—either standing, sitting, or lying still—and mark that. Shape longer holds: Keep the rewards coming as long as she holds still. Although some might argue that the marker word releases the dog from what she is doing, I've coached many dogs to hold longer Stays by reinforcing them for holding still. Here are three ways to encourage your dog to Stay:

a. **Wait until your dog holds one position. Lift your face in a smile but hold off on marking the moment for a full count of "one-one thousand." Mark, reward, and then stand back up. If she's holding still, mark again. Still holding? Or did she get up and put herself back down? Good. Mark that. If she's like most dogs, she'll like the game and prompt you to keep the food flowing. Such a smart girl!**

b. **Progressively lengthen the pause between each reward: one second, two seconds, four seconds, then six . . . If your dog's overexcited and keeps snatching at the treats, work on Leave It first (see page 160). Don't let her snatch treats, but keep the rewards flowing as long as she's holding still and staying calm.**

c. **Ask your dog to Sit, show her a treat, and wait until she's holding still to mark and reward. Slowly lengthen the time she must hold still, and reward her for Staying for longer periods of time.**

Step 2: Say and Signal

Gather your marker, mat, and a handful of treats and take your dog to her Learning Zone off-leash. Wait for whatever position she offers, then say and signal "Stay" with a flat palm in front of her face. If your dog Sits and holds still, reward her after two seconds; if she continues to hold still, continue to reward her, progressively increasing the time between rewards. If she gets up, no harm, no foul. Just ignore her until she settles into the position. When she does, reward her again, and again and again. One of my dogs wouldn't get up. She kept scootching around in front of me as though saying, Look, Ma, look—I'm still Staying! Aren't I smart! When time's up, use a release word like "Okay" or "Go Free" to let her know the game's over—at least for now!

Step 3: Proof and Generalize

Use Stay all over your home, while you open and shut the door, while someone else cooks dinner or sets the table. Practice around the kids, the cat, delivery people. Make it fun and use tasty treats, and before you know it, distractions that would have unraveled her will anchor her to the floor! Use Stay before you toss a toy, again at the dog park, or before she's allowed off-leash. Stay will become its own reward!

If your dog is easily distracted, work gradually and only practice when you can give her your full attention. For example, try a few Stays with the TV on, then with someone watching TV, then with someone watching TV and eating a sandwich. Choose whichever stationary posture (Sit, Down, or Stand) is most comfortable for your dog. As you practice, increase the duration and distractions separately before taking Stay out into the real world.

Step 4: Varying Reward Pattern

After you've been at this for a week or two, you'll be ready to start varying rewards. Mix up the treats so she'll never know what's coming. Sometimes reward a long Stay with a game, tug, toss, or chewy. Sometimes just exclaim "Good!" Other times have her Stay before seeing her friend—the release to socialize is its own reward. Mix it up! Make it perplexing and fun.

Step 5: Freedom and Priorities

Stay at a distance is a challenge, but most dogs catch on quickly. By this time, your dog's cooperation will be self-reinforcing. Here are two ways to work on distance control and prioritizing with Stay:

a. Ask a friend or family member to step on your dog's leash or tie it to something immobile, like a stair banister. Position your dog and say "Stay." Leave the room, gradually increasing the time, distance, and distractions you add while out of the room. If someone is with your dog, they can settle her calmly. If you return to find your dog has moved, stay calm. Relocate your dog in the original pose, stand nearby as you count back from ten, and then praise, reward and release her calmly.

b. Outside, secure your leash to a tree or pole at a safe distance from any roads or foot traffic. If you have a yard, secure what I call a tree line: a rope or tether attached to one or more trees or posts that will enable you to secure your dog discreetly at unpredictable times. While some dogs figure this out, others think they're free to go once the leash is removed. Say "Stay," gradually increasing the time and distance.

GO TO YOUR MAT

Everybody wants to belong: Dogs and people like to feel welcomed and appreciated. To help your dog feel acknowledged and clever in any room or situation, organize a special place for her with her own mat and some toys. Take it with you when you travel for your dog to use like a security blanket.

Here's how you teach her to love, cherish—and stay—on her mat. Gather your marker, your dog's mat or bed and rewards, and go into her Learning Zone off-leash. Put the mat down, step back, and see what happens.

Step 1: Mark the Moment!

Encourage your dog's next move in one of three ways:

a. **Stand calmly and wait until your dog steps on her mat. Decide now if you want her to be completely on her mat or if part on/part off is good enough for you. I like all or nothing, but that's just me. If waiting to capture the moment is killing you, try shaping the skill step-by-step.**

b. **Shape this skill by marking and rewarding incremental steps onto the mat, even if that means one paw at a time. Mark and reward one paw, then two. Now hold out for all or nothing. This learning curve is exciting for both dogs and people. It can go very quickly or take a few sessions for your dog to understand that all four paws on the mat are what you're asking for.**

c. **Put her mat down, lure your dog over to it, and mark the moment all paws line up. If your dog knows Stay, it's likely she'll start offering you both behaviors simultaneously. Nice. Lure her over, pause, then reward her when she holds still.**

Step Two: Say and Signal

With all your tools and goodies, go to your dog's Learning Zone off-leash and point to her mat as you say "Go to Your Mat." Does she go? Super. Mark and reward. If she Stays, keep rewarding. If she doesn't go, repeat yourself, but don't stare. Wait patiently. I always bring in a nail file to keep myself busy while my dog considers her options. Once she goes onto her mat, I pause promptly and mark and reward her. If she knows Stay, practice it on her mat. You can also introduce other positions (Sit, Down, or Stand).

Step 3: Proof and Generalize

Set up mats in all the rooms you share. Mats should be on the edge of a room, near your sitting areas but not in the middle of footpaths. Put a toy basket nearby or leave her chewies on the mat. Hide some treats just out of reach so you can reward your dog each time she chooses to go to the mat on her own.

Now practice sending your dog there. Stand near the mat, point, and say "On Your Mat." Look at the mat, not at your dog. If she goes, mark and reward her; don't worry about her Staying there now. If she blows you off, all is not lost. Go and do something nice for yourself. Try again later, standing closer to the mat at a time when your dog is hungrier (and thus more attentive), more tired (and likely to want to chill), or less distracted (it's hard to be still when life is swirling all around you). If your dog is too excited to focus, try feeding her on her mat and making On Your Mat the go-to plan before offering anything your dog loves (toys, food, love).

Step 4: Varying Reward Pattern

After a week or so, you'll notice that your dog starts to gravitate to her mat on her own—it makes her feel good. Like an armchair in a kitchen. Begin to phase out your treat reliance by rewarding your dog with toys and love when she goes to her areas willingly.

Step 5: Freedom and Priorities

As your dog grooves with her mat, bring it around with you. Heading to a friend's home? Taking your dog on a train, plane, or ferry? Going on vacation? Don't forget your mat! I bring one or two dogs to the coffee shop with me each morning; I have a nice, flat, extra-large mat that comes with us every time. A little bit of home follows us wherever we go!

COME

Come is everyone's golden chalice, that magical word some people think symbolizes our ultimate connection and control over dogs. Well, I think that's a whole lot of phooey. Come is way overrated. If your dog doesn't Come on a dime, don't worry—she still loves you.

If you've pressured your dog to Come the second you speak, and get all weirded out and wicked when she doesn't obey, there's your first clue why your dog thinks Come means run. Come symbolizes your descent into madness—monster Mommy (or Daddy). Let me show you a better way.

Think of Come as the phrase equivalent of "Huddle!"—a quick and exciting invitation to reconnect. It's a great way to transform the word "Come" from a demand you think your dog must obey to a game that she can't wait to play!

Gather your marker and rewards, and take your dog into her Learning Zone off-leash.

Step 1: Mark the Moment!

You'll start this lesson backward: teaching your dog that Come means you're together, not apart. Here are a few ways to get started:

> Stand calmly and capture the moment your dog Sits or Stands in front of you and looks up. Mark the moment and hold her collar gently as you pop a tasty treat into her mouth. That's all she has to do to win the prize. Big rewards are a' coming!

> If your dog's super bouncy, you might want to shape the Come, marking her for either standing near you, sitting in front of you, or looking up. Once you've got all three behaviors separately, start waiting for two together—any two, then all three at once.

> Lure the Come by waving a treat in front of your dog's nose, stepping back, and guiding her into a Sit in front of you.

Step 2: Say and Signal

Go into your dog's Learning Zone off-leash with her mat and treats, and say and signal "Come" by throwing one arm or two over your head in what I call the human exclamation point. Mark, praise, and reward your dog the moment she arrives. If she offers a Sit, super; if she doesn't at first that's okay, too. Even if she jumps on you, don't sweat it initially; we can shape that out later. Embrace her enthusiasm! As she grows more reliable, hold out for a Sit before marking and rewarding her arrival. Celebrate your togetherness. Change your position and say "Come" again! Mark and reward her Coming and Sitting near you—good dog!

Step 3: Proof and Generalize

Once she's got all that down, bring Come out of her Learning Zone, where the word will be in competition with other distractions. Remember what you're asking: that your dog leave something she's enjoying to reconnect with you. Give her good reason! Say "Come" whenever offering your puppy a treat or toy. Say "Come" as you run playfully in the opposite direction. Say "Come" when you shake treats or squeak a toy. Come for dinner, Come when someone is at the door, Come for pats, food, and goodies.

Come can start to lose its appeal if you continually call her for nothing, though, or for things she'd rather avoid like a scolding or isolation. She may blow you off for better activities—even well-mannered dogs do that from time to time. Don't lose your cool! If she's off on a tangent, go collect her. Then let it go—after-the-fact corrections backfire every time. There is no way she'll want to Come again. Amp up the fun using a target wand or disc to make focusing around distractions a game.

Step 4: Varying Reward Pattern

Vary your food rewards and include other incentives like toys and attention. Encourage your dog to Come as you walk into the kitchen for a meal or up to the kids' room to wake them for school.

Step 5: Freedom and Priorities

Ready to take your show on the road? If you're able to find a fenced area or can use a twenty-five- to fifty-foot light line, practice Come off-leash using lots of enthusiasm, your marker, treats, and/or a target wand. When practicing on-leash, use a no-pull harness when possible to avoid any strain on your dog's neck or your arm.

FOLLOW

An outing with your dog should leave you less stressed, not more. If your dog views your walks as more of a strength-building exercise than a leisurely stroll, reevaluate what's going on. Does the

COME GAMES TO ADD EXCITEMENT

Come should always invite a fun reconnection. Here are three games that are sure to bring your dog back to your side in a flash. Just do the activity and wait for your dog to notice and run over before you highlight her enthusiasm with the word "Come"!

WHAT'S IN THE GRASS?

Pretend you've found something in the grass. Ignore your dog and channel your pretend find. I guarantee she'll want in on it! See her running over? Say "Come" and reward her with a treat, toy toss, or a dig.

RUN AWAY

Bait your dog with a treat or toy, then say her name and "Come" as you run away. First, stop after ten feet, turn, and wait until your dog's on all four feet to reward her. Then lengthen the distance and dart in unexpected directions!

HOLD BACK

Ask a friend or family member to play with you. Stand on opposite sides of a room, porch, or yard. Have your helper hold your dog as you show her you have a treat or toy, then walk away. When you turn, kneel down and call your dog to Come. Have your friend pause while your puppy or dog struggles to break free. After a count of three to five seconds, have your friend release your dog to Come to you. You can vary the length and angle for this game, too.

sight of the leash rev your dog up? There's a clue. Aside from my personal view that leashes are one of the worst (although necessary) inventions of modern history, you and your dog have to come to some agreement on how to act with one.

Gather your marker, mat, and rewards, and take your dog into her Learning Zone off-leash. You read that right! Although this word is a companion to leash walking, your walking word must be taught off-leash first. Your goal here is not just that your dog Follow you, it's to get her to want to Follow you!

Step 1: Mark the Moment!

Encourage your dog to Follow in one of three ways:

a. **Walk around your dog's Learning Zone. If it's too small, add a room or use a larger but still familiar room. Capture the moment your dog shows interest and follows along. If she's not interested in you, make this session an aerobic activity—dance, swing your arms, skip! Have fun, use treat cups, and become someone your dog wants to follow!**

b. **Shape any interest she shows in you: a glance, a few steps headed in the same direction. Gradually wait for more. Mark and reward one step in your direction, then a few steps, then two steps and some eye contact.**

c. **Lure your dog to your side (either side you want, but one side initially) by holding the treat at her nose level. Mark and reward a few steps, then more steps, then vary the distance from three to ten feet between each reinforcement.**

Step 2: Say and Signal

With treats, mat, and/or your clicker, go into your dog's Learning Zone off-leash, instruct "Follow" as you slap the side of your leg and start forward. If your dog doesn't respond in three seconds, say it again and throw some enthusiasm into it! Mark and reward her cooperation, slowly increasing the distance between rewards.

Step 3: Proof and Generalize

Once your dog responds to the direction and signal, practice Follow around your home. Ask friends or family to make noise or use appliances as you say, signal, and reward her cooperation. If she's confused or distracted use a target wand to help her focus. Slowly add more distractions, vary the distance you walk (still inside or in a hallway), and increase the length of time you walk together.

While you're at it, set up an obstacle course with various distractions (e.g., laundry baskets, chips, children), and include other words in your walks like Leave it, No, and Down.

Step 4: Varying Reward Pattern

Vary your food rewards and include other incentives like toys and attention. Begin to attach a light drag lead; at first letting her drag it along as you walk about, then picking it up loosely as you go.

Step 5: Freedom and Priorities

Find a fenced area or use a twenty-five- to fifty-foot light line to practice Follow off-leash with lots of enthusiasm, your marker, treats, and/or a target wand. Use a no-pull harness or head collar when possible to avoid straining. Clipping on her leash, say "Follow" and make an effort to keep the leash as slack as you can. If your dog strains forward, stop and wait until she looks to you to continue. If she lunges, change direction, then mark, praise, and reward her for being back at your side.

Remember that your dog is an individual as intelligent and curious as a young child. Freedom will always call to her. When possible, let your dog lead you or enjoy an off-leash romp, especially at the end of a cooperative walk. Follow her lead or release her on a long line or in an enclosure to go her own way.

IMPULSE CONTROL

Impulse control is a worthy goal—no matter how many legs you walk on. It can be especially tough to exercise, however, when life

LET'S GO

Let's Go is Follow's cousin, a more general direction that can be used when your dog's exploring off-leash or on a long or retractable lead. Let's Go doesn't demand your dog be at your side but lets her know when you're changing direction or heading home.

gets distracting. To help your dog improve her self-control, teach her these words in her Learning Zone to show her what they mean.

NO

"No" is another one of those magical words that dogs are supposed to know from birth. For a lot of dogs, "No" is their middle name—Fluffy No, Sparky No, Daisy No, Rosco No. But when overused, No loses any meaning.

No should be taught as a word, just like any other. No says "That's not a good idea," or "Our family doesn't do it that way," or "Bad choice." No doesn't condemn—it instructs, then redirects. Say it in a calm tone, and direct your dog to a better alternative.

(Note: Your dog must be older than six months to learn this direction; before that she's just a puppy—a delightfully clueless little infant who's not capable of learning right from wrong. Be patient.)

Before you go into your dog's Learning Zone with all your usual paraphernalia, set up the space by laying her mat in one corner with her favorite chews and toys and something you'd rather her avoid, like socks, paper towels, or a tissue basket in another corner. In a slight change of procedure, put your dog on a familiar leash or light four-foot drag leash attached to a no-pull harness or head collar if you're using one.

Hold your dog's leash as you walk into her Learning Zone. If she knows Wait, use it at the stair or threshold. Then let her proceed in.

Step 1: Mark the Moment!

If she goes to her mat and grabs her things, mark and reward. Awesome. If she stops when she notices the temptation or goes straight for it, pull back. The next thing you do is important: step forward and yell or stamp the object like it's poison. Do not look at your dog, just stamp on the object as a warning for her to stay away. When you're done, escort her to her mat, mark and reward, and sit with her like that event was the scariest moment of your life to date.

Step 2: Say and Signal

If this exercise stresses your dog, vary it with other, more fun lessons or tricks. Vary the temptations, and add the word just before your leash tug. Always redirect your dog to her mat and toys. She may start looking up when she notices something unfamiliar on the floor or may just look for her mat and toys. Good! You're on your way.

Step 3: Proof and Generalize

Practice No in increasingly more distracting areas of your home. Ask friends or family to make noise or use appliances as you say "No" and redirect her to her mat and things. Try placing temptations on furniture and tabletops. Redirect any interest she expresses—don't wait for your dog to steal—by then you'll be too late. If she stares at the table or countertop, say "No," then pull back or block her. Lastly, yell at the furnishings or countertop. Got a dishwasher-obsessed dog? Catch her channeling the dishes and stop her in her tracks with No. Don't correct her—that wouldn't make any sense. Just yell at the dishes, and then move on with her like you just leapt over death's door. Hurry to her mat, sit and hold a bone if you've got the time, and mark and reward her for being still.

Step 4: Varying Reward Pattern

Now your goal is to phase out the object-correction move. After berating 6–10 inanimate objects, you should see that No is alerting your dog to step away or pull back when you say it. If your dog doesn't go straight to her mat, or look up for your direction, direct her to her mat and her toys.

Step 5: Freedom and Priorities

As you and your dog grow steadier with No, use it when you socialize and encourage her to listen at gradually increasing dis-

Blocking involves stepping between your dog and a distraction. Without a leash, it can be a calm reminder that your dog needs to use better impulse control. Add the directions No or Leave It, depending on the situation.

tances. Use No to stop her from investigating something you'd rather she not and No to bring her focus back when she's too distracted to listen.

LEAVE IT

Leave It says you have to leave that thing now, although you might be able to have it later. I like to use Leave It when teaching my dogs to pause before taking a treat or eating their meal. It's also good to practice when playing with friends. Leave It is remarkably easy and fun to teach and learn.

Go get two types of treats, one your dog likes, and another she loves, grab your marker and mat, then go into your Learning Zone off-leash.

Step 1: Mark the Moment!

Stand calmly with the less-enticing treat in your right hand and the tastier of the two hidden behind your back in your left hand. Hold out your opened right hand six to eight inches in front of her nose, but close it as she reaches for the treat. If she paws, barks, or bites, remain calm. The second she pulls back, mark the moment and reward her with the treat from your left hand. Once your dog catches onto this pause-don't-grab game, hold the tastier treat in both hands. Next, put the lesser treat on the floor, near your foot and tasty treat hidden in your left hand. If your dog makes a dive for the first treat, cover it with a hand or foot and wait for her to pause and pull back to mark and reward.

Step 2: Say and Signal

Grab your various treats and mat, and head back into your dog's Learning Zone off-leash. Repeat the same sequences, adding "Leave It" just before you present each reward. Encourage your dog to make eye contact with you after hearing the cue. If she doesn't, see if a "*cluck, cluck*" will bring her eyes up.

Step 3: Proof and Generalize

Practice Leave It in increasingly distracting areas of your home. Ask friends or family to make noises as you practice your sequences. Once your dog's reliably pausing before grabbing the food in your hand, try Leave It with food on low coffee tables, using a high-level treat to reward her self-control. If she's quick, attach a short hand or finger lead to step on if you need to. This is also a good time to introduce other pets to her Learning Zone and encourage self-control with Leave It and high-end food rewards.

Step 4: Varying Reward Pattern

Begin to phase out your treat reliance by using other things your dog finds exciting, like toys, freedom, and play to reward her self-control.

Step 5: Freedom and Priorities

Use Leave It when you socialize, too. Work at great distances with a long line as you encourage your dog to respond from two, four, and ten feet away from you. Use Leave It when passing friends or leaving social play groups. Use Leave It with tempting smells, leashed dogs, and wildlife. Make sure Leave It lifts your dog's tail by pairing it with food, a fun game, like Tug or Carry, or some enthusiastic loving.

UNDER OR BACK

Everyone needs a happy place: a corner of the world where they can feel safe and relaxed. Well-loved kids look to the hug of a parent or a hand to grasp when life feels unsafe. Dogs need something similar.

Provide your dog with a safe place either under your legs or behind you when she feels unsettled or out of control. She'll breathe easier knowing you're out in front taking the heat no matter what's happening. Here's how to teach it.

Sit down and call your dog over to you. Your dog will sit in one of two places: on your feet, pressed up against your side, or under the space created by your legs. There is no one right way to sit near you per se. Resting against you or sitting on your feet is just fine when life is calm. But when life gets unpredictable, your dog's response often depends on her position. If she's in front of you, she'll respond more impulsively. But if she's in your shadow, she'll be more likely to watch (and mimic) your reactions.

To teach your dog to get behind you, practice in your Learning Zone during non-distracting times. Say "Back," then wait to capture or lure her behind you with a treat or toy and instruct Stay when she's standing in your shadow.

Follow the Five-Step Strategy for the sister direction, Under, too. Gather your marker, mat, and rewards, and take your dog into her Learning Zone off-leash.

Step 1: Mark the Moment!

Sit on the edge of a chair so there is a wide-open space between your bent knee and the chair itself.

a. Wait until your dog climbs into the space or under your legs. Capture the moment by marking and rewarding her the very instant she does.

b. Shape your dog for even tiny steps in the right direction. Mark and reward her if she comes to your side, then wait for a little more—maybe comes to your side and drops her head, then comes, drops her head and bumps your leg, then comes, drops, bumps, and lays down. Eventually, she'll put it all together!

c. Lure your dog under your legs, then mark and reward her. Continue to practice until your dog goes under in one fluid motion.

Step 2: Say and Signal

Say and signal "Under" by pointing beneath your legs. Wait until your dog goes there to mark and reward. Continue to practice this step until your words and signal excite your dog, but only do three Unders per session. Also use this time to practice Down and Stay—you'll eventually use all three directions at once.

Step 3: Proof and Generalize

Practice Under around your home. Under while you're watching TV; Under while the kids are playing; Under while you're eating breakfast. Practice using Under with increasingly more distractions.

Give your dog a special bone or chew to keep her busy.

Step 4: Varying Reward Pattern

Phase off treats and encourage your dog Under with toys, chews, and plain old love and reassurance. Under will soon become your dog's comfort zone; a place to emotionally reconnect and fill her loving cup.

AWAY

Away is related to Back. It tells your dog to move Away from the door, a visitor, or even you when you're busy. Away says "I'm present but not accessible, so please go off and do something else." Introduce this word in your dog's Learning Zone: say "Away" and toss a favorite toy or treat behind her tail. Vary the surprise: Sometimes toss a treat, other times a toy or chew. Now position a toy basket in her Learning Zone and try to land your toss in the basket. End each Back or Under lesson with a fun Away game until your dog catches on.

Step 5: Freedom and Priorities

Practice Under around distractions both in and outside of your home. Bring treats and toys to guide your dog and a mat if that would help steady her. A savory chew toy will help entertain and calm, too.

Ten Terrific Tricks

Learning can be addictive. It should be fun to do and enjoyable to watch. And what's better at getting everyone's tails wagging than teaching some tricks!

I'll end this chapter with my top ten. Choose the ones that come naturally to your dog, introducing each in her Learning Zone until they connect, then practicing in increasingly more distracting areas. To see many of these tricks in action, visit Modern DogParenting.com/Tricks&Games.

PAW AND HIGH-FIVE

The classic Paw can be easy to teach if your dog or puppy is naturally expressive. Hold out a treat six inches in front of your dog's nose and wait. If she tries to snatch it, close the treat in your fist, reopening your hand only when she pulls away. Eventually she'll get fed up and start batting you with her paw, at which point you mark, open your hand, and reward her. Once she's putting that together, prompt her by saying "Paw" and holding out your flat palm at her elbow (aka her hock) height.

You might notice that I've left out a few tricks, including Give Kisses, Speak, and Up, Up. I love these tricks and teach them in chapter 7 as part of an overall Good Manners protocol. A dog who Speaks needs to learn to Hush; to teach a dog Off, she must also learn to identify Up, Up. Give Kisses is adorable; nipping is not.

If your dog's less paw-centric, wait until she's lying down. Hold a treat in front of her paws, closing your fist if she lunges or grabs for it, and wait. Eventually she'll get bored and bat your hand—mark it, open your fist, and reward her! As soon as your dog catches on to this cause and effect routine, your problem won't be how to encourage her to do it, it will be how on earth to get her to stop!

At this point you can spin off and teach things like High-Five (just present the treat and say "Paw, High-Five" as you gradually angle your hand vertically) or Wave (present the treat, say "Paw, Wave" as you pull the signal back, and wave it in front of your dog's face just before her paw touches your palm).

To teach your dog to stop, ignore the pawing unless you've asked for it. Also teach her Not Now by holding out a reward, asking for Paw twice in a row, then saying "Not Now" and waiting until her pawing stops. Mark the moment it does, and reward. (If your dog or puppy is so persistent that she's drawn blood, see the Spray Away correction explained in the next chapter.)

BELLY UP

This is my favorite greeting trick, and kids love it, too. Most dogs do it naturally, so it's a cinch to learn. If you're in the habit of scratching your dog's belly, say "Belly Up" each time she prompts you by rolling over. Say it while bonding after a play session, watching TV, or greeting each other. Now use it when your dog greets other people: Offer a treat to encourage her down and onto her back.

ROLL OVER

While this is a more complicated move, dogs who love rolling around pick it up quickly. Does your dog roll in grass or goo? Here's your silver lining! If yours is less inclined to go Belly Up, work at this one slowly or select a more natural move to work on.

Introduce the concept in your dog's Learning Zone or at a quiet moment when it's just you two. Guide your dog onto her back; a belly scratch usually does the trick. Now take out a treat and swing it to one side of her face, and mark the moment she rolls to her other side. Reward her and celebrate when she's right side up! Now you can move on to a more formal introduction of this trick.

Shape this trick in your dog's Learning Zone. Lay down her bed or ask her to Down on a carpet or cushion. Show your dog a treat and say "Roll" as you move the treat from her nose, down under her chin, and around by her shoulder. If she rolls onto her side to get it, everybody wins! Reward and praise. For the first three days, all she'll need to do to get this trick right is to lay on her side. On day 4, she needs to give you a little more. Continue to shape by saying "Roll Over," luring her with a treat, and waiting for her to roll her legs into the air with her head down. Yeah! What a genius. By day 7, encourage her to roll over by saying "Roll Over" first, then "Over" as you swing the treat across her face to the opposite side. To call this one from a standing pose, use your target wand (see chapter 2).

BOW

Each time your dog stretches, gesture with a wave of your arm and say "Bow." Reward her with praise, toys, or attention. Other natural behaviors can be put on cue this way, including Shake (as in, when wet), Sneeze, and Clean Your Paws (lick, lick).

DANCE

If you've got a dog who's as happy on two legs as four, she'll be a natural at this trick. The only rule is that she must keep her front paws in the air—no cheating by holding on to you!

Hold a treat six inches or so above your dog's nose, and wait until she's airborne—even a moment—to reward her. Gradually lengthen the time your dog must remain airborne to get a treat. Wait until she's jumping with gusto to say "Dance!" Don't overdo it, though! Keep your Dances under seven seconds, and save this trick for dogs older than nine months. Once your dog stands or hops excitedly, add variations like Disco Dog, Two Steps Forward, and Walk Like a Lady—depending on your dog's flair for theatrics.

CRAWL

Crawl is another fun one for kids and dogs. Some dogs Crawl naturally; if yours does, praise her like she just invented the move. Say "Crawl" and present her with attention, food, and/or toys. To prompt your dog to Crawl, ask the kids to make a tunnel with their bodies by crouching down or bending their legs at the knee. You could also use a children's play tunnel or a shortened Agility tunnel. Lure your dog through initially, then add the word "Crawl" as she catches on!

CARRY

Some dogs love to carry stuff around; others, not so much. If your dog is mouthy, teach her to Carry by using her toys first. When playing one-on-one, wave a toy in front of her face and encourage her to grab it. If she does, encourage her to hold onto it as you run forward, staring straight ahead. Stop after five to ten steps and say "Give" as you wave a treat in front of her nose. As she catches on, prompt with the word "Carry" and encourage her to hold the object for longer periods. You can ask her to Carry other things, too—a box of spaghetti when you're bringing in the groceries, kindling for the fire, the kids' lunch boxes. Say "Give" to prompt a mouth-to-hand delivery. Perfect this one, and she can even help you collect the laundry!

TAKE, IT'S YOURS, CARRY, BRING, AND DROP

Although I went over Bring and Drop in chapter 5, I'll reintroduce them here to show how you can use single directions to shape a variety of fun adventures.

Each time you offer your dog a toy or bone, say "Take" and

praise her for the simple act of reaching out and receiving it. If it's hers, say so—"It's Yours," and let her keep it. Pat and praise her, but do not force your dog to give up everything all the time. That's silly. You'll just encourage her to take things and hide with them. Instead, encourage her to bring it to her place or take it to a person: Clap, point, and send her by assigning words to different people and places—"Take It to Daddy," "Go to Your Mat."

When you're asking her to Take something of yours, have your treats and marker handy, and supervise her enthusiasm. Say "Take," but be ready to wave a treat by her nose and say "Give" if she starts to run, clamp, or shake it.

Practice Carry by sending her to another person or to a place, and escorting her in the beginning. If you're sending her to a person, ask the person to call her the moment they hear you say their name.

Can you see the potential here? This is a great way to teach your dog to help you with your chores (she can learn to shuffle the laundry or deliver notes) or even get super fancy and teach her things like Fetch the Paper or Get Me Some Juice (from the fridge!). The

WHAT'S AN OBJECT, REALLY?

We people sure do have a funny attachment to things. I say it like I'm an exception, but I'm not. Dogs—and the rest of the animal kingdom—can't register our infatuations. Imagine how funny we look screaming over a crushed remote or a lace heirloom doily the circumference of a large orange. I know you might be mad or sad when your dog messes with your prized objects, but try to contain those feelings. Getting angry won't turn back time and will only create more stress. Can you guess what stressed dogs do to relieve their tension? Yup—they chew, and they don't just chew a little . . . they chew a lot.

fun thing about teaching your dog to handle, carry, and deliver things is that she'll be more in tune and less destructive even when you're not around!

BANG

Related to Belly Up and Roll Over, this is the classic Dead Dog trick. Your dog should be comfortable resting on her back or side and know a solid Stay with a hand signal before you begin.

In your dog's Learning Zone or a quiet room, gently pet your dog until she's comfortably on her side or back. You can also lure her into this position with a treat or toy. Once she goes willingly, add the direction—say "Play Dead," "Bang," "Time for Bed," etc.—before settling her into position. Then flash a quick Stay (if she knows this direction), pause for one or two seconds, then mark, reward, and release. Gradually increase the length of time she's to hold still, then slowly stand up. Move into more distracting rooms and start to give the direction from a standing position.

SIT PRETTY/BEG

I love this one! I don't ask all dogs to do it, but if a dog routinely rocks back on their hind legs, they're made for it! To help your dog balance, build up your dog's strength and coordination. Let your dog rest her front paws on your forearms as she leans to balance on her hind legs. Lure her into this position with a tasty food treat, and after a week, introduce Stay to gradually increase the time she can pose!

These family-friendly instructions may not be enough to land you an agent, but if you're interested in more trick training, there are many books devoted to it—I even wrote one of them! As your dog gets more trick-savvy, use a target wand or disc to encourage her cooperation at a distance.

So there you have it—and you thought teaching your dog was going to be a drag. Dogs are such eager students when we believe in their brilliance, encourage their cooperation, and motivate learning with inclusion and rewards. Who wouldn't love learning with you?

7

All Good Manners
Start at Home

Nothing succeeds without toil. (In modern-speak,
Success is dependent on effort.)
—SOPHOCLES

Whether you're holding this book while a puppy nibbles on your shoelace or have a problem dog who's destroyed your home or a newly rescued adolescent who's giving you a run for your money, this chapter will give you a new perspective on the frustrations many people experience.

Using a fresh approach that flips bad behavior into a reward for greater self-control, you'll be amazed at how you can reshape your dog's behavior without nagging or quashing his self-esteem. Since different issues crop up at different stages of a dog's development, we'll take a look at the whens, wheres, and whys, too.

Of course, frustrations are a very personal thing. What's a problem for you could very well be endearing—or even a necessity—to someone else. A needy, licking, play-obsessed dog could be a nightmare in one household and a blessing in another.

Decide now what's really important to you. If you like your dog jumping all over you when you come home, that's fine. You could teach him to jump only with permission so he saves his jumping just for you, but if you don't care that your dog jumps on others, you won't catch me waving a finger at you. If your dog loves to dig and you live on the beach, clearly that's not an issue, but if you're an avid gardener (like me), then read on to find a solution you can both live with!

At the End of Your Leash?

This phrase has two meanings. First, the obvious: Who is at the end of your leash? A young puppy, an adolescent dog, a rescue, or a mature dog that needs some polishing? How you condition or rehabilitate new habits is very dependent on your dog's age and life experiences. See just how in the Age and Stage categories listed below.

These words are also a twist on the phrase "At the end of your rope." If you're feeling a little frazzled, you may be at the end of your leash. I've been there, too. Breathe easy—shaping better habits doesn't need to be a struggle. I'll map everything out for you.

Age and Stage Categories

Before we jump into individual behaviors, take a look at how your dog's age and life experiences influence his outlook. Although most impressionable in puppyhood, dogs—like people—learn throughout their lifetime. Studies show that the brain generates new memories whenever a dog has a new adventure. Great news for adult rescues and older dogs who can—and should—learn new tricks!

YOUNG PUPPIES (UNDER SIX MONTHS OF AGE)

Puppies are a blank slate, at least where people are concerned. Curious and playful, they test all sorts of rituals to see what will get them more fun, food, and love.

If there's a puppy in your home, you have a golden opportunity. You get to decide what behaviors will give your puppy what he wants. Want a dog that Sits for attention? Ignore the jumping, reward the sitting. Want a quiet dog? Don't rush in when he's barking his head off.

The best—not the only—time to start your Happy Dog Adventure Story is the day you bring your puppy home. The next best time? Any day thereafter.

ADOLESCENTS (SIX TO EIGHTEEN MONTHS)

Adolescence isn't a pleasant time, no matter your species. For people it can last ten to fifteen years; for puppies it's over in a year or two. What a bargain. Adolescence is a time of curiosity, limit testing, insecurity, and adventure seeking. It marks the birth of otherness and individualization. Oh, joy!

You can tell adolescence is heading your way when you get the look. The in-a-minute look after you've called his name, the you've-got-to-be-kidding look when you interrupt socialization hour, or the have-we-met? expression when you want to show off a trick. But if these looks erupt during your dog's six to eighteen-month stage, then good. You're right on track! Adolescents have to push back to grow up happy.

Through his very predictable routines, your adolescent—like everyone else's—is showing you that he has enough faith in your unconditional love for him to test it. Maybe this doesn't feel good to you, but it is good, period.

How you process and handle this time is equally important. Start by tracking your puppy's fall from grace:

Counter and furniture jumping should occur between four and six months, when your puppy takes notice of you and models your

THE THREE WAYS ADOLESCENTS ACT OUT

TANTRUMS

In chapter 1, we went over your dog's basic needs (to eat, drink, play, sleep, and go to the bathroom) and learned how if a need isn't met, your dog will be all out of sorts, like a toddler, but with big teeth. You should be able to identify a puppy tantrum when you see one—tantrums look similar no matter the species. Puppies nip when kids might cry, but both thrash, destroy, and race around like crazy, wild things. Some tantrums can even lead to aggressive reactions, like snarling and snapping. Don't worry—you don't have a Cujo in the making, you just have a puppy who needs more structure. He's probably overtired, which is the number-one unmet need that keeps my phones ringing.

Some people argue that all this acting out demands discipline, but I argue right back: No! A tantrum puppy is an emotional tornado— you can no more control it than you can control the weather. I'll detail how to deal with your puppy's reactions (see chapter 8), but the first step in calming his tirades is to organize a schedule around his five basic needs. Once your puppy is old enough (somewhere between six and twelve months on average) to regulate himself, teach him how to deal with the necessities of everyday life, like eating when he's hungry, figuring out what to play with or chew on, and when to take a nap.

BACKTALK

At five to nine months, you're going to have to suffer through some canine backtalk. We all do. Try not to lose your cool—walking away won't mean you're giving in. If your dog barks at you, jumps from behind, or pretends like you've never met when you request a Sit, pocket whatever treat or toy you might be offering and ignore him. Offer the treat and your attention to someone else in your house— even your partner or kids—your puppy won't know the difference.

He'll only see that someone else is getting the prize that should have been his.

After a while, your puppy will want back into the family circle. When he Sits or acts in a civilized manner, welcome him. Offer a different prize: a chewy, puzzle toy, or maybe a five-minute play break. Try to focus on what your adolescent does right, and voilà—he'll start doing right more often!

STRESS

Funny enough, life is as stressful for the maturing adolescent dog as it is for most kids. It's a brain-hormonal thing—there's too much happening in his head. Surprisingly, most adolescents don't like being alone. They act out or get into trouble when given too much freedom. Leave your puppy alone, and don't be surprised when you get home at the end of the day and get the look—the look a teenager gives you when you come home from a long weekend and ask why your home smells like beer, the patio furniture is on the roof, and the car is turned upside down. The look of stress. This behavior begs for boundaries but can lead to all sorts of trouble when disciplined without insight.

Generally, after nine months, dogs relieve stress through destructive chewing, mindful marking, hyperreactivity, barking, digging, and even self-mutilation. They do these things more if left alone unsupervised. Your homecomings may get your dog revved up in an overly dramatic reaction, a sign of what I call hyper isolation anxiety (HIA). HIA results in hyperactive jumping, barking, or nipping behaviors. If you need help resolving these issues, read on!

behavior. Yes, we can and should teach him not to jump, but jumping is a good sign of normal development.

Alert or demanding barking for an out-of-reach toy, a visitor near your home, or a need to get to a potty area signals a can-do spirit, which emerges between five and eight months, or in the case of überconfidence, even earlier. Teach your adolescent other ways to ask for help, and condition him to everyday noises and interactions.

Real destructive chewing happens around seven to eight months. And it happens quickly—an adolescent can tear a pillow, shred newspaper, or leave lasting teeth marks on a table leg in five seconds flat. Feeling furious is normal; getting mad after the fact is pointless. I'll show you how to handle your frustration.

Adolescence is a bit chaotic. Come to think of it, stop reading this minute, call your parents, and apologize for yours. . . . But seriously, you'll get through it—all good parents do. I've had wild, misbehaving adolescent dogs. One, named Hootenanny, is now our family's sweetheart. She's been voted Best Dog Ever by everyone from the postman to our neighbor's once dog-phobic seven-year-old. Reflect on your own adolescence, and show some empathy when your dog acts out. Above all, be patient: Growing up is hard work, especially for your dog.

MATURE DOGS (OVER TWO YEARS OF AGE)

Mature dogs are set in their ways, much like grown-ups. It's not that they can't change—many would welcome a break from the rigors of always being on high alert—but the truth is, it's less about changing your adult dog's behavior and more about modifying your own reactions to it. Your dog's going to do whatever gets

WHO'S YOUR DOG'S BEST TEACHER?

You might think you have the most influence on your dog's behavior—and you do, sort of. But I want to go deeper. Your dog's best teacher is himself. Through trial-and-error and cause-and-effect, your dog makes his own best decisions, testing out different routines to see what effect—if any—they have on his day. Want to influence him? Great! Read on.

Rescuing a dog is a wonderful thing to do—I've rescued all but one of my dogs and have never ever regretted it. If I've caught you before you've taken the leap, learn as much as you can about each candidate's history. If you've already rescued your forever dog, you probably know the answer to a lot of these questions already: How old was he when he was found? Where is he from? Was your candidate abused or neglected? Is he afraid of men? Children? Does he socialize well with other dogs? Considering his age and how his past experiences might be playing out in your home, can help you shape a rehabilitation plan that's effective and supportive.

him food, fun, and attention, but whether the attention is negative or positive doesn't matter much. In fact, the more frustrated you get, the worse your dog's behavior may become. Why? Because—like kids—dogs internalize our frustrations. Consider the dog who barks at the doorbell. If you yell "BE QUIET," he'll not only interpret your loud shouts as barks, but he might think there's real danger: *Bell rings, my people (who are otherwise calm and friendly) jump and shout!* You don't have to be Pavlov's dog to put that one together.

If you're reading this book eager to teach your older dog a few new tricks, be encouraged. If you can control yourself, your dog will eagerly learn anything you want him to and will be overjoyed by the extra love and positive attention.

Seven Common Behaviors (That Can Annoy Any Dog Lover)

On the next page you'll find a table of common dog behaviors—things dogs do not because they're trying to dominate you or even get your attention (although certain habits may take that path), but because they, like children, are impulsive when ignored.

I've listed seven of the most common things we humans like to complain about. Dogs do other, more appalling things, too—like roll in poop, sniff crotches, and lose control of strong emotions, reacting aggressively or with tremendous anxiety—but I've pushed the heavy stuff to chapter 8. Flip ahead if you just can't wait.

Meanwhile, grab a pencil and go through the table below. Circle the behaviors that relate to your dog and cross off the ones that don't. I've left the last row blank for you to write down what you'd like your dog or puppy to do differently. If he's jumping,

TABLE 7.1

BEHAVIORS	HOUSE SOILING AND MARKING	JUMPING	CHEWING	NIPPING	BARKING	DIGGING
Include	General housebreaking for puppies and older dogs; marking	Greetings; counter cruising, furniture, strangers	Exploratory, destructive, landscaping	Playful, tugging on clothing	Alert, protective, boredom, demanding	Inside, outside
Why does my dog do it?	Confusion, stress	For fun, to get closer to your face, to give warning	To experience new things, because of tooth pain, boredom	Unmet need, fun, puppy play, self-expression	Instinct, protective, fun	Fun, boredom, to get to something underground
Options	Paper training, go outside, mark outside or designated area indoors	Energy expressive trick, grab toy or bone, puzzle toy, Belly Up, hold Sit/Down, Stay	Chew own toys/bones, play with puzzle toys, toy basket, Retrieve and Tug	Kisses and soft mouthing	Speak and Hush	Dig area
What should my dog do instead?						

should he Sit or grab a toy? If he's chewing your table leg, write down what you want him to chew instead.

Rewards

To overcome these common frustrations and help your dog form good habits, he'll need encouragement to ditch his delights and adopt your vision. Sometimes that'll take some preplanning—like buying fun toys for dogs that like to play or chewies for dogs who get their ya-yas crunching and munching—but in the end, rewards are a very personal thing, for dogs *and* for people.

Personally speaking, I have a soft spot. Can you guess what for? It's not fine jewels, shopping, or even dining out—although I do love a good meal. It's babies—wrapped in fur, feather, scales, or skin—I really can't get enough. I read stories in the toddler room at church, often bringing our pets to help soothe the kids with separation anxiety (they suffer, too). I volunteer at the elementary school—not in my own kids' grades, but in the library with the younger kids.

What's with my fascination—are there certain personalities I gravitate toward or relationships I hope to sustain? Ah, no. That'd be weird. What I'm addicted to is learning: seeing a frightened animal grow more trusting through play, laughter, and shared food. Fearful pets respond really well to hand-feeding—the better the eats, the faster they shift their focus. Remember Peter the Pig's story in chapter 1? I also enjoy shaping choices through encouragement, whether it's teaching a dog to choose a toy over a tablecloth or a hamster to bite a celery stick instead of a child's outstretched finger. Learning in motion is my ultimate reward. Good dark chocolate is a close second.

So what about your dog or puppy? If you had to rate his top ten rewards, what would they be? Most love food, but even that has a spectrum: I have one dog who'll do a backflip (almost literally) for a Cheerio or food pellet, and another who wouldn't look up for anything short of the gristle off a steak bone; one of my dogs loves his squeaky bee, another loves her ball. Sometimes it's hard to keep straight, but each of my dogs is clearly motivated by their own special thing.

I've included a list of things your dog might enjoy. Grab your pencil and circle away.

Dried kibble or cereal

Toy toss

Smelly treats only

Dog-to-dog interaction

Choice meat bits

Going outside

Special toy

Sight of leash

Tug game

Freedom

Digging

Pulling on leash

Encourage More Than You Discourage

If you're geared up to have a dog who behaves, channel this simple formula: Encourage more than you discourage. If your dog's a barker, encourage quiet. Is your dog still having accidents? Encourage pottying in the right spot. Same goes for digging, chewing, scratching, and jumping.

"How? Please tell me how," you say. Well, don't just think about the opposite behavior, *obsess* over the opposite behavior. Obsessively reward silence, obsessively reward not digging or digging in the right place. Find ways (I'll help you!) to encourage opposite behaviors so your dog forms those habits, and you'll be on the road to having a much a happier dog—and a much happier you!

Channel Your Dog's Mischief

Dogs learn through both avoidance and delight, which can be confusing. Sometimes you'll just want to yell at your dog. That'll feel good for about three seconds. But nobody likes being yelled at, so while your dog will stop whatever he's doing right at that moment, he won't necessarily know what caused your squawking in the first place. And then you'll feel guilty, and that's awful. Take Posey, the sock-obsessed border collie puppy.

When Posey's parents yelled at her for grabbing socks, she

THE ANIMATED PEZ DISPENSER GAME

PEZ toys—the refillable character dispensers with small, pellet-like candies—have made a huge comeback. My kids love them, and so do I. I feel like a hamster every time I fill one up. Anyhow, here's a fun and remarkably effective learning game to play with your dog or puppy throughout the day. You are the PEZ dispenser, releasing food pellets from a pocket or pouch whenever your dog does something you like.

See him Sitting quietly in front of you? Good boy! Is he laying on his mat? Walk over and dispense a reward. Is he chewing his bone? Awesome!

Ignore anything you find annoying: barking (wear earplugs), jumping (cover your face or leave the room), staring, pawing, scratching at your leg . . . ignore, ignore, ignore. No eye contact, no touch, no shouting.

Encourage more than you discourage, and play the Animated PEZ Dispenser Game to transform your relationship overnight!

stopped. But when I replayed a video of this interaction, it was clear that Posey's dropping the socks in surrender was actually a startled reaction to yelling-induced fear. Since Posey went back to the sock minutes later, we all agreed that yelling startled her but didn't leave any lasting impression.

Before meeting with me, Posey's family had tried spraying all their socks with bitter apple, a nasty-tasting spray. I recommend that, too—it can be a great way to discourage chewing one object, while encouraging a more acceptable toy, what the pros call habituation. I asked them how that was going. Apparently, Posey liked the deterrent spray—to her, it was a condiment. Bummer.

All was not lost, though. Posey's breed is known to be quick witted and industrious. Instead of correcting her over and over for what she was doing wrong, I urged her parents to focus on what Posey was doing right. They got her a basket and filled it with soft, sock-like squeak toys and taught her to retrieve the squeaks by name using the approach outlined in the pages ahead, as well as the laundry trick on page 194.

Out with the old habit, in with the new!

Problem as Reward

Before we shift into resolving your frustrations, let's talk about how you might use them as rewards. Make a list of all the behaviors that annoy you, from barking to peeing, digging to jumping—straight down to marking. Choose a word—one word—that gives your dog the license to go ahead and do it. Why? If your dog needs or loves to do these things, telling him he can't would be like telling a drummer to keep his hands still. By putting your dog's needs and/or passions on cue, you can direct them. Dig here, not there; bark now, not then; chew this, not that.

Once you have word control, the sky's the limit. Not only can you let your dog live his dream (sometimes), you can use his passion as his reward (instead of food, for example). Got a dog who loves to bark? Great, he gets to bark after a cooperative walk or a quick Come. Does your dog like to dig? What better way to bond after lesson time! Channel your dog's passions, link a word to the action, and you'll both be better off in the long run.

Watch for special boxes in each section that follows for tips on how to use each Problem as a Reward. See if you can cleverly redirect your frustrations into praiseworthy actions!

Potty Training

Here's the world's oldest pet project. Teaching your dog where to potty and, more specifically, where not to, is the most important focus from day one. If you're feeling frustrated, you're in a historically long line of good company. Don't overthink it, and please try not to get angry! Just come up with a plan and stick to it. I'm here to help.

WHENS AND WHYS OF HOUSETRAINING

Puppies don't have a lot of bladder control until they're four to five months old. Until they do, they need to go out every one to three hours and often once or twice during the night, too. This is a problem if you're a working puppy parent or you cherish eight uninterrupted hours of sleep. In this case, create a puppy zone with a playpen, crate (left open), corner area with papers for pottying, and bowls and toys to occupy your puppy when you can't be around.

Puppies also need to potty after a good long snooze, directly after eating/drinking, as well as after isolation, excitement (play or chewing), or stress (barking for an hour straight). With little fanfare or attention, take your puppy to his potty area at his scheduled time or after these intervals.

ESTABLISH A ROUTINE

Dogs like routines. The more black-and-white, the better. Decide if you want your dog to go outside or on papers. If the goal is out-

PROBLEM AS REWARD: HOUSETRAINING

WORD(S): Get Busy

MEANING: Potty here, now.

USE: Anytime, anywhere you want your dog to potty. It helps your dog focus on emptying his bladder in unusual places, especially when traveling, visiting friends, and in bad weather.

HOW: Tag along each time your new puppy or dog goes to his potty area. As he's getting into his potty pose, say "Get Busy," without hovering or staring at him while he does. When he finishes, praise calmly and give him loving attention. Within two weeks, your puppy or dog will hear "Get Busy" and potty if he needs to.

REWARD: Initially withhold any petting or attention until after your puppy potties. Some dogs respond well to food rewards, too, while others are distracted by them.

side but you're starting on papers, put the papers down by the door you'll use to take him out.

Either way, follow the same routine: Each time you think your dog needs to potty or he's acting fidgety, take him to his pre-established potty place. Say "Outside" to direct your dog to the door or "Papers" if that's what you've chosen and "To Your Spot" to direct him where to go. Use the same path, go through the same door, and stop only when you get to the designated potty area.

Visit ModernDogParenting.com/FreeDownloads for more on creating a housetraining routine.

ENCOURAGEMENTS

To help your dog learn where to potty, focus on nothing else for three to five days. Feed him, yes; give him some toys or an occasional pat, sure; keep track of his whereabouts in case he goes to the door or starts to look like he's going to potty, definitely; but the lion's share of your love (for just a few days) comes after a properly placed pee or poop. Wait until your puppy is finished relieving himself, then kneel down calmly and offer some good clean loving. (Anything too hyper might startle, not support, the process!)

RESTRICT FREEDOM

Once you're back inside, limit your puppy's freedom. Roll up rugs if you can or section off a space that's rug-free. Decorate the edge of the area with beds, bowls, and toys (dogs like to potty at the edge of their enclosure). If you can't be nearby, crate or enclose your puppy or dog in a small area. This is not a forever deal, but housetraining is super important. Stay focused; get organized.

COPING WITH ACCIDENTS

Don't freak out if your dog has an accident. Most do. Some will have an accident or two at random times for many months. Don't worry. If you catch your dog as he's preparing to go, make a strong noise to see if you can startle him to stop. Calmly flip back to your happy, direction voice, say "Outside" or "Papers," and move him in that direction. If it's after the fact, let it go. Clean up any mess with an odor-neutralizing spray when your puppy isn't around so he doesn't spin clean-up duty into a game.

Still puzzled by your dog's accidents? Target the whens and whys. Are they happening at night or when you leave your dog alone to run an errand or after a good long chew? How could you work around that? Be mindful and present when your dog chews or plays with toys or other pets, place your puppy in a more restricted area when you're busy, crate him at night or set your alarm to get up. Young puppies have no bladder control—sometimes just taking away the water bowl after 7:30 P.M. or restricting feeding after 5:00 P.M. can do the trick!

TRY NOT TO WORRY

I get many frantic calls about dogs still pottying inside from time to time. Sometimes the solution is as easy as thinking through when, where, and why it's happening; other times a few lessons are needed to get your dog or puppy refocused on your plan. Either way, the answer to your problem is never far. There is nothing your dog's doing that hasn't been done before, and no housetraining problem that can't be solved with an extra dose of patience, structure, and positive reinforcement.

Marking

For too many, the word "marking" is a four-letter word. Dogs whose motto is "I pee, therefore I am" may use marking to alleviate frustration—after barking to ward off a roaming dog or delivery person—or to relieve stress, fear, or separation anxiety. If this sounds all too familiar, determine why and when your dog marks. Does your dog bark, then mark when he sees what he considers an intruder from the picture window? Block that room and offer your dog puzzle toys, secured tugs to play with when you're busy or gone, and feeding games to calm his excitement. Marking dogs are smart and self-activated. They also benefit from more exercise, directed lessons, and dog sports.

If you've got a worrywart on your hand, a dog who paces and frets when left alone, try to keep him with you when you can, and establish a special quiet zone or enclosure for when you're out or busy with other things. Choose an area away from noise, light, and distractions, and decorate it with comforting blankets and inspiring toys, chews, and puzzles. Leave on calming music (my dogs and my kids are both addicted to our Pet Tunes Bluetooth

PROBLEM AS REWARD: MARKING

WORD(S): **Hit It**

MEANING: I know you've peed already—what you're doing is marking, and that's cool if you need to do it, I guess—just do it here.

USES: Outside on walks; if your dog potties indoors, places pads around his favorite marking spots.

HOW: After his morning pee, notice if your dog sniffs areas intently and then pees just a bit to leave his mark. Say "Hit It" as he lifts his leg or she kneels to leave some pee-mail.

REWARD: A multiminute mark-off can be a nice gift during an otherwise cooperative walk or lesson.

Speakers), and limit the drama when you come and go. Regardless of what's motivating your dog's marking, praise and reward his good habits and use odor deterrents or obstacles to discourage a repeat performance.

Jumping

The silliest advice I've ever heard suggests that dogs jump to be dominant and should be punished for doing so with kneeing, paw stepping, and electric shocks. Who came up with the idea that to teach dogs to behave right, you have to hurt them?

Jumping is as natural a behavior for dogs as hugging is for kids. And we seem to enjoy it when our dogs are little for many of the same reasons. But little kids who hug don't become serial huggers post-puberty, and neither will your dog if you gently guide him away from the habit. It's easier than you think!

First, ask why your dog is jumping. Maybe it's because he likes to see your face—and everyone else's—when you come in the door. That's understandable; during any lucky puppyhood, dogs get their fill of face-to-face interaction. Little puppies love to smell our breath, lick our face and ears, and nibble on our hair, and at least initially, we like it, too. But as dogs get older and bigger, face-to-face contact can get obnoxious or interruptive. We react, dogs find our reactions entertaining, and the vicious cycle of action-reaction clicks into place.

Puppies and dogs also like to jump on things—mostly for curiosity's sake, but our reactions fuel their excitement. Consider your dog's perspective: We, their parents, are always looking at countertops and tables; it's only natural for them to want to know what's up there. Jumping on the furniture? That's also a no-brainer. When a dog's explorations are rewarded with forbidden treats and untold comforts, dogs remember.

Fortunately, there are remarkably easy ways to redirect your dog's jumping habits. Before you begin, however, you must be able to answer two questions:

Why is your dog jumping?

What would you like him to do instead?

If these questions are stressful, read from the list that follows for clues.

ATTENTION

Attention jumping is almost impossible to ignore when puppies are young. They are so darn irresistible. I'm a total sucker. Even if you can resist carrying your tiny puppy around, it's unlikely that your friends or family will follow your lead. Don't get too mad. Your puppy's not going to learn a lifetime of bad habits in the first two weeks he's home.

It helps my clients to know that all babies' brains grow better and faster when surrounded by love and laughter than by frustration and stress. No matter who's yelling at whom, if the yell is

TEACH THE FOUR-PAW RULE

To make your goal official, tell everyone that your dog or puppy is learning the Four-Paw Rule. If nothing else, admirers will be distracted long enough for you to slip your puppy a toy and drop some treats on the floor to keep him on all four paws. Quickly kneel down if you're able, and if your puppy is still leaping brace him calmly by sliding your thumb under his collar so he's unable to launch upward.

loud enough for you to hear, it's loud enough to affect your puppy. The bad vibes will sink in. So keep smiling and loving and rewarding your baby when he's got four on the floor and use your sweetest voice to encourage your family and friends to get on board, even if you have to bribe them.

GREETING JUMPING

If you want to encourage better greeting habits, you'll have to remember where good manners start. (Hint: At home.) Encourage your family and friends to ignore your puppy when he jumps, and redirect him to his toys if he's excited or a chewy if he's anxious. If your dog's a true Mexican jumping bean, leave on a light drag lead so you can step on or hold it until he quiets down. I call this transitional excitement and find that it only takes one to three minutes to subside if you don't pay attention to it. Remember, your dog can't tell the difference between negative and positive attention.

Practice some off-leash lessons around the door when no one is there, and teach your dog that the bell means a yummy treat if he holds a Sit-Stay. Go to the door when no one is around, flip back to chapter 6, and practice Stay, Back, and Leave It. You'll be more prepared when people come a-knocking! Here are some more helpful tips:

Strategically place a cup of treats by the door. Now go to the door at various times of the day to practice when nobody is there. Shake the cup, wait for your dog to Sit, then mark the moment and reward him. Practice Sits by the door over and over and over until your dog races ahead of you and prompts you with the behavior. See if you can shake his focus with an occasional door knock or bell. Call out "Who's there?" or "Anyone home?" or "Daddy's back!" Don't follow the phrases with anything but a shake of the cup and the same old routine. Cup shake; dog Sits; you mark, treat, and praise. Pretty soon the doorway will inspire self-control, no words necessary!

Teach your puppy that he'll get more treats, toys, and attention if he Sits next to people instead of in front of them. Practice this one when you come home: Wait until your puppy calms down, then teach him a new phrase—"Say Hello"—as you lure or guide him next to you, rather than in front of you. Pet him with long, soothing strokes collar to tail so he'll remember how good it feels. Practice with visitors, family, and friends, too: It's your new greeting system. Next to, not face front. To see it in action go to ModernDogParenting.com/ProblemSolving.

COUNTER CRUISING

Dogs start jumping on counters around five months of age. It's a great sign of normal development. Yeah! Counter cruising shows that your dog is watching you and wants to be just like you. The problem is, the counter isn't really a place for dogs. You know that, but your dog doesn't—at least, not yet.

Designate a where-to-go and what-to-do-when spot, like I suggest in chapter 6 with the Go to Your Mat direction. Lay down a mat close—but not too close—to your table, cooking zones, and foot path to your table. Tie a chewy to the mat so it can't be carried off, and reward your dog with treats and love when he stays put.

Discourage any interest he shows in the countertops. It's your countertop, and he's not invited. Period. Like kids with coffee or teenagers with alcohol, the answer is just no. Don't make a huge stink; just block your dog's access with an object or your body, leave on a short leash or finger lead so you can remove him calmly, and redirect him to his bed and toys. If you throw a fit every time your dog sneaks a peek, he might get the message that you're guarding something valuable and wait to check it out when you're gone.

Your dog also can't learn to ignore the counter if treats keep falling from the ledge or if he can successfully swipe a bagel when your back is turned. Here are some other quick tips:

> If you can't supervise, close off the area or put your food away; dogs learn quickly that they can counter cruise when alone.

> If the kitchen is your dog's area, try rigging an unpleasant occurrence should he get onto the counter. Some dogs find Tabasco or wasabi sauces distasteful—a piece of bread can be soaked and left out to give an unpleasant surprise. Motion detectors can also echo an unpleasant alarm, or mouse traps can be set and covered to snap—but not to trap your dog—when he surfs for leftovers.

> Look to the Impulse Control section of chapter 6, specifically teaching No, and keep your counters clean.

FURNITURE

If you like your dog on the furniture, don't let anyone tell you that you're going to ruin him for life. I've got five dogs—rabbits and cats, too—and everyone's welcome up onto the couch to snuggle from time to time. It gets a little crowded on movie night, but you can feel the love, and that makes me happy.

The only time you shouldn't let your dog on the furniture is if he growls or snaps at you while he's up there. Call a professional for help if that's the case. While I go over aggression in chapter 8, snapping and guarding spaces is pretty serious stuff. Reality is, he can bite.

If you don't want your dog on the furniture, that's okay, too. Designate a go-to spot close by and remove him patiently, calmly but very consistently, every time he gets up. If you're sitting up there on the sofa, calmly use your leg to block access or leave him on a short finger or hand lead to guide him off and onto his mat without grabbing his neck. Inconsistency really doesn't work here, though. If your kids drag your dog up and you drag him down, you're going to have one mixed-up puppy.

If your goal is teaching your dog or puppy to stay off the furniture:

Place a mat or dog bed near your chair or couch.

Tie a bone on his mat so it can't move far from that area.

Only look, pet, reward, sit with, engage, etc., your dog when he's on his mat or bed. As often as possible, mark the moment he's on his mat with your special word or clicker, and reward him when he's on his bed with or without a chewy.

Never, ever look directly at your dog if he jumps on the furniture. Promise me. Never, ever. Drama inspires more drama, so no wild yelling fits of frustration unless you want a repeat performance day after day.

If your dog's resting or standing on the couch and staring at you, stay calm. This is the oldest dog-training-human trick in the book, although it releases new frustrations in you. Calm down, I tell you! Running at or chasing your dog off the furniture will only excite or hyperfrighten him so he runs around your home like his tail is on fire. Keep your eye on the goal and get a grip.

To cope with the classic dog-on-the-furniture move, walk sideways or backward over to him and gently lead him off by his collar, or preattach a short lead or finger lead if you find it helpful. Say and signal "Go to Your Mat." See chapter 6 for full instructions. If your dog won't stay put, attach a short leash to an immovable piece of furniture and secure it if there won't be too many distractions and you'll be nearby to supervise. Give your dog a bone or chew so he learns how to busy himself when you're present but not accessible.

If your dog is cozy-obsessed and has access to the furniture when you're not home, block his favorite resting spots for now. Lay a gate over the area or pull out a tarp and tuck it into the cushions when you're gone. Eventually, the high ground will lose its appeal, especially if you cozy up his own mat with a velour blanket, favorite chews and puzzles (tie them down so he can't move them), and a T-shirt or two perfumed with his favorite-people scents. Soon, he'll see his mat as the best resting spot of all!

PROBLEM AS REWARD: JUMPING

WORD(S): **Up, Up and Off**

USES: **Sometimes, dogs need to jump, like when hopping onto a grooming table or into the car. Did you know you can teach your dog to jump with your permission? If you long for a hug but don't want your dog leaping onto you when you come in from work, or you love snuggling on the bed or sofa but don't want him there every single second, teach him to jump on permission with "Up, Up" and "Off."**

HOW: **Use a tapping signal and "Up, Up" to tell your dog where to jump, e.g., on your leg or chest, onto the furniture, into the car. When it's time to get off, calmly say "Off" as you toss a ball or treat to the floor. Redirect your dog to another activity or ask him to Sit so you can praise that.**

REWARD: **Up, Up can be a reward for cooperating with your rules. A jumping love fest is great fun after a walk or lesson and Stay practice!**

If the jumping in your home is out of control, try a few discouragements that your dog won't necessarily think are coming from you but can't help noticing every time he chooses to jump.

Fill a small travel-size spray mister with a deterrent spray or vinegar diluted with water. Place a bottle by the door or in other jump-centric locations. While you do not want to spray your dog in the face, create a vapor mist around you or your counters or furniture that's unpleasant and easily avoided.

Sometimes the easiest way to deter a dog is to step into the space he'd otherwise jump into. Good blocks just happen—no words, no eye contact. After a pause, direct your dog to a toy or bone.

Chewing

All dogs chew, some more than others. If you get chew toys your dog enjoys and pay attention to him when he's chewing his things, it's unlikely you'll have too much of a problem. Discover what your dog likes, buy multiples, and spread them around your home, tying some to his mat as you reward him with treats and attention for staying there. If your dog chews while you're out, you might have a separation anxiety problem; that's a bigger deal. We'll cover that one in the next chapter. But for your run-of-the-mill destructive chewing, and for offshoot frustrations like the infamous Grab-'n'-Go, look no further. Solutions ahead!

WHENS AND WHYS OF CHEWING

When, where, how, and why is your dog chewing? If it's during his first year, your dog's in a teething phase. If he's a rescue or a Nervous Nellie, chewing might help calm his nerves. Active dogs like the repetitive nature of chewing, especially on slow days. Protective dogs like to chew when frustrated by too much unpredictable

ACCEPTABLE DISCOURAGEMENTS

Carefully crafted discouragements can encourage your dog to think on his own—to make the right choice based on the effects of his actions rather than your negative response to them. Dogs—like children—learn through cause and effect, trial and error. If an action—say, jumping or crotch sniffing—results in less attention and something unpleasant, those reactions will be abandoned for something that works. If grabbing a toy or Sitting gets approval and rewards, then those will quickly become your dog's go-to responses when greeting visitors, family, and friends! Here are some acceptable discouragements I use:

STEP BACK

If your dog's in an enclosure—crate, pen, or tethered—simply step back if your dog jumps, or barks or nips to greet you. I know he's excited, but even excited dogs can hold a Sit. Step forward when your dog is on all four paws and breathing calmly.

SPRAY AWAY

Get ten small, handheld mist pumps—the kind you'd use for travel. Fill each with a spray deterrent and strategically place them around your home. Anytime your dog is crowding or jumping, calmly spray a vapor mist around you or anyone's torso to discourage jumping/crotch sniffing. These misters also discourage nipping and chewing. Say "Shhh" just before you discreetly spray the object of interest.

CLOSE SHOP

Dogs often jump, paw, bark, and claw in a frantic attempt for some face-to-face action. To short-circuit any routines you find unpleasant, simply close shop. Quickly fold one or both arms over your head to block all access to your face, and drop your arm when your dog Sits or stands calmly.

activity. Most dogs chew anything from bones to wood—some even like metal and rocks. If you grab these things away from your dog, however, he won't stop liking them—that's impossible. He'll just covet his prizes and hide them from view.

It's better to teach your dog to exchange things you don't want him to have than to get upset when you find him chewing something you'd rather he not. See chapter 5 for lessons on Give and Drop. Meanwhile, here's what you can do now:

Find bones and chewies your dog likes. Buy a big supply and freeze or store what you're not using.

Place or tie your chew toys in specific areas so your dog never has to look around to find his things.

Mark, praise, and reward your dog each time you find him chewing his toy. Good boy!

Stuff ten hollow plastic toys or bones with a mixture of soaked dry food or treats mixed with sweet potatoes and freeze them. Give them to your dog when you leave or are too busy to play.

Stop yelling or getting mad at your dog when he destroys or chews stuff. I feel your pain—firsthand, I really do—but it's one of the risks you take when you raise a puppy. Some puppies only go for the bones you give them, while others are born with a fetish. Paper fetishes are tolerable, but I've had puppies addicted to leather and shoes, and one of my current puppies—Mojo— seems to like painted wood furnishings.

Keep small spray deterrents around your home for easy access. Calmly say "Shhh" and discreetly spray the things your dog chews or is chewing, e.g., when he grabs a wire, a table leg, or a shoe. Always approach him at an angle, spray the object, and redirect your dog to his area and his own chewies. Don't stare, yell, or get mad—you'll only teach him to go back when you're not around to protect the prize.

Tie acceptable chews to the things your dog routinely chews.

PROBLEM AS REWARD: CHEWING

WORD(S): **Bone or Chew**

USES: **Dogs need and relish a good chew. Fill your home with a supply of satisfying bones, and you're guaranteed to have a happier dog.**

HOW: **Each time your dog looks bored or you catch him channeling your shoe closet, say "Find your Bone" and lead him to his mat or toy basket. Clean up and/or spray things you don't want him to touch with a deterrent spray. Keep doors shut. If your dog ritually goes for an item, tie one of his chewies to it so it won't get kicked or carried off.**

REWARD: **Dogs love to chew on rainy days, after exhilarating walks to help them settle down, and during busy or chaotic times for the same reason. Offer a new or tasty bone after a cooperative walk, a Stay around distractions, or a difficult lesson to reward his concentration.**

Grab-'n'-Go

If you ask me, dogs who play this game are brilliant. They're the Harry Potters of Doglandia. When they're bored, which might be too often, these dogs start the family's engine by grabbing someone's most prized treasure—be it a stuffed toy, Nintendo controller, oven mitt, or tool—and rouse the entire household into chasing him to retrieve it. It's a hoot—at least for the dog! No matter how heavy the discipline, nothing can beat the thrill of the chase.

To cure this addiction, teach your puppy or dog the new rules of the game. Decide what game you'd rather he play: do you like retrieve, kickball, or tug-of-war? For the rules of these games, flip to chapter 5.

In the meantime, gather up all the objects your dog would ever think to bait you with, a handful of yummy treats, and some more acceptable toys, and lead your dog into his Learning Zone or a small room. Your goal here is to teach the Grab-'n'-Show versus the Grab-'n'-Go game. Within a few days your dog will learn that

a. he can pick things up.

b. some of the objects he can keep, while others are delivered in exchange for treats, praise, or rewards.

In your Learning Zone, drop a forbidden object on the floor. Your dog will either snatch it or ignore it. Praise whatever he does. If he snatches it, pull out a treat and say "Give" as you wave it in front of his nose. Are you teaching him that it's okay to grab things? Ah, no. He already thinks that. You're teaching him to bring you things for a reward—it's helpful, really. Reward your dog when he drops the temptation—offer one of his toys or play Tug.

By introducing many of the previously forbidden objects, using food to coach Drop, and encouraging more organized interaction, your dog's attitude will shift from wanting to steal, covet, and provoke, to bring and share!

If your dog still has a strong penchant for baiting games and forbidden objects, see the concept of "No" in chapter 6.

Nipping

Dogs are very mouthy, especially as puppies. They use their mouths like people use their hands: to explore, play and socialize with friends, and experience all sorts of sensations just by wrapping their mouth around it. Nipping is a healthy social interaction, too—at least from the dog's perspective. But with people it isn't. How's a dog to know?

If your puppy's a nipper, here's what to do as well as what not to do. If your dog's older than six months and still nipping, read this section, then flip to the aggression section of Chapter 8 to focus on why the habit is still lingering and what you can do to stop it once and for all.

Here's what *not* to do:

> Don't jam, shout, squeeze, or poke your puppy or dog. Bullying has been shown to lead to aggression. Although your puppy probably won't snap at you, he may snap at other pets, kids, or nurturing adults. Aggressive handling teaches your dog that bullying works.

> Don't forget how important routines are. Overtired puppies get nippy. Puppies and adolescents also get nippy if they have to poop or feel hungry or thirsty. Flip back to chapter 1 to review your dog's needs chart and make sure his mouthing isn't a cry for help.

> Don't overstimulate your puppy. Even outgoing pups get overwhelmed if socialized for too long. If your puppy is extra nippy, he's likely due for some quiet time. If your puppy's a social scaredy-cat, expose him to new situations and people in short spurts. Keep outings short and confidently greet people and other dogs—you want your dog to mimic you, not hold back. If he's confident, ask new people to reward him with food or discreetly place food/toys for him to discover. Regardless of your dog's personality, if people-centric situations cause more nipping than tail wagging, remove your dog unless you can calm him down. Sometimes good food will help his mood, other times only solitude, comforting music, and his own special chewy will do the trick.

HELPING YOUR NIPPER STOP NIPPING

To teach your puppy not to nip, you've got to find something to encourage him to do instead, like giving kisses. Licking doesn't come naturally to most dogs, as it requires a different set of muscles. Dab your hand with butter, broth, or yogurt and say "Give Kisses" as your puppy licks your hand.

Until your puppy is about twelve weeks old, gentle mouthing is a loving sign most often seen in litters between puppies and Momma or other loving grown-up dogs. Allow gentle mouthing by letting your hand go limp. Direct him to a toy/bone and praise him if he offers you Kisses.

If he mouths too roughly, quickly shout "Ouch" or "Off" (without staring), as you encourage your puppy to remove his mouth from your skin. If you jerk away, he might think you're playing and grab harder and faster next time.

Carry or place tiny handheld spray deterrents around your home and discreetly spray the part of your body or clothing your puppy's grasping. If you remember to say "Shhh" just before you spray, soon just "Shhh" will warn your puppy off—no spray necessary.

A light leash can also be left on his collar or harness to gently move your puppy from your body or anyone else's and to redirect him to an alternative activity.

In my home we have a "three strikes and you're out" rule for any and all wild, people-focused nipping rampages. If one of our puppies is out of control, we ask if there's anything he needs, like food, water, or a nap—if there is, we help out with that—and how we can redirect him to a fun toy or activity.

If our puppy still flashes his pearly whites, then a grown-up will calmly take him to his quiet area (where he may actually bark for five minutes straight—a sign of an overtired puppy) and leave him in his zone with a favorite chewy to soothe himself with.

Barking

If your dog likes to bark, he likes to bark. I can't help you there. Asking a barker not to bark—or yelling or isolating him when he's in the middle of barking his head off—will only confuse him,

PROBLEM AS REWARD: NIPPING

WORD(S): Gentle

USES: If your puppy is a crazy nipper, you'll need to phase out this habit. Teach gentle mouthing before insisting that he redirect his impulses altogether by asking him to grab a toy when he's feeling nippy. Puppies should be discouraged from mouthing after six months.

HOW: If your puppy is in a nippy mood, ask yourself if he needs anything like a walk, rest, or food before you address his mouth. If nothing pans out, and you have the time, sit on the floor and let him nibble on your hand/arm. Stress "Gentle" as he does so, and "Good, Gentle" as long as he doesn't apply pressure. Try not to move your hand, as this will prompt hard nips. If he clamps down too hard, say "No" or "Ouch," and remove your puppy from your hand as described on page 227.

REWARD: Sitting on the floor is a great way to bond with young puppies after a lesson. Soft mouthing is how young puppies connect with those they love. Don't get too bent out of shape.

which will lead to more barking, not less. The good news? There is something that will help, and I'm here to tell you what it is.

BARK ON CUE, HUSH ON DEMAND

The Problem as Reward word-to-action strategy will be especially handy if you've got a barker. In this case, you'll want to teach your dog Speak and Hush. Speak lets him know that it's okay to bark, and Hush tells him when it's not the right time.

To get your dog to bark on cue and Hush when told, think of how you could get yours to bark now—now, as in, this very moment. What would guarantee it? A doorbell, isolation in a crate or gated enclosure? Being restrained from entering the dog

PROBLEM AS REWARD: BARKING

WORD(S): **Speak and Hush**

USES: **Many dogs enjoy voicing their opinions. Put barking on cue, so you can quiet him, but let him bark himself out, too, from time to time.**

HOW: **In the car, park, or backyard, say "Speak," run around with your dog, and bark, too. When you're done, or he's done, quiet him down with "Hush" and a jackpot of yummy rewards.**

REWARD: **If barking is a passion, use a bark-fest as a reward for lessons or after/during walks and social adventures.**

park? Get a visual, and then make it happen. Grab some prized treats and/or toys, your clicker if you're using one, and let's get started.

Rig the situation that'll prompt barking, then say and signal "Speak" (I open and close my fist). Look at your dog eagerly, say "Speak," signal, and even bark yourself to encourage mimicry. Now wait! The moment your dog barks—even just vocalizes a bit—mark and reward. Do it! He'll be as confused as you are, especially if you've been yelling at him to be quiet his whole life, but trust me on this. Keep practicing this direction until he's excited barking when you say "Speak." Once you've eliminated any pausing in confusion, vary both the timing and type of rewards—sometimes after one bark, sometimes after four, or eight, or three. Mix it up to keep your dog or puppy on his toes.

Now for the Hush . . . the direction you've been waiting for! Set your dog up to bark like before, so he knows what's coming. Start with Speak, but after a few barks, bring your index finger to your lips, stand up straight, and say "Hush." Look straight up to the ceiling and ignore your dog 100 percent until he stops barking.

Even if it takes a year (which it shouldn't). Once your dog pauses—even if just to catch his breath—mark the moment and reward. Once he grasps the Hush direction, he'll grow as eager and addicted to hear it as he will any other word, although in the beginning it can be a little slow going.

Don't bring your Speak and Hush routine out of lesson time until you've got both down pat. Practice these skills often, and within five to seven days, your dog should be responding to both.

WHENS AND WHYS OF BARKING

Now let's get down to the real reason your dog's barking, how you can use his new skill to Speak and Hush on cue, and discover what else you can do about it. Dogs don't bark for nothing. See if you can figure it out: Is your dog barking to get your attention or in frustration at being left alone or unable to get what he wants? Those are the easiest types of barking to control, by the way. Consider yourself lucky. Is your dog a protection barker—leaping up, even from a deep sleep, to alert you to approaching sounds? Maybe he fashions himself your border patrol guard, keeping watching inside and/or out. If you have other dogs in your home or neighborhood, maybe your dog is a copycat barker, with little idea why he's getting so worked up.

How you cope with your barking problem depends a little on your dog's breed type and personality, but even more on what's prompting him to bark in the first place. Refer back to chapter 2 to help figure out what the different types of barks mean.

Attention/Frustration Barking

Here's the easiest barking problem to solve. If your dog or puppy barks to get your attention, leave the room. If you can't, put headphones on and ignore him. If your landlord's threatening eviction, go stay with your parents or at a hotel for the weekend.

With the following plan, you'll get a handle on your barking problem fast!

Help your puppy decide on a new way to get your attention when he needs you. I teach mine to Sit and look up at me; I also give them love and treats for hanging out on their mats, chewing bones, and playing with each other—anything but barking. Whatever you choose, pocket your dog or puppy's meal—the whole meal, if you're able to—and feed him when he's quiet.

Play the Speak-Hush game, and once your puppy learns Hush, say it inside. Follow up with something else your dog can do to keep his mouth occupied, like chewing.

If there is a time your puppy or dog is just crazy, like when you come home from work or the kids are active, highlight that hour with a special chew, game, or puzzle toy. Give your dog something to look forward to that doesn't involve rambunctiousness or barking.

Protection

Protective dogs can often go from a dead sleep to up on their feet and barking in .01 seconds flat. It's impressive. Dial back the evolutionary clock to the time when we lived in caves or small villages and the protection dog had widespread appeal. Nowadays, not so much. Few people need or want to be alerted to subtle fluctuations in the airwaves, and that's the problem. Shouting at your dog comes naturally, but it makes the barking worse. Now your dog thinks you're alerting, too. The message is bark more, wag less.

To stop your protection barker from becoming a chronic barkaholic, help him get used to ordinary sounds even as you teach him Speak and Hush. Socialize your dog or puppy as outlined in chapter 5, and link everyday sounds to lessons and games.

Once your dog has learned Speak and Hush, try this move in Real Time. (Keep high-quality treats in your hand or pocket and in strategic places around your home so you're ready whenever the bark happens.)

> **Say "Speak" when he alert barks, and bark with him. You read right. Bark with him for about five seconds.**

> **Say "Hush" and wave a treat in front of his nose. Mark and reward him when he stops, even if he goes right back to barking. Do it again, and again and again. After a few trials, withhold the treat until your dog gives you a full two-second bark pause, then three seconds . . . now use the pause to redirect your dog to a game like Tug, Bone, or other games he'll enjoy.**

> **If you need some leverage, secure a light drag lead to his collar or harness and redirect your dog to something else far away from the scene or space that provoked his barking. You can also use the line to prevent him from pacing or racing back and forth if that's his habit.**

The ultimate goal is that your dog barks for a few seconds, quiets down on Hush, and redirects his excitement to a toy, ball, or chew. It can take a few weeks, but keep the vision in your mind. You'll get there.

Border Patrol Guard

This is a tricky one. A lot of dogs left out without supervision adopt this pastime, keeping your home and/or yard free from "perceived" invaders. At its worst, Border Patrol (aka territorial barking) can lead to impulsive aggression when your or another dog breaks free from his home or enclosure—a reaction to stress discussed in chapter 8.

The truth is, a lot of dogs have this problem. Most people do not see it coming. The dog that playfully dragged their person around and was allowed to jump on and tackle people and other dogs slowly evolved into a mature dog with little self-control. My neighborhood is filled with many wonderful dogs who are less than wonderful when left alone on a tether or in their fenced yard. One barks when left outside from six A.M. to nightfall; another tears up and down her fence barking at passersby or my kids on their bikes. My kids are now too afraid to ride their bikes in their own neighborhood, which is a total bummer. Another stands chained to her stoop and barks at every noise. I know these dogs—I like these dogs. But I also feel sorry for them, and worry for the safety of my family and passersby.

Here's what I have to say about this issue:

Portion out food when your dog alerts to you instead of the distraction. Buy an electronic treat dispenser if you can, and activate it around the time you know your dog goes on duty. When you leave home, leave puzzle toys, stuffed Kongs, and bones to keep him occupied.

Dogs who assume this role are rarely bored, as their "job" as border control keeps them busy. If this sounds like your situation, consider your neighbors and then your dog. Isn't there something a little more fun and less agitating your dog could do to pass his time?

Make an effort to redesign his playscape. If your dog runs the fence line, is it possible to segment your enclosure to not include the street-facing portion of the yard, or at least block it unless you're out there to chaperone your dog? If the reactionary barking happens inside, could you organize the floor plan to keep your dog away from any red zones when his reactivity peaks (like when you're at work or in the evening)?

Copycat

Copycats crack me up. They really have no idea why they're barking. The problem is, sometimes they can't channel their off switch. If one dog barks at a noise, he'll generally stop when the noise passes, but not so the copycat barker who barks on and on. If one dog barks for help retrieving his ball, the copycat barker will, too. It's enough to drive anyone bananas. Fortunately, the copycat barker's not all that committed to the activity. Practice the Speak-Hush game, then use it to direct your dog to a chew or toy.

Digging

Most dogs—not all, but most—like to dig. It's especially addictive to puppies, as I imagine certain video games are to young children. Repetitive, empowering, conclusive—fun! Some dogs dig for a purpose, others for pure delight. Here are various reasons a dog likes to dig: what fits your situation?

A dog will dig when there is nothing else to do. It's fun.

If he hears a creature tunneling around, he'll dig to see if he can catch it.

When it's hot, a dog will dig into the cool dirt to prevent over-heating.

Tethered or penned dogs dig in desperation—or at least that's what I imagine—if left alone outside with nothing to do and no one to be with. That's sad. I hope that's not your dog.

If your dog is passionate about digging and you're not a fan, create a sandbox or get a kiddy pool and fill it with sand. You could also section off an area of your yard for digging, or take your dog to the beach or woods to get his fix. It can be a great way to bond after a long hike or walk.

To help your puppy with his digging habits:

If your dog's tearing up your yard, block access to those areas when possible. If you can't do that, try filling his holes with 1/4 cup of red pepper flakes, rocks, and/or a few of his own poops to discourage more digging.

PROBLEM AS REWARD: DIGGING

WORD(S): **Go Dig and All Done**

USES: **To teach your dog digging is okay in certain areas.**

HOW: Go dig with your dog in certain areas like a sandbox or wooded pathway. Say "Go Dig" as you go there and "All Done" when you're ready to quit.

REWARD: There are few greater rewards for passionate diggers than a communal excavation.

If boredom or stress from being locked outside is to blame, inspire other fun pastimes like puzzle activities, chewies, or hangman, where you tie a rope, plastic, or stuffed toy to a branch or banister so it hangs at your dog's head level and will swing when pulled.

If you're a gardener, take this lesson from me: When my Whoopsie was eight months old, I thought I'd it be fun to have her help out in the garden, so I taught her to Dig. Easy trick, though not the best timing. An enthusiast for any new adventure, she was too young to contain her impulses. After helping me with some pepper plants, she returned to the spot later to unearth them. Happy puppy, not-so-happy Mommy. Moral? Wait until your dog's over the adolescent hump to involve him in any outdoor landscaping projects. Dogs just don't know the value of a good bulb.

8

Embracing Your Dog's Emotional Tornadoes

The greatest thing in this world is not so much where we stand as in what direction we are moving.
—OLIVER WENDELL HOLMES

know . . . crotch sniffing, stool swallowing, rolling in goo . . . Just be grateful you're not a dog. Sometimes your dog's obsessions are undeniable—if not a little hard to stomach—but you don't need to overthink everything your dog does.

Other behaviors, though, are heartbreaking: biting, trashing your bedroom when you're out, growling at children . . . It's natural to hope that love can cure all, or—when that fails—that a round of reprimands will dampen her impulses.

In this, our last chapter, we'll look at some of your dog's most baffling concerns. If what you're doing now isn't working, let's see if we can discover what will. Bad behavior is often just a cry for help, an emotional tornado of sorts, so start by looking for the message beneath your dog's mischief. Parenting is, at the end of the day, a commitment to love your whole child and to support her on her journey. Accepting your dog unconditionally and learning how you can calm her stress is the only way to shift her awareness and escort her back into the safety of your forever-loving heart.

Please, Just Stop!

One day, your dog's going to do the unfathomable: She's going to go for that decaying roadkill; obsess over dirty diapers, used sanitary napkins, cat poop, etc.; or ram her muzzle into your visitors' nether regions.

While this might come as a surprise, your dog's not doing these things to spite you or even to get your attention. She's doing these things because they make her feel alive. They make her feel marvelous.

On the rare occasions that you catch your dog in the midst of her rude and crude behaviors, your reprimands will fall like a wet blanket. She can't fathom your frustrations, and even if she could, she wouldn't want to. What is a loving dog parent to do?

Here's a list of common complaints, and some clues for how you might redirect your dog's most obnoxious obsessions. To see many of these suggestions in action, visit ModernDogParenting .com/ProblemSolving.

STOOL SWALLOWING

The funniest thing about stool swallowing is that it's the reason we employed dogs in the first place. We didn't have outhouses around our campfires—we had dogs! Dogs who gladly inhaled all clues of our whereabouts and rolled in other animals' scents to mask their own. Pure brilliance! And yet, here we are in the twenty-first century trying to sell our dogs on the gross factor. They're not buying it.

Of course, I'm the first to climb on the Stop Stool Swallowing

Now bandwagon, however fruitless it may be. With kids in and around my home, I'd rather not have any stool swallowers lolling about.

Here are tricks that have worked for my family, as well as my clients:

Feast Factor

Dogs, like kids, eat more junk when they're hungry. Target your dog's stool-swallowing adventure hour and feed her ahead of time.

Taste Deterrents

Is it possible that anything could taste worse than poop? Apparently, yes—at least to dogs. Meat tenderizer is a popular option, as well as other powders and pills you can pick up from your veterinarian. Add these to meals and cross your fingers.

Pick Up Poops in Private

Avoid letting your stool-obsessed dog watch you pick up poop. Although I know that *you* know that the deposits will be trashed, for all your poop-impassioned dog knows, you're collecting them for an ultimate feast.

Toys

It's hard to search for stool if you're busy chasing, playing, or carrying a toy. Use toys to direct other activities, and try tying one on a string to bounce along and distract your dog on your walks.

WHINING

Whining is a bother, but it's natural—at least in the beginning. Your dog will whine whenever she's caught between a want and a can't. She wants to reach something, but she can't get to it. She wants your attention, but she can't have it. She wants to be free, but is tethered or behind a fence. If whining mobilizes your help, it can quickly shift from an involuntary behavior into a habit.

While whining may seem low scale on the list of possible canine infractions, it's annoying and will get worse over time. Whining can become a dog's go-to reaction anytime she's not getting her way.

To help the incessant whiner, keep these things in mind:

Keep Your Eyes to Yourself
Don't look at a whiner: If whining draws you to her cause, the whiner whines more.

Button Your Lips
While I know it's temping, don't shout at a whiner. If you do, your whiner will stop momentarily. But silencing the whiner by shouting scares an already nervous or edgy dog, which leads to more . . . can you guess? Whining. Arghhhhhh.

Whiner Rehab
To rehabilitate your whiner, focus on when she whines: Does she whine to get out of the crate, for attention, to go outside? Think through what you'd rather she do instead. Now either ignore the whining (earplugs or headphones and music help) and respond when she stops, or teach your dog a different method to get what she wants, like retrieving a toy (which would plug the whine) or doing a trick.

LEASH LUNGING

I hate leashes. I really do. They are a necessary evil, I'll give you that, but I apologize to my dogs each time I clip one on. That said, I always try to make our outings a cause for celebration. I pack yummy snacks, favorite toys, and my dogs' mats when I expect them to lie still. I pack my clicker, too, or use a word marker to reward their self-control and focus.

Maybe you've got a leash-reactive dog or you want to prevent leash issues in your future. Kudos to you! Whatever you're hoping for, this section will shed some light.

Before we begin, imagine this situation: Someone you love calls you in a happy voice, saying "Come here—I want to show you something," just seconds before forcefully grabbing you by your shirt collar and pulling you off balance.

What would you do? The sweet, inviting voice says "Follow me," releasing the love hormone, oxytocin. But when you feel the collar pull, a flood of the stress hormones cortisol and adrenaline gets released, too.

Two very conflicting impulses arise. No matter how much you love the puller, your reaction would be reflexive and automatic: to pull back, and pull back hard. That's known as the opposition reflex, and dogs have it, too.

Here are some things to consider as you condition better leash manners with your dog:

Comfort Wear

Use restrictive wear that calms rather than stresses your dog. Flat or choke collars can leave your dog feeling frantically asphyxiated and restrained. Flip to chapter 2 and consider a no-pull harness or head collar.

Off-Leash Walking Skills

In chapter 6 we learned positive and fun walking skills that should be introduced both indoors and off-leash. Start there to give both you and your dog happy memories of walking side-by-side.

Target Wand

Throughout the book I've referred to target wands to direct your dog's attention. Here is another perfect opportunity to use one. As first discussed in the Follow section of chapter 6, use a target wand on cooperative leash walks to keep your dog focused and excited to stay with you. Your dog's meal is especially useful as extra motivation when using your target wand on walks.

Stop and Go

Teach your dog that checking in with you is really, really important. Like a little kid checking in with their parents before they leave a store or venture ahead, teaching your dog to stay with you is a necessary part of living in this modern world. Fortunately, teaching this skill is pretty straight-forward.

After teaching your dog to Follow you in chapter 6, pack your dog's all-time-favorite toys or goodies, and take her to a low-distraction area of your yard or neighborhood. Start out using your cooperative walking direction (e.g., Follow), talk to your dog, and reward her cooperation. If she races ahead, stop dead in your tracks. She may pull like a sled dog; just dig in your heels and wait. When she looks back, mark with a clicker or word like "Yes!" and reward her. Continue praising her as you move forward, rewarding her from time to time with whatever she enjoys, but stop and encourage a check in anytime she's more focused on something in the environment than you. Initially proceed after a second of eye contact, then 2 seconds, then 4 seconds, then vary—sometime 4 seconds, another time 10, then 6, then 14! And mix up your responses too—a treat or toy or enthusiastic praise. Dogs love the unpredictable reinforcements as much as we do! Vegas anyone?

RED ZONE

If one thing—road construction or another dog approaching, for example—is particularly distracting for your dog, ask yourself if she's afraid, excited, or defensive. If you don't know, ask a dog-savvy friend or hire a professional to judge. Whatever is prompting her reaction, you'll need to determine your dog's red zone (where her reactivity peaks) and walk outside it to get her to focus on you rather than what's distressing her. As she grows more accustomed to the distraction (what the pros call habituation), move steadily closer to her red zone.

DOOR DASHING

Back in chapter 2 we discovered that dogs view their home as their den and their immediate surroundings (yard, block, or neighborhood) as their territory. However, there's one big difference between the dens of old and our new, modern housing system: the door. Second only to leashes, the door can cause big frustrations. Unable to navigate freely through it, dogs' tensions rise as they're forced to watch the world go by instead of engaging with it.

Unless conditioned not to, most dogs will develop a break-free mentality anytime the door opens. Sound way too familiar? Here are some easy tips that'll help:

Deconditioning

Activity around the door sounds the alarm. Some dogs race over for fun, some to spot trouble, others to warn off intruders. No matter what your dog's thinking, the first step in rehabbing your door dasher is to decondition her to door activities.

Start by playing a recording of your doorbell sounds at low volumes during play and meal times. Once your dog has completed her first steps of the Five-Step Learning Strategy in chapter 6 with any of her word directions, including Sit, Down, Stay, or Come, ask a helper to open and shut the door while you practice steps 3 to 5 in distant rooms, while gradually moving closer to the door. You're teaching your dog to focus on words over distractions.

Throughout the day, call out familiar phrases that you say when someone's coming in like, "The Kids Are Home!" "Who's There?," and "Honey, Could You Get That?" or simply knock on the wall or tabletop to stimulate your dog's response without any follow-up or reaction on your part.

Counter Condition

Link all door and greeting sounds to positive activities and good behavior. Knock on the wall, then ask your dog to Sit and reward that. Call out to an imaginary visitor as you signal and reward your dog for giving Paw. Ask a friend to open and shut the door while you feed or play Tug with your dog. Gradually move these games and counter conditioning rewards closer and closer to the door until voilà—you can do them when you or your visitors come in.

Impulse Control

Now you're ready for the big leagues: asking your dog not to race out an open door. There are many fun ways to go about this, but remember to stay cool. The more frantic you act, the more excitable your dog will become.

Use a high-end reward and marker to highlight your dog's cooperation, i.e., staying inside, even when the door is left open. Start by reviewing Sit from chapter 6. Teach your dog to Sit before you let her through any important passageways, including—but definitely not limited to—the main door. Make a master list of all the thresholds, doors, and passageways you can use to practice. If your dog is crated, start with going in and out of her crate; then try before approaching or letting your dog out from behind a gate (indoors or out) and getting in and out of the car, dog park, kids' room, animal hospital, day care, or friend's house. Sit is the go-to behavior for just about everything—so much so that Sit becomes a reward in and of itself.

Initially, leave the door open a crack as you encourage your dog to Stay and focus her on a toy, bone, or target wand game. Gradually open the door more and more, and encourage your dog to Sit and Stay as you walk back and forth to the open (but still visitor-less) door.

Let your dog drag a lightweight leash or clip a short hand lead to her collar whenever she has free access to the door to enable you to step on the leash or hold her steady should a visitor stop by. Secure a station lead to something immovable nearby but in sight of the door, as described on page 54, or use a crate or gate zone in view of or near the door to help your dog grow more accustomed to door activity. If securing her on a lead or in an enclosed area, help your dog get used to being secluded by having a helper open and shut the door while you give a bone to, play with, or feed your dog.

Review the Name Game to guarantee that your dog will focus quickly and move to you if she escapes. Remember this one? Shout your dog's name and move away from her, shaking a treat cup if you have one. Reward with praise or treats the instant she looks at you. YES!

If your dog is still too hyper when company comes, be sure to leave her with a toy or bone while you answer the door, and do not let her participate in hosting activities until she's calmed down.

CROTCH SNIFFING

Next time you're at the dog park, watch how the dogs greet each other. Hint: Dogs don't do face-to-face, paw-shaking how-de-dos. Instead, their nose shifts into high gear, scanning bottoms and fur to get a proper visual on their friend's age, sex, and status. How? It's an olfactory thing—something people study and think on but never fully comprehend.

I won't bother outlining how your dog would prefer you greet her, but suffice it to say, it's not eye-to-eye. Cut your dog some slack—she's not sniffing anyone's nether regions to be rude—and reroute your scent-starved canine with these tactics:

Redirect

In chapter 2 you learned that your dog is nearsighted and depends on smell to identify everything. Teach your dog to sniff hands to Say Hello, as first directed on page 33, by adding a surprise bonus to visitors' hands versus other smell-centric zones. Leave a bag of treats taped to the door or near your entranceway to ensure that family and friends come bearing gifts that'll focus your dog's attention in the right place.

Displacement Activities

Leave a basket of toys and/or bones by your entranceway and shift the greeting drama to a game or chew when you or anyone else comes in the door. Since crotch sniffing and door dashing often go hand in hand, refer to the section on page 242 for a more thorough explanation of how to redirect your dog to toys during greetings.

Spray Away

Place small spray bottles by your entranceway or in your purse to discreetly spray a vapor boundary around yourself or visitors should your dog make a move to zero in. Without looking at or paying attention to your dog, redirect her to her toy basket or bone.

Block or Stop

Block your dog's access to a visitor's body by calmly but consistently stepping in front of her when she angles for the nether regions. Combine this approach with others for a unified solution.

While many of the above habits are annoying, few dogs have a problem with their behavior. Whiners can get addicted to whining if it gets a reaction, leash pullers to straining unless taught to walk politely, and door dashers will always dash unless taught to Wait. Reshape these habits, or choose to live with them. It's up to you.

In the next section, I touch on heavier drama—emotional tornadoes that are no fun for anyone. Dogs who rely on aggression or OCD-like behaviors to soothe overwhelming fears or frustrations aren't happy about it. Although you may be near your breaking point, understand that the worst stress is being experienced by your dog. See what you can do to help.

Modern-Day Dramas

Dogs sure do have a lot of drama to deal with in today's world. Crammed into smaller spaces, there are both more of us and more of them than ever before. But dogs need freedom and time to explore. With less of it, some dogs are stressing out. In this section,

THEN AND NOW

Back when I was a kid, the most frustrating thing my dog did was dig up my mom's flower garden and tip the neighbor's garbage can—which she did, every Tuesday. Dogs didn't demolish their homes because few were allowed inside. They didn't dig or claw at the furniture or chew holes in the wall during thunderstorms because they were forced to cope outside on their own. I always knew where to find my dog after a storm—under our front porch.

And when people yelled or frightened their dog, or when dogs felt uneasy with a visitor or a kid, they did what dogs can't always do in today's world—they fled the scene.

Modern times have pulled this free-ranging lifestyle right out from under our dogs. Those who once happily trotted about inside now find themselves stuck there and longing to get out. Dogs who once roamed their neighborhoods, socializing with all the things and people in it, now tour their surroundings restricted on a tight tether and pulled in directions they'd never think to follow.

Tensions can, and often do, mount, unless we sell our dogs on all the pluses of modern times—like the wonderful food, toys, puzzles, games, organized fun, and adventures they can enjoy. If your dog's more nervous than happy or reacts defensively instead of with acceptance or joy, consider the modern stresses that might be weighing on her mind and how you can help her learn to tolerate, cope with, and even enjoy the world you share.

we'll look at more dramatic reactions, from aggression to separation anxiety, phobias, and OCD-like behaviors, and how you can help your dog cope without losing your cool. Science shows that love and laughter can heal most wounds, whether they're inside your dog's head or self-inflicted.

Inedible Gulping and Other Compulsive Behaviors

The reactions listed below differ from normal reactions in that they are unprompted by real-world events: The fly-snapper catches bugs that aren't really there; the dog ingesting pebbles isn't hungry, per se; and the obsessive licker is neither injured nor stung. All these repetitive behaviors have an obsessive-compulsive slant commonly seen among other species, including humans.

Purebred dogs seem to suffer more from OCD-like disorders than mixed-breed dogs, which suggests that light chasing, inedible gulping, and related behaviors are—at least in part—inherited disorders, not ones that are learned. Many of the routines listed below, however, can emerge as outlets for stress, boredom, or from cross-wiring in your dog's brain, and have little explanation. Some of the most common interruptive, often idiopathic or OCD-like behaviors out there include:

INDELIBLE GULPING	**Eating nondigestible stuff, like acorns, pebbles, fabric, and paper.**
SHADOW AND LIGHT CHASING	**Chasing both natural and unnatural shadows and streams of light.**
LICK GRANULOMAS	**A self-mutilating behavior where a dog will continuously lick one spot until it becomes an open and/or infected sore.**
FLY SNAPPING	**This dog will look like she's battling a swarm of flies, except**

there won't be any bugs. Funny looking, at least initially, this behavior is worrisome when it's a regular and involuntary reaction.

TAIL CHASING

Equally adorable, at least on paper, is the tail chaser. While it's a cute trick, it isn't as cute when your dog is unable is control this impulse.

Dr. Karen Overall, a respected, board-certified veterinary behaviorist, suspects that 2 to 3 percent of pet dogs suffer from OCD-like behaviors. She suggests that each case be isolated and examined to determine the interplay of nature (genetics), nurture (home life), and overall neurological elements (brain chemistry).

Forgive your dog if she has an OCD-like condition. You'll probably need more help than this book can provide. Speak to your veterinarian and/or a reputable behaviorist. If medication helps to soothe your dog's inner compulsions, then use it. That's what good medication is all about. Here are some other tips to consider as you move forward:

Purposeful Attention

If they're anything like their human counterparts, dogs who suffer from OCD-like behaviors are both smart and driven. While that may be no consolation to you, offer your dog some goal-oriented activities to earn your attention and fulfill her need for repetitive, focused activities. Dog sports like Agility, Flyball, and Freestyle come to mind. You don't have to engage in competition; I've run fun classes for the not-so-competitively inclined. Search for a group like that in your area.

Exercise

Perhaps it goes without saying, but the less energy your dog has, the less she'll have to expend on compulsory outlets.

SEIZURES, STEREOTYPIES, OR ALLERGIC REACTIONS?

OCD-like behaviors are not yet fully understood. While some in the medical community consider and treat these idiopathic behaviors as petit mal epileptic seizures—petit because they only affect an isolated area of the brain versus grand mal seizures, which affect multiple brain lobes—many argue other causes. Behaviorists and scientists alike reference stereotypies, repetitive and often emotionally soothing behaviors observed in understimulated predatory zoo mammals, which could also be used by dogs to relieve boredom and purposelessness. Others suggest the interplay of allergens (e.g., to wheat or flea/tick preventives) or sensory infections, primarily affecting a dog's sight or hearing, as possible causes for such behaviors.

Both OCD-like rituals and seizures have a similar look and feel, as though your dog's mind has been taken over. While dogs experiencing seizures should be isolated until their electrical firestorm has passed, some OCD-like behaviors can be calmed through redirection to an alternative, yet incompatible, activity.

Speak to your veterinarian about how to manage your dog's extreme reactions.

No-Drama Reactivity

Many dogs seem continually starved for attention, mine included. It's not necessarily a bad thing—they are like kids, after all—but use your dog's everlasting need for loving to inspire good manners and self-control. If your dog gets the lion's share of your attention for acting out, self-inflicted and/or obnoxious OCD-like behaviors can become ingrained and habitual.

Redirect or Block

When possible, redirect or block ritualized or OCD-like behaviors. Use a high-end food reward to lure your dog out of a room or area that could be triggering her reaction. Find an appropriate, incompatible routine, like Tug, Fetch, or Find It (explained in chapter 5), or see if some calm interactive petting or a walk will refocus her mind.

Dog Aggression

Dog aggression baffles most people. It's startling to see a dog's face shift from sweet to suspicious or full of rage. When this happens, it's hard to know what to do or how best to reassure your dog. Why are dogs' reactions so intense?

I'm here to help you understand why, as dogs mature, many show aggression when dealing with overwhelming feelings of fear or frustration. Aggression occurs less in younger dogs or puppies because, until their hormones start flowing, dogs are what professionals call socially inhibited. The young of any species are too unsure of situations and of their experiences in the world to make a stand.

Without the freedom to leave stressful situations or work out their differences, more and more dogs are feeling the kind of stress that leads to aggressive responses. But when it's broken down, aggression isn't that startling at all. Remind yourself over and over and over again that dog aggression is just a reaction to intense feelings of fear and frustration. Think of aggression in human terms: What would you do if someone grabbed something dear to you? How do you feel when someone hugs you too hard, plays too rough, or talks too close? Dogs can't talk, and while many do posture as a way to communicate their feelings, aggression is the only other resource they have to make a point.

Aggression does have different levels, some less intense and worrisome than others. Dogs who signal their mood with warning postures and purposeful stares or growls are showing tremendous self-control. If your dog shows aggression without actually biting you or someone else, the prognosis for calming her confusion is good; there's a lot you can do to refocus her mood.

Once a dog begins to maim or injure, however, aggression becomes a more serious topic, and one that is beyond the reach of this book. If your dog is harming others, speak to your veterinarian and/or hire a professional to help you. I've listed some resources in the bibliography.

I'll leave you with an overview to help you both understand and think through a positive approach for dealing with dog aggression, whether you're coping with your own dog's intense reactions or protecting yourself or a loved one from an aggressive dog.

TYPES

Some dogs have strong attachments to food, toys, and sleeping spaces. Known as resource guarders, these dogs use aggression to protect their personal space from others. Children, who seem more like prey animals than people to the undersocialized dog, are often targeted.

If this is happening under your roof, get the right kind of help. Ignore anyone who tells you to discipline or shock your dog. She's protecting what, at least in her mind, is rightfully hers. Negativity will intensify her aggression, and a softer person or child will bear the brunt of her response.

DID YOU KNOW?
DOGS COMMONLY GROWL AT EACH OTHER

Dogs growl at each other when roughhousing or protecting their stuff. Growling at people, however, is a different story. People don't like being growled at. Most dogs revere people too much to make a fuss, but if your dog missed that memo, flip to page 252 for quick tips on resolving this issue, or call a professional for help!

THREE WAYS TO CHEER UP ANY DOG

Whether or not your dog is aggressive, here are three great ways to deal with a variety of stressful situations:

JOLLY ROUTINE

When dogs are unsure of how to handle themselves, they nip and jump in hyperexcitement, shrink back in fear, or charge forward assertively. People often react impulsively, too, shouting at their dog or kneeling to pet and soothe. The tenser you act, the more nervous she'll be.

If the goal is to help your dog feel more comfortable with all that life has to offer, adopt a jolly routine with signature words, treats, toys, and pats: "What a wonderful dog!" "Who's my pretty girl?" "What a handsome, good boy you are!" Fish out some yummy treats or a favorite chew or toy to help your dog see that when unpredictable things happen, good always comes from it!

DIZZY WAITER

Here's a funny game to play with food lovers, hoarders, and bowl-possessive dogs. It's a great way to teach impulse control and get your dog comfortable with you during mealtime.

Take two similar bowls: your dog's food dish and another like it.

Make a big fuss over preparing her food, but only put one piece or spoonful of kibble in her dish. Put the remainder in the other bowl.

Waltz over to her meal area with both bowls, ask your dog to Sit, then place the nearly empty bowl at her feet.

Your dog's going to be baffled. She'll eat the one kibble, then look at you like you've lost your mind.

Encourage her to Sit again, then give her a few more pieces of kibble and walk away.

Come back and add a few more. Keep waltzing back and forth, making her Sit each time.

You can do this a couple of times a week to keep your dog on her toes and let her know that all good things come from you!

CHAMPAGNE FOR EVERYONE!

After rescuing our little puppy mill dog, Bamboozle, we noticed he was a wreck whenever anyone arrived at our home. He'd bark and bare his teeth even as his tail curved beneath his belly. It was pitiful. To help jolly his mood, I developed a game called Champagne for Everyone!, although any word or phrase will do. The point of the game is to link the door and anyone who comes through it with happy thoughts instead of scary ones. You can play, too!

Each time you open the door—even when it's just family arriving— say "Champagne for Everyone!" Shake a treat cup or squeak toys, then throw the reward to the floor so that your dog will look down instead of up at the looming visitor. After a couple of weeks, you should see your dog's attitude toward the door change from unsettling to happy, and she'll start looking down instead of staring suspiciously into anyone's face!

Other dogs react aggressively when protecting their perceived space (aka their territory), either indoors or outside. Unfortunately, this perception gets reinforced every time someone passes by—in the dog's mind, they warded off an intruder. When someone actually does enter their territory, however, this dog may hyperreact, often viciously. This startles many people—from delivery people to dog walkers, who are surprised when their off-leash dog gets attacked.

Some dogs also respond aggressively around moving objects like skateboards, bicycles, joggers, and small animals (which can include small companion dogs). This type of aggression is known as predatory aggression and can quickly become ingrained. Why? Same as above—the jogger jogs on, the vehicle motors by, and the animal runs away. Tethered or fenced, the predatory dog struggles to break free. Beware if she does! This dog is driven to outrun most anything man can create. And prey can only be stopped one way: with a quick, clamping chomp.

Phobias

Thunderstorms have been around since the dawn of time, but many of our dogs' widespread phobias are fairly new on the evolutionary timeline. Fireworks, loud machinery, wood floors, amplified music, transportation vehicles on the ground and in the sky, appliances, and even the beeps of our handhelds . . . it's enough to drive many dogs to distraction. How you cope with each phobia will vary, but organizing a program based on consistency and emotional support is necessary to acclimate your dog to all of life's distractions. Here are some tips that may help; you'll find others at ModernDogParent ing.com/ProblemSolving.

ATTITUDE IS EVERYTHING

Dogs pick up a lot of cues from their people. If you've got a phobia-suffering dog, your attitude can make or break her future. While it can be excruciating to watch your dog or puppy melt into a fear-induced tizzy, it's important for you to stay calm when she's upset. Your reaction will dramatically affect your dog's behavior. If you're indoors with your dog when her reaction is triggered, either keep her on a leash with you if she's comfortable with that or, if not, go into a small, quiet room with her and sit calmly. Read a book, answer some texts—act like nothing is upsetting you. If your dog will take treats, give them to her.

I sat just outside a closet with a foster dog I named Tulip who freaked out during thunderstorms. I'd catch up on my emails while she hid beneath my sweatshirt while the world—in her mind—was coming to an end. Our little closet time did seem to calm her tremendously, so much so that she could tolerate shifts in weather without the need to hide!

COUNTER CONDITIONING

Many of your dog's worries can be soothed by linking them to food or other cherished activities. Is your dog afraid of wood floors? Or loud music? Start counter conditioning slowly at low intensity or volume by using your marker or target wand to pair her phobias with positive experiences.

GRADUAL DESENSITIZATION

If your dog is afraid of noises, sights, or physical sensations, soothe her by introducing the stimulus at lower volumes, greater distances, or different angles. Milo, a Shiba Inu mix terrified of wood floors, had developed a superstitious ritual—a pitiful little 180-degree pivot and backward moonwalk across all wood floors—after slipping while chasing his toy. The ritual soothed his anxiety but affected all aspects of his life.

Milo was a targeting fool, so on a hunch, I bought a slat of Pergo flooring from Home Depot. I taught him to target that and slowly counter conditioned him to step on the Pergo, eventually desensitizing him to his fear of walking across wood floors.

Separation Anxiety

I hate leaving home. I don't like leaving my family or my dogs or my fireplace or my kitchen table. Once I'm out the door, the thrill of adventure takes over, but that initial thrust is never easy. Knowing my dogs would rather come than stay makes it a little rough, too.

If your dog suffers from separation anxiety, she's in good company. I'd go so far as to say she's in the majority. How you handle it—whether you feel guilty or sad like me—and help your dog tolerate being left behind is the focus of the pages ahead. Here are some good things to remember:

DOGS HATE SILENCE

Silence is stressful. It spells *h-o-m-e a-l-o-n-e*, and dogs know it. Few dogs like being left behind. Ease their isolation stress by filling your home with everyday sounds like fans, music, or TV. I've gotten both my kids and my dogs addicted to Pet Tunes, which soothe me, too.

DOGS GET BORED

Left alone with nothing to do, your dog may zero in on your scent, then do what dogs do, namely chew, soil, or shred. It's aggravating, but can you see the loving message behind her focused mischief? She misses you! Don't waste your time getting angry. There is *no way* your puppy or dog can go back in time. She'll just link your frustrations to both the separation and your reappearance, leading to . . . can you guess? More anxiety when you leave. More anxiety leads to . . . guess again? More stress-relieving activities, chewing, and home destruction. There's a better way.

DIRECT THE FUN

If your dog already has pronounced separation anxiety, make helping her overcome it your priority. There are many books devoted to the subject; my favorite by Malena DeMartini-Price, CTC, is listed in the bibliography, as well as other sites and periodicals. Meanwhile, see if you can help get your dog's tail wagging when you go. Stuff her food into Kongs and puzzle toys, use interactive feeders like the Pet Tutor and follow other suggestions in this section to comfort her when you can't be home.

INTERRUPTIONS ARE STRESSFUL

Dogs enjoy full rest cycles, which last two to four hours (two hours for puppies with small bladders and pups under sixteen weeks, longer for more mature dogs). If you're gone during the day, hire dog walkers to come every three to four hours. Rousing your dog too often can increase separation stress, as she has to relive it over and over on a tired, fussy brain.

Dogs are most alert in the early morning and late afternoon, around dusk. Plan activities and fun adventures then. While a midday outing can relieve the bladder and offer time to stretch, you're not obligated to run a mini marathon during your lunch break. I take my dogs out to potty, then sit quietly on the porch answering texts and calls while my dogs stretch, relax, and chew their bones in the sun. Within the hour they're taking another snooze, which ends around the time my kids get off the bus, ready for fun.

LESSON TIME

Self-control is exhausting! Focused lessons take concentration. These mind-over-matter exercises can lead to delightful snoozes while you're away.

ENERGY BUSTERS BEFORE DEPARTURE

Plan your energy-busting activities in the morning and late afternoon. Sometimes your life will lay itself out this way—perhaps you like to walk/jog at those times anyway, or your kids have practice and you can spend time with your dog while you wait—other times you'll have to work it in, especially on the weekends when everyone gets busy. Flip back to page 122 for suggestions on activities that will tire your dog out before you go.

ADVENTURES

All dogs love adventures. A trip to the dog park or a walk around the block can refresh their outlook. If your dog loves connecting with people, a town trip or pet therapy class can give them a whole new leash on life! Is your dog sporty and energetic? Consider taking her on a hike or signing up for an Agility, Flyball or Freestyle class.

Low-Energy Departures and Arrivals

Don't make a big to-do of your comings and goings. Yes, dogs get excited when there's any activity around the door; yes, it feels good to be so welcomed, but we're talking routines here. Overexcited greetings aren't symbolic of love, they're symbolic of . . . well, overexcitement. When you're on your way out, the overexcited dog has nothing to do with her enthusiasm except displace it. Most dogs go for high-odor items like garbage, clothing, frequently used furniture, or shoes. Can you blame them?

Overexcitement on the way in is no good, either. While it feels great to you, it jars your dog mentally. What if one day, the sound she was sure was you coming home turned out not to be you? What can she do with her now frustrated excitement? Right—go find a high-odor prize on which to displace it.

Stay cool when you go. Pick up your keys, kiss your kids good-bye, toss a treat, toy, or bone your dog's way, and leave. Coming home? Check yourself at the door and promise not to react if something was destroyed, chewed, or soiled. Enter calmly, put your things down, check your phone or e-mail, then pet your dog when she's calmed down. If you're worried she may need to potty, take her out calmly but don't reconnect until she's settled down.

INTERVENTION

Separation anxiety can be a very confusing disorder to understand and resolve. Working with a qualified behavior counselor can help you to get your dog through the process. Does your dog suffer each time you leave? Medication may be recommended and can help. If you've tried other things to soothe your dog's worries, speak to your veterinarian or a specialist and consider all your options. As an associate certified dog behavior consultant with the International Association of Animal Behavior Consultants (IAABC) I have studied the effects of medication on stress and feel medications can help a dog cope when necessary. And coping is a good thing, because we can't change this modern world.

So there we have it. We've completed our Happy Dog Adventure Story, discovering that dogs are much more than just pets who float in and out of our lives. Dogs are like children in their complete adoration and devotion. When treated like family, they not only live with us, but they make a deep and lasting impression on our hearts.

Bonus Chapter:

A Dog Parent's Guide to Health and Happiness

Our task must be to free ourselves . . . by widening our circle of compassion to embrace all living creatures and the whole of nature and its beauty.
—ALBERT EINSTEIN

Nothing screams "parenthood" louder than a sick or suffering child, no matter how many legs they walk on. As far as good behavior goes, setting a schedule, teaching manners, and offering appropriate displacement toys won't count for much if your dog has an upset belly or other aches and pains.

To make sure your dog-child gets just the right amount of TLC, use this bonus chapter to discover how to keep them healthy and happy. Ahead you'll find tips and strategies for grooming, parasite protection, exercise, and nutrition.

WHY DOES MY DOG ROLL IN GOO?

Dogs love scents like people do, although what passes as perfume to them leaves much to be desired for us. Decaying frog guts, rotting vegetation, and dried insects are just three of their favorites. What could be more exciting than coming upon such earthly pleasures? Rolling in them to bring the scent home.

Squeaky Clean

Although you might like your dog super clean, you'll likely stand alone on this one. Dogs, like kids, prefer a little dirt under their collar. Even when raised indoors, puppies will choose soil to sidewalk every time. Whether you're looking for tips on giving your dog a quick rinse or you'd like a month-by-month maintenance schedule for grooming and bathing, you'll find what you need in the pages ahead.

HEALTHY COAT, HAPPY DOG

Do you know what type of fur your dog has? There are seven coat types. See table 9.1 to pair yours with similar breeds. The last column suggests brushes for each fur type.

FINDING THE RIGHT BRUSH

Finding the right brush for your dog is important. It should remove your dog's unwanted hair and relax him, too. You might need a few tools to do the job right.

In table 9.1, I list the ideal brushes for different coat types. Here is more grooming trivia to keep in mind in order to select the right tools:

Bristles vary in stiffness. Get a brush with bristles that reflect your dog's coat: For soft and silky coats, use soft and flexible bristles; for coarse, rough coats, find a brush with equal resistance.

TABLE 9.1

COAT TYPE	BREED EXAMPLES	IDEAL BRUSHES
Silky/Feathery	Afghan hound, borzoi, Yorkshire terrier, Maltese, Havanese	Slicker brush, hand mat, dematting comb
Double Coated, short coat	Labrador retriever, Akita, Siberian husky, Rottweiler	Shedding blade, short pin brush, grooming glove
Double Coated, long or thick	Collie, chow chow, spaniels, Great Pyrenees, German shepherd, golden retriever, Australian shepherd	Undercoat rake, shedding blade, long pin brush
Smooth, single coat	Beagle, boxer, dachshund, greyhound, vizsla, German shorthaired pointer, whippet, bull terrier, pug, bulldog	Soft bristle brush, grooming mitt
Wiry	West Highland white terrier, border terrier, Parson's Jack Russell terrier	Firm bristle brush, slicker brush
Corded	Puli, Komondor	Your fingers will do

Brushes also vary in bristle length. A short coat (think whippet, vizsla, bully breed) requires short, tightly packed bristles. Long coats tangle and do better with longer, more widely spaced bristles.

When choosing a detangling rack for your dog, match the pin length to the thickness of your dog's coat.

Although special shedding tools can come in handy, routine brushing keeps tangles in check and reduces both the grooming bills and the need for shaving (necessary if the tangles become . . . well . . . untangleable).

YOU SHOULD SHAVE THICK-COATED DOGS IN THE SUMMER

Some people think they're doing their thick-coated dogs a big favor by shaving them when it gets hot. Affectionately called a smoothie, a summer shave is perhaps the worst thing you could do to your dog's coat. Like shearing a sheep, smoothies should only be practiced when a dog's coat is completely matted.

Cutting a dog's undercoat as a practice, however, is a different story. Double-coated breeds need both layers of fur—the undercoat, which is soft and neutral-toned, and the coarse top coat, which has dramatic, sun-blocking pigments to regulate the dog's body temperature year-round. A seasonal shave traumatizes normal hair growth, and after a few rounds can result in patchy regrowth and a damaged top coat—the very layer that naturally deflects heat.

HOW TO BRUSH

To get your dog addicted to grooming, stuff your pockets with his favorite treats before you take out the brush. Ask a friend to assist you as you first pair the sight, smell, and feel of the brush with yummy snacks. Use gentle, calm strokes to condition your dog to the grooming process and keep him still. Keep the sessions short.

Some dogs—especially those with sensitive skin—react defensively to the brush. One of my kids does, too. Reactivity, no matter the species, is frustrating. If your dog runs from your grooming basket, buy a soft, comforting baby brush from the drug store. Then use the tricks listed above to recondition a more happy association.

BATH TIME BLISS

Some dogs love swimming; others won't go out if it's so much as drizzling. Regardless of your dog's feelings about water, an occasional bath is necessary. Here are five steps to get your dog's tail wagging every time he heads for the bathroom:

1. **START SLOW** Let the fun begin outside the bathroom. Bring your shampoo or home mixture out while playing with or feeding your dog in the kitchen. Leave it open by his food bowl so he develops a positive association with the smell. Identify it with a cue like "Bath Time!"

2. **RACE YA!** Put a spin on the Name Game described in chapter 6 using your treat cup and the word "Bathroom" as you move quickly or run in that direction.

3. **DRY RUNS** Explore the tub or shower without turning the water on. Place a plush towel or mat on the floor of the tub/shower to steady your dog, and scatter some treats, toys, or favorite bones around. No water yet!

4. **DRIP BY DRIP** Let your dog get used to the sound of running water by turning on the faucet just a little bit. Continue to play on his mat and offer food.

5. **TIME TO GET OUT THE SHAMPOO** Once your dog is used to the sound of running water and is more excited to explore the matted surface sprinkled with treasure treats, introduce the concept of "You're Going to Get Wet." For some dogs, baths are never going to make their top ten fun activities list. Although you might feel frustrated, pretend to stay calm. If your dog's not a fan, use as little base water as possible, cover his ears and eyes when you're dousing his head, and massage the soap through his coat gently while you soothe him with music and/or your voice.

AN IDEAL BATH SCHEDULE

If you're a clean freak, brace yourself: Your dog should not be bathed often. For some breeds—like double-coated, wiry, and corded dogs—a few times a year will do, and for others, a monthly rinse will be all you need to help limit the grime. Dirt does not collect in dogs' pores like it does in ours, simply because they haven't got very many. Instead, dogs' hairs are covered in a protective oil, so when they do get dirty, the dirt dries and literally rolls off. Brushing your dog can speed this process along, but routine bathing strips him of his natural oils and leaves his coat dry, dirty, and smelly.

But that's not the worst of it! Overbathing affects his skin, too. Dogs' skin, like ours, does more than keep the blood in—it also shields them from bacteria, viruses, and infection. To do this, however, your dog's skin must maintain a certain balance, or what's known as a pH level. Chemicals in commercial dog shampoos can wreak havoc on your dog's skin, as will using human brands (we have a different pH level). Using the wrong products will immediately affect your dog's coat and hair regrowth, alter his odor, and eventually cause skin conditions that lead to infection and illness. Yikes!

When choosing a proper shampoo, try to stick to formulas with natural products. Look for ingredients like saponified oils; sodium hydroxide (aka lye and caustic soda); coconut, olive, pine tree or jojoba oils; aloe vera; herbal extracts such as rosemary, peppermint, eucalyptus, rosemary, lavender, sage, and cedarwood; and vitamin E.

Avoid products that contain harmful ingredients, including but not limited to artificial colors or fragrances, formaldehyde, isopropyl anything, cocomides, sodium sulfates (SLS or SLES), parabens of any type, phthalates, methylchloroisothiazolinone (already banned in Canada and Japan), polyethylene glycol (PEG), or mineral oil. These chemicals are known carcinogens and cause immediate diarrhea, eye damage, and skin irritation that can lead to illness.

Still sold on a weekly bath? Know this: Once you've stripped the oils from your dog's coat, he'll start to smell and look shabby,

TOMATO JUICE TAKES OUT SKUNK ODOR

Ah, no, but it will leave your dog a pretty shade of pink. If your dog meets the wrong end of a skunk, buy a commercial cleanser or create your own by mixing ½ quart hydrogen peroxide, 2 tablespoons baking soda, and 1 teaspoon Dawn liquid dish detergent.

which might lead you to think "More baths, try conditioner, cut the hair!" You're essentially washing your dog's natural radiance away. Stop the vicious cycle.

Parasites and Preventions

Parasites—whether feasting on the insides or outsides of your dog—are the ultimate downer. They feast on dogs, especially those with weak immune systems like the young, old, or ill. If you suspect your dog is suffering, reach out to his veterinarian ASAP—many parasites carry other, more serious diseases. Here are some common parasites and key tips to avoid an infestation.

SKIN PARASITES

Keep in mind that external parasites live for only two reasons: eating and procreation. Their favorite foods are blood and skin cells. Narrowing in on their worldview will help you reduce your pet's exposure to parasites and, in turn, your own.

Fleas

These flightless jumpers get around. They prefer warmer temperatures and high humidity, but are found around the world. During their approximately hundred-day life-span, fleas jump from host to host with rapid determination; they are a homeowner's worst nightmare. Eggs, once laid, roll off the host and settle where they land, inside or out. Each egg releases a worm (scientifically known as a pupa) that evolves into a flea that eagerly bounds away, searching for blood.

Fleas can cause a host of diseases and deficiencies including flea allergy dermatitis, hemoplasmas, iron-deficiency anemia, typhus, and Bartonella (spread by cats and also known as cat scratch disease). In the past, fleas were responsible for spreading the bubonic plague.

Ticks

Ticks relish warm blood and will feast on any mammal—they're not picky. They lay eggs on the ground, and from these eggs emerge hundreds of new and hungry ticks.

If you're out in nature, stick to well-maintained trails. The University of Rhode Island offers a fabulous resource site (TickEncounter.org) that outlines the different habitats various species of ticks prefer. Some like dense brush, while others prefer tall grasses. Think you're safe on the pavement or sidewalks? Ticks can be found there, too. Ticks ride on their hosts, feeding until they're full, and they can drop off in the most unexpected places, which can also include inside your home.

If a tick bites you or your dog, Lyme disease is but one of the viruses you could contract. Ticks also transmit anaplasmosis, ehrlichiosis, Rocky Mountain spotted fever, cytauxzoonosis, and—only in humans—tularemia and tick paralysis. Perhaps most disturbing is that one tick can transmit a "cocktail" of multiple viruses at once. During high tick season, be on the lookout for these pests. If you can remove a tick within twenty-four hours, it may not have had enough time to transmit any viruses.

Flea and Tick Prevention

Before I had kids, I spent hours researching, preparing, and applying nontoxic remedies on my pets. I used flea combs after each walk and picked through their coats meticulously every night. I congratulated myself on avoiding commercial mixtures, but during that decade, both my dogs and I got Lyme disease, and we had a flea infestation that took months to resolve.

After giving birth to human kids, I have much less time and far bigger concerns. Though I've not been a fan of using chemical preventatives more than necessary, I've learned the hard way that prevention is both healthier and cheaper than treatment. Now, in addition to yard treatments and herbal sprays, I use deterrent collars, monthly oral preventives, and even topical applications in the worst months.

The key word for any pet lover to keep in mind is "repellant." The products you should use need to repel fleas (ticks, too), not simply kill them after they bite your pets.

Mosquitoes

Little needs to be said about these charming insects. Responsible for spreading yellow fever, malaria, and filariasis, the mosquito has other recent claims to fame, namely heartworm and

MYTH BUSTER
ONLINE OR STORE-BOUGHT PRODUCTS ARE JUST AS GOOD AS MEDICALLY PRESCRIBED TREATMENTS

Online and store-bought preventatives are often far less effective—as noted on their labels—than those purchased through a reputable veterinarian. Although the convenience of online collars and remedies can't be argued, buyers beware. Some online vendors sell expired treatments that are ineffective and may actually be more dangerous to your pet than the pests they're protecting against. If that weren't enough of a concern, combining some collars with certain medications, or using a product if a dog is pregnant, can be a deadly game. It is imperative that you speak to your veterinarian before deciding on a product or combination of deterrents.

IT'S OKAY TO USE BUG SPRAY ON MY DOG

You can't use people bug sprays on your dog. DEET—the most common ingredient in our repellants—is highly toxic and will make your dog sick if he licks his fur after the bug spray is applied. Most bugs target ears, so apply a nontoxic repellant to that area or purchase a mesh bonnet, which can be found online.

West Nile virus. Although there is no vaccine for West Nile, heartworm, the most threatening mosquito-borne disease, can be easily prevented with a heartworm prevention medicine.

Mites
Mites feast on dogs all the time, but there are good mites and bad mites. It's important to know the difference.

Demodex Mites
Demodex mites pass from mother to pups. All dogs have them, and they're not contagious. They live a relatively uninterrupted life in dogs' hair shafts and may only become problematic when a dog's stressed, ill, or injured. A resulting demodectic mange infection usually begins as localized demodectic mange, on the face and eyes with hair loss and red scaly skin. If the infection spreads unchecked, it's known as generalized demodectic mange. Topical treatments are the norm; in extreme cases medication would be prescribed. Demodectic pododermatitis is a foot mange infection and develops if the skin is left open due to a wound or excessive scratching/licking from allergies or boredom.

Sarcoptic Mites
These mighty-mites are unwelcome—and highly contagious—guests. They burrow into your dog's skin and cause extreme itching and hair loss—a condition known as sarcoptic mange. Initially navigating to open areas on your dog's ears, elbows, and belly,

they'll spread everywhere if left untreated. Treatment involves dips, injections, oral drugs, and ointments.

Cheyletiella Mites

These mites are also contagious and feed on the skin. Their street name is "walking dandruff," as they cause skin to flake off. As a parasite, they're similar to fleas and are often treated with similar products and preventatives. Although the irritation is less severe than with the other mites, it can be more dramatic in young animals who have weaker immune systems. Skin scraping and stool samples can reveal their presence; if swallowed, these guys can pass through your dog's digestive system unharmed.

INTERNAL PARASITES

Equally unpleasant are the internal invaders—the parasites and worms that sneak in and infect your dog's organs and/or digestive tract, leaving him weary or ill. Certain parasites cause little or no reaction in healthy dogs, but stressed, old, or young dogs may suffer greatly. Some worms, if left untreated, can even be life threatening. If you see creepy things crawling in your dog's stool or notice persistent diarrhea or vomiting, take him to see his veterinarian ASAP. Here's a quick rundown of what he/she might find:

HOOKWORM **Hookworms feast on your dog's blood, causing anemia and energy loss. Since they can enter through the mouth or the skin, they can also cause skin rash and infections.**

WHIPWORM **Living in the large intestine, whipworms cause watery diarrhea and/or bloody stools.**

TAPEWORM **Tapeworms enter your dog's system through infected rodents or fleas. They come in a few varieties, one of which—echinococcus—can infect people, too.**

ROUNDWORM **Roundworms live in the intestines and generally only cause problems in young puppies. As most dogs are born with roundworms, don't be too surprised if your puppy becomes symptomatic—signs include gas, potbelly, and belly aches. If left untreated, however, the early infestation can stunt growth. If you see any of these symptoms, take your puppy to see his doctor.**

HEARTWORM **These worms grow in the main blood vessels of the heart and, when mature, affect the transportation of blood to the various organs. A routine blood test will reveal heartworm, although other symptoms like abnormal breathing and heart rate, shortness of breath, dry cough, and even fainting can tip you off. This fatal disease can be prevented with oral medication, or treated aggressively with injections, rest, and supportive antibodies and/or transfusions if needed.**

Treatment for Worms

Treatment for worms involves oral medications known as de-wormers. Many heartworm pills available today also target other worms.

SINGLE-CELLED ORGANISMS

These guys live in your dog's intestines and are transmitted through ingested poop and contaminated soil or water.

COCCIDIA Most dogs can live with coccidia, tiny one-celled organisms, without any signs or symptoms. Reactions most often happen when young puppies are stressed or ill, especially just after they leave their litter. When reactions do occur, they cause watery diarrhea, vomiting, belly ache, and dehydration. Coccidia can be transmitted through stool or by eating an infected animal or their poop.

GIARDIA This parasite can be picked up by both dogs and people when drinking contaminated water. With dogs, it's generally not life threatening unless the dog's immune system isn't strong. The surest sign your dog is infected is foul-smelling diarrhea, greenish mucous, and/or bloody stool.

Treatment for Internal Parasites

Although parasites can and do live harmoniously in your dog's intestines, some types need to be treated. Antibiotics are the general rule of thumb if your dog is infected.

Routine TLC

Dogs, like young kids, depend on you to stay on top of their personal hygiene. Unkempt dogs with tangled, parasite-infected coats, or nails that are too long to be comfortable have a lot more on their minds than you. A good dog parent is a responsible dog parent.

TEETH

There is a lot of buzz about doggie dental health these days. Should you give your dog bones, or avoid them altogether? Is brushing your dog's teeth necessary, or will this just stress him out? What about oral gels and sprays? Have they come up with braces for dogs yet?

Well, no one has invented doggie braces yet, but dogs can

suffer tooth decay and infections. Decades ago, dental problems were rare as dogs had shorter lifespans and generally hung around outside gnawing on discarded bones and sticks, which kept their teeth strong. Dogs (and people) live a much different lifestyle now, and many veterinarians and breeders—concerned about the quality of bones sold—recommend plastic substitutes that many dogs ignore. Before we touch on safe alternatives and preventative tooth care though, here's some doggie dental trivia to keep in mind.

> Puppies lose their first set of teeth between four and six months of age. Tiny deciduous teeth fall out and are replaced by an adult set. If a baby tooth doesn't fall out, it may rot and/or throw off bite development. Speak to your veterinarian if your puppy has two teeth growing where there should only be one.

> Your dog's gums should be pink; neither white nor red.

> Signs of infection include white or angry red gums, swollen gums, foul breath or drooling; secondary symptoms may include a loss of appetite or increased drinking and peeing.

> Excessive tartar (or plaque) can also host infections; you might see a tumor on the gum or notice a loose tooth. Bring your dog to

MYTH BUSTER
I CAN USE MY TOOTHPASTE TO BRUSH MY DOG'S TEETH

Well, no. You shouldn't. In fact, avoid people products altogether. Fluoride, a known toxin, can poison dogs if ingested in high doses and has the reverse effect on a dog's teeth as it does on a person's, breaking down the enamel.

the veterinarian immediately if you notice these symptoms. Infections in the mouth spread quickly to the entire body.

Chewing is a proactive way to prevent tooth decay. Find bones your dog enjoys.

Caring for Your Dog's Mouth

An entire industry has cropped up suggesting that toothbrushes aren't just for people anymore. While you can condition your dog to tolerate your probing, it might not always be necessary. You can find plenty of oral gels and sprays that work as effectively as a toothbrush if you follow the manufacturer's instructions. Ask your veterinarian for suggestions.

If you're sold on brushing, brace yourself for some initial resistance from your dog. To get him comfortable with the brush, lather it with peanut butter or a similar spread for the first week. Let him lick it for a while, then gently roll it around before you attempt a rhythmic swish.

EARS

A healthy ear has a neutral odor and looks clean and pink. A waxy ear has a lot of buildup. Wax blocks the natural airflow into the ear, which is not good. Bacteria and other parasites can lodge in the earwax and multiply. Allergens can get trapped, too. Although genetics play a role in ear health, you're the key player now. If you find your dog is predisposed to waxy ears, wipe out his ears weekly with hydrogen peroxide or a specially formulated solution; your veterinarian can suggest one for you. If your dog is a swimmer and prone to ear infections, ask your veterinarian for a drying solution. Be mindful not to flood the ear canal with water when bathing your dog.

If you see thick black/dark brown wax accompanied by redness, crusty skin, and a bad odor, or if your dog is scratching his ears continually, suspect an infection and seek medical attention immediately. Ear infections can become systemic and very dan-

CAN I USE A COTTON SWAB TO CLEAN MY DOG'S EARS?

No. Your veterinarian would not approve. Dogs have a vertical canal that drops right into the eardrum. Jabbing their ear can cause irreparable damage to their hearing as well as their balance. Use premedicated wipes or soft cotton dipped in a prescribed solution or hydrogen peroxide to clean the outside of the canal regularly.

gerous in a short time. What might have been treated with a quick round of liquid eardrops can become a serious infection that is a big, expensive ordeal to contain.

Your veterinarian may find ear mites, or more commonly just an infection caused by a blocked canal. If not cleared immediately, bacteria and parasites can settle in, requiring a round of medication.

EYES

Check out your dog's eyes when he's indoors and relaxed. Hopefully they're bright, symmetrical, and free of hair and goop. If your dog has hair around his eyes or matted fur blocking his view, it will need a trim. If you don't have a steady hand, take your dog to the groomer for a clip.

If your dog's eyes have discharge; are clouded over, bulging out, or squinted; or if he's pawing at or rubbing his face on the ground, there's an issue that needs immediate attention. Conditions that your veterinarian might find include inflammation, pink eye, ingrown eyelid, injury, irritation, prolapse of the third eyelid, corneal ulcers, cataracts, glaucoma, or progressive renal atrophy.

The Third Eyelid

Dogs have a third eyelid called a nictitating membrane that cleans dirt off the eyeball—like windshield wipers. See if you can find it by offering your dog a treat and gently pulling down his lower lid. A thick, naturally pink membrane should rise over his eyeball. An angry red or white nictitating membrane indicates irritation or illness.

NAILS

Cutting a dog's nails is tricky business. If managing your dog's nail growth gives you the heebie-jeebies, most groomers will take care of it for a small fee. If you're brave, here's the quick skinny.

All dogs' nails have a fingertip—known as the quick—that the nail covers. You don't want to cut that. "Quicking," or cutting your dog's tip, is kind of like cutting your fingertip off. It's going to bleed and be painful. Avoid this drama with the following tips:

Use treats, toys, and a comfy blanket to settle your dog before clipping. Find a well-lit corner, and make sure you're both positioned comfortably.

Choose scissor-like tools instead of clippers, and use a grinder, which acts like a nail file. Guillotine-like clippers are difficult to maneuver, crush the nail, and can cause pain.

Think like the nail. Cut around parallel to the quick, not vertically across it, in a rounded shape. Trim up one side and down the other.

If you can, trim your dog's nails every couple of weeks. As dogs instinctively lean forward when their nail tip touches the ground, long, uncut nails will throw your dog's weight off and make him more prone to musculoskeletal problems.

ANAL SACS

Dogs have two little kidney-shaped sacs on the edge of their rectum. When all goes as planned, they secrete a distinct odor each time your dog poops. With some dogs—especially overweight ones—these sacs become impacted, which puts a lot of pressure on their rump. If not pinched and expressed by hand (a lovely task your veterinarian can help with), impaction will cause swelling and infection. How can you tell? The surest sign is rump dragging, which is funny to everyone but the dog. With his hind legs outstretched, he'll drag his bottom around the floor to relieve the pressure. Dogs also scratch at the base of their tail—a symptom that can be confused with a flea problem. Talk to your veterinarian about how to prevent or cope with this condition.

Fun and Fitness

With canine obesity on the rise—more than 50 percent of America's dogs are overweight—focusing on fitness should be every dog parent's priority. In fact, when people ask me how to get their dog to stop digging or looting the laundry basket, my favorite answer is, "Take him for a walk!" Dogs behave a lot better when their energy's all used up.

Before you start a fitness program with your dog, however, check in with your veterinarian to be sure your approach is mindful and measured. Like people, dogs can pull muscles or ligaments if pushed too far, too fast. Although you might be conditioned to run for miles, your dog should start slow to build up his stamina.

Puppies should not be pushed into an organized exercise regime until nine months of age, when their growth plates are fused and they're nearing maturity. Stress on growing bones can lead to more than just muscle strain—it can stunt growth. Talk to your veterinarian before you get started.

I'M WORRIED MY DOG WILL RUN AWAY FROM ME.

Well, that's a good thing to worry about. Even the most well-mannered dogs can get distracted. Always use a leash near streets, and play in enclosed areas or use a long line to give your dog a sense of freedom as described in chapter 2.

Other fun ways to get your dog moving include playing in the yard, swimming, visiting a safe and well-run dog park, and scheduling playdates. Dogs will enjoy any activity you do together: going for a hike, mountain biking, walking on the beach. . . .

If competitive canine sports sound fun, you'll have plenty to choose from. Check out Agility, Freestyle, and Flyball for starters, then Google "canine sports" and let your imagination run wild. Just remember to start gradually, with short outings and easy adventures.

First Aid

Accidents can happen when you least expect them. Knowing what to do in the moment can save your dog while you transport him to his veterinarian. Here's a proactive plan covering common injuries.

Heatstroke

Always provide your dog with access to shade and water. Never leave your dog in the car when the sun is out; he'll bake. Dogs don't sweat—they release their body heat through panting, an inefficient system at best. Symptoms of heatstroke include heavy panting, fainting, disorientation, vomiting, and diarrhea. Immediately wrap your dog's neck, ears, and nether regions in wet towels to bring his temperature down gradually. Do not give him ice or cold water as it may shock his system.

Bleeding

Internal bleeding and external bleeding both require immediate veterinary attention. If your dog has symptoms that include white gums, vomiting, or coughing up blood, suspect the worst, but stay calm. Carefully move your dog into the car and drive him to the nearest animal hospital.

External bleeding requires calm handling and attention, too. If the blood is gushing, elevate the area and apply constant pressure, laying each bandage on top of the next, versus ripping one off to add another. Find a veterinarian or emergency animal hospital immediately.

Choking

Dogs can choke on many things. While they have a powerful gagging reflex that ejects most objects caught in their airways, your dog may still be unable to dislodge something. If that's the case, you'll have an emergency on your hands. You, or someone trained in doggie CPR, need to act fast. Drive to the nearest veterinary hospital. To see canine CPR in motion, visit Modern DogParenting.com/Health&Wellness.

Broken Bones

This painful injury must be handled with great care. Dogs in pain will try to escape and hide. Even the most docile dog will bite when injured. Get a leash on this dog fast. Stay calm, and steady your dog. If you suspect a spinal injury, maneuver your dog onto a flat board before taking him to the veterinarian.

Snakebites

Many dogs don't have a clue when it comes to snakes. The best prevention for injuries like this are a solid recall and a leash when hiking in snake-populated areas, and when possible, work with a snake handler to develop a healthy fear of snakes in your dog.

If your dog gets bitten, stay calm. Try to get a visual on the type of snake that bit him. Immediately wrap the wound with a strip of cloth or bandanna. Apply constant pressure to slow the spread of the venom, and bring your dog to the nearest veterinarian.

Foxtails

Foxtail seeds easily latch on to a dog's fur and become embedded in the skin. These seeds are bad news. If not removed, they may burrow into the skin and lodge in your dog's central nervous system, wreaking havoc in his brain, lungs, or other organs. Check your dog's coat routinely during the seeding season (May through

December), removing anything easily grasped, and bring any embedded seeds or abscesses to your veterinarian's attention.

Burns

Curiosity—in the form of an overturned teacup, a chewed wire, an exploratory sniff of a toxic chemical substance—sometimes leads to serious trouble in the way of burns. If you find that your dog has been burned, stay calm, note the cause, and bring your dog to his veterinarian or an emergency animal hospital.

Good Nutrition

Knowing how and what to feed your dog can get very confusing, but considering that most dogs in other parts of the world still scavenge—garbage tipping, rodent killing, or thieving—to survive, anything you provide is a step up. At least your dog won't be living one meal to the next.

Before typing "dog + diet" into your web browser, brace yourself. Dog diet advocates have created a controversial brew, and while most arguments will sound pretty valid, choose the one that feels most doable for you. Seriously, now: If only we gave our own nutritional intake so much thought!

All diets are good for some of the dogs some of the time. My dog Hope, a scruffy shelter dog, had a belly full of reoccurring kidney stones. Although the shelter was ready to put her down, I adopted her and, on a veterinarian's suggestion, gave a raw food diet a try. It was an instant cure. I tried the same diet on Whoopsie Daisy, my Labrador retriever, and she vomited for a week.

Nowadays my home is a veritable delicatessen, with twenty paws gathering around the dinner table at mealtimes. Since my eldest dog suffers from chronic ear infections, she gets nutritionally balanced home-cooked meals, while the rest of the dogs get a dry food base mixed with a variety of fresh fruits and vegetables (melons, apples, sweet potato, broccoli, carrots, peas, and beans), as well as yogurt, fish oil, eggs, or sardines. Do I need to do this? No, but it makes me feel good, and you won't catch them complaining!

Here's a quick summary of the various diets available to you and your dog—select one that works for you and doesn't make your dog sick. Get input from your veterinarian as to what he/she thinks would be best for your dog.

DRY Processed kibble is the most cost-effective way to feed a dog. Added preservatives ensure the food won't rot. There are many different types; ingredients do vary. Look beyond the clever packaging to discover the healthiest recipe you can afford.

CANNED This type of dog food also contains preservatives so it does not need refrigeration unless opened. There are many different types of canned food. As most cans are 75 percent water, you need more to fill your dog up. Ingredients matter a lot. Some poorer-quality cans use indigestible protein sources that pass through your dog. Whether you choose to feed your dog canned food exclusively or use it to liven up a meal, choose one that is labeled "100 percent nutritionally complete" (U.S. brands) or "complete and balanced" (European brands).

FREEZE-DRIED Now on the rise, freeze-dry companies take raw, natural foods, cook them at a low temperature, and seal them in airtight packaging. You can do this on your own, although it's time-consuming and labor-intensive. Many brands of quality dog food are offering this option to their consumers.

RAW The raw food craze is often linked with the acronym BARF, which stands for biologically appropriate raw food. This diet consists of raw meat, bones, and organs, and can be made or bought. Fans of this diet claim it's superior to processed foods. Critics claim it's nutritionally unbalanced and unsanitary to handle.

HOME-PREPARED MEALS Home cooking is certainly an option, although preparing meals for your dog is different than making

WOULD MY DOG BE HAPPIER ON A MIX-AND-MATCH DIET PLAN?

No. Although people claim variety is the spice of life, drastic changes in diet give your dog the runs. Their shorter intestines demand a relatively consistent diet. If you need to change your dog food, do it gradually over eight days to avoid belly aches and diarrhea.

dinner for people. Dogs have certain nutritional needs that must be understood, or they'll end up with all sorts of ailments. If you want to home cook, speak to a canine nutritionist or research online.

SEMI-MOIST If you scan the shelves of most supermarkets, you're likely to find a semi-moist food fashioned into the shape of a pork chop or hamburger patty. Avoid the temptation. Although they might get your dog's tail wagging, they're junk. Devoid of anything remotely healthy, they can be used as treats, if you want, but I wouldn't recommend that, either.

So there you have it: all you need to know to be a good dog parent. Without good health and a hearty diet, nothing else really matters. If you're like me, you'll take pride in seeing your dog in good shape, and others will know just by looking that your dog-child is well loved.

What Keeps You Going?

The hardest part about dogs is that they don't live forever. After two to three years, they're all grown up, and unless you're rescuing an older dog, the two of you will grow delightfully set in your ways. As the years pass, you'll collect memories and pictures that will freeze the time that passes all too quickly with our beloved dogs. It's hard for anyone who has ever loved a dog to believe there is a time that you could live without them.

I have an old dog. Her name is Whoopsie, short for Whoopsie Daisy. I cannot fathom the day when she won't be there to greet me at the door or send me racing for a towel to wipe up yet another spill caused by her perpetually wagging tail. I want to end my book with our love story. She's been with me through two marriages, three moves, countless pets, and the births and raising of my kids. Her tag reads "The Buddha at our feet." And she is my Buddha, my own personal talisman. Let your life be filled with as many great adventures.

See you out there!

FROM FOUR TO SIX TO SPANDEX:
WHAT MY DOG TAUGHT ME ABOUT AGING

Recently, I went to the mall—which is remarkable only in that it's a bi-seasonal event in my household, on par with visiting the dentist. I'd rather take my kids down to the lake or walk with my dogs, but sometimes shopping is inevitable.

The real shock wasn't that I entered the mall, however—it came in the Macy's dressing room when I slid on a pair of size 6 jeans and could not, for the life of me, button the waistband.

I know. The world is full of sorrows and stress; people are starving and homeless; world leaders can't get along. But still. I have a closet full of sixes. I'd already gone from a size four to a size six, and I just could not do it. I opted for spandex.

So now, instead of dressing in perky capris in lively colors, I've shifted to spandex skirts that fall below the knee. It's a different look. "Elegant and dignified," I reassure myself as I look in the mirror.

Top this off with the fact that my hair is graying. And the wayward strands are not elegant and tame, lying flat, capturing light and adding to my appeal. No. My grays are kinked and unruly. The type a witch would wish for.

With my newfound obsessions for baking pies, planning kid-centric activities, and perusing cooking magazines, I've become undeniably middle-aged. So the question is: Where to turn for a good role model?

Hollywood is no help, unless it's to challenge the promises of plastic surgery and snake-oil treatments. New Age magazines don't offer much beyond momentary hope or spiteful schadenfreude—your choice.

Is it ever okay to just be aging? I longed for an alternative.

And then it hit me. Literally. Sitting on the couch watching a *Modern Family* rerun, I was sidelined by the tail of one of my most trusted companions: my thirteen-year-old dog, Whoopsie Daisy.

Whoopsie started life black as a bat and energetic as a freight train. Her hobbies included ocean swims, Frisbee, and soccer games in which she served as a goalie few could outkick. She'd accompany me to my dog lessons to serve as a distraction dog and to my group classes, where she would instinctively coddle the puppies who refused to venture out of the corner. A certified therapy dog, she required no leash in the nursing home or the schools we visited as she sensed where she was needed most.

But Whoopsie is older now . . . speckled with gray, battling the bulge, incontinent, and arthritic. Flashing her images of the currently popular meme of dogs dressed in underwear, I whispered that her day for needing an undergarment might come. She planted a wet one straight across my face.

"Someday," I called out to my kids while sopping up her piddles, pointing to the true meaning of love, "you'll be doing this for me!"

Even peppered with white, sagging, and sore, Whoopsie has one part that's never changed and that has become my symbol, my amulet, my meditative image for aging. It is her wagging tail. It flags me calmly in the morning when I lie next to her on the chaise, routinely knocks over coffee cups, and scatters LEGOS as it waves a cheerful hello to whoever approaches her. Its joyous spiral propels her forward even when it seems that her body bemoans every step.

Though she hasn't the words to express it, her enthusiasm for community sends a message stronger than any I've heard or read of. It seems whether you're a dog, a person, a flower, or a tree, aging shows little mercy to those along its path. You sag, you ache, you dribble and droop, but as long as keep your tail up and wagging, you'll be surrounded by enough love to propel you forward.

ACKNOWLEDGMENTS

Every night at dinner my family holds hands and mentions something we're grateful for. As I put the finishing touches on my book, I envision holding hands with an enormous circle of dog lovers, each grateful for something unique. Let me start!

First, I want to thank you, my readers, for choosing this book. It's hard enough to care for oneself these days—to share your time and love with a dog is commendable. Choosing a positive path is first-rate.

I'm so grateful to all of the voices that have guided me throughout my life. My journey continues in the wake of so many inspirational thinkers. Temple Grandin stirred me early on to embrace my unique dog obsession and run with it; I've never looked back. In my early twenties, Job Michael Evans, Carol Lea Benjamin, Ranny Green, and others invited me into their circle. It was a great honor. Stanley Coren was and continues to be my icon for writing about and living this dream.

To others I've met along my path, your work will continue to shape my thoughts: Karen Pryor, Ph.D.; Dr. Ian Dunbar; Jean Donaldson; Patricia McConnell, Ph.D.; Dr. Nicholas Dodman; Dr. Brian Hare; Steve Dale, CABC; Pat Miller, IIACAB; Terry Ryan; Dr. Sophia Yin; Turid Rugaas, PDTE; Malena DeMartini, CTC; Wes Anderson; and all my friends and colleagues at IAABC. There are others, too, past and present.

Finally, my life's song would be nothing without my sturdy foundation of family and friends. I love you all. Thanks especially to Olivia Powell, my niece and first reader. Your edits were spot on and your tireless availability was beyond reassuring. You might not have known much about dogs to start, but you sure do now! And a special hug to my daughter Lindsay who is both an editor and a writer in the making. You have my complete respect! Thanks for always pointing out my misspellings and helping me think of new words when the chosen ones didn't fit!

A final shout-out to Deborah Schneider, my agent at Gelfman Schneider/ICM Partners. You took me in when I was just a puppy, and now look at us! Thanks for introducing me to my editor, Daniela Rapp at St. Martin's Press. It's so easy to write for professionals who are, at day's end, just as crazy about dogs as I am!

BIBLIOGRAPHY

My passion for dogs and people has been influenced by many be-haviorists, trainers, and scientists; their work has created a trail that anyone can follow! Compiling a full list would take a book in itself! Below, I've referenced those who have made the greatest impact on this book. To access my continually growing list of helpful blogs, podcasts, and articles, connect with me online at ModernDogParenting.com. See you out there!

HELPFUL BLOGS AND ONLINE RESOURCES
American College of Veterinary Behaviorists, *Decoding Your Pet*: Psychology Today.com/Blog/Decoding-Your-Pet

Animal Health Foundation, *Animal Health Foundation Blog*: AnimalHealth Foundation.net/Blog

Brian Hare, *Dognition*: Dognition.com

Brian Hare, *Dr. Brian Hare*: BrianHare.net

Center for Canine Behavior Studies, *Center for Canine Behavior Studies*: CenterForCanineBehaviorStudies.org

Ethology Institute. "Do You Know What the Dog's Twist Behavior Means?" Ethology Institute Cambridge. ethology.edu/do-you-know-what-the-dogs-behavior-means

Francine Rattner, "How to handle a dog with OCD tendencies." *Animal Health Foundation*. 24 December 2012.

Hal Herzog, *Animals and Us*: PsychologyToday.com/Blog/Animals-And-Us

Ian Dunbar, *Dog Star Daily*: DogStarDaily.com/Blogs

Jean Donaldson, *Plantigrade*: 209.200.229.183/Blog

Jennifer Arnold, *Through a Dog's Eyes*: PsychologyToday.comBlog/Through-Dog-s-Eyes

Jessica Pierce, *All Dogs Go to Heaven*: PsychologyToday.com/Blog/All-Dogs-Go-Heaven

Joan Mayer, *The Inquisitive Canine*: InquisitiveCanine.com/Blog

John Bradshaw, *Pets and Their People*: PsychologyToday.com/Blog/Pets-And-Their-People

Linda Brietman, *The Pet Docs*: ThePetDocs.com

Malena DeMartini, *The Experts in Helping Dogs with Separation Anxiety*: MalenaDemartini.com

Marc Bekoff, *Animal Emotions*: PsychologyToday.com/Blog/Animal-Emotions

Mark Derr, *Dog's Best Friend*: PsychologyToday.com/Blog/Dogs-Best-Friend

Maureen Backman, *Mutt About Town*: MuttAboutTown.com/Blog

Nathalie Mosbach, *K9 Consultant*: K9Consultant.Blogspot.com

Nicholas Dodman, *Dr. Dodman*: DrDodman.org

Patricia McConnell, *The Other End of the Leash*: PatriciaMcConnell.com/TheOtherEndOfTheLeash

Robert E. Bailey and Marion Breland Bailey, *Behavior Matters*: BehaviorMatters.com

Robert E. Bailey, *IQ-Zoo*: UCA.edu/IQZoo

Stanley Coren, *Canine Corner*: PsychologyToday.com/Blog/Canine-Corner

Steve Dale, *Steve Dale CABC*: SteveDale.TV

The Pet Professionals. *Vet Teaches How to Give CPR to Your Dog*: www.YouTube.com/Watch?v=c5ixBuM_Ew0

Wes Anderson, *Smart Animal Training Systems*: SmartAnimalTraining.com

BOOKS AND ARTICLES

American College of Veterinary Behaviorists. *Decoding Your Dog: The Ultimate Experts Explain Common Dog Behaviors and Reveal How to Prevent or Change Unwanted Ones.* New York: Houghton Mifflin Harcourt, 2014.

Appleby, David, John Bradshaw, and Rachel Casey. "Relationship between aggressive and avoidance by dogs and their experience in the first six months of life." *Veterinary Record* 150. 2002: 434–438.

Arman, Koharik. "A new direction for kennel club regulations and breed standards." *Canadian Veterinary Journal* 48. 2007: 953–965.

Arnold, Jennifer. *In a Dog's Heart: What Our Dogs Need, Want, and Deserve—and the Gifts We Can Expect in Return.* New York: Spiegel & Grau, 2011.

———. *Through a Dog's Eyes: Understanding Our Dogs by Understanding How They See the World.* New York: Spiegel & Grau, 2011.

Arrowsmith, Claire. *Brain Games for Dogs: Fun Ways to Build a Strong Bond with Your Dog and Provide It with Vital Mental Stimulation.* Ontario: Firefly Books, 2010.

Bailey, Jon, and Mary Burch. *How Dogs Learn.* Hoboken: Howell Book House, 1999.

Bartlett, Melissa, et. al. *Teaching Dog Obedience Classes: The Manual for Instructors.* Hoboken: Howell Book House, 1986.

Behne, T., et al. "One-year-olds comprehend the communicative intentions behind gestures in a hiding game." *Developmental Science* 8. 2005: 492–499.

Bekoff, Marc. *The Cognitive Animal.* Oxford: Oxford University Press, 2009.

———. *The Emotional Lives of Animals: A Leading Scientist Explores Animal Joy, Sorrow and Empathy—and Why They Matter.* Novato: New World Library, 2007.

Bennett, Pauleen, and Vanessa Rohlf. "Owner-companion dog interactions: Relationships between demographic variables, potentially problematic behaviors, training engagement and shared activities." *Applied Animal Behavior Science* 102. 2007: 65–84.

Berns, Gregory. *How Dogs Love Us: A Neuroscientist and His Adopted Dog Decode the Canine Brain.* Boston: New Harvest, 2013.

Bradshaw, John. *Dog Sense: How the New Science of Dog Behavior Can Make You a Better Friend to Your Pet.* New York: Basic Books, 2011. Print.

Brown, Steve. *Unlocking the Canine Ancestral Diet—Healthier Dog Food the ABC Way.* Wenatchee: Direct Book Service, 2009.

Carpenter, M., et al. "Social cognition, joint attention, and communicative competence from 9 to 15 months of age." *Monographs of the Society for Research in Child Development* 63. 1998: 1–143.

Casey, Rachel, et al. "World learning in a domestic dog: Evidence for 'Fast Mapping.'" *Science*. 11 June. 2004: 1682–1683.

Coren, Stanley. *Do Dogs Dream?: Nearly Everything Your Dog Wants You to Know*. New York: W. W. Norton & Co., 2013.

———. *How Dogs Think: What the World Looks Like to Them and Why They Act the Way They Do*. New York: Atria Books, 2005.

———. *How to Speak Dog: Mastering the Art of Dog-Human Communication*. New York: Atria Books, 2001.

———. *The Intelligence of Dogs: A Guide to the Thoughts, Emotions, and Inner Lives of Our Canine Companions*. New York: Free Press, 1994.

———. *The Modern Dog: How Dogs Have Changed People and Society and Improved Our Lives*. New York: Atria Books, 2009.

———. *The Pawprints of History: Dogs and the Course of Human Events*. New York: Atria Books, 2003.

———. *Why Do Dogs Have Wet Noses?*. Toronto: Kids Can Press, 2008.

———. *Why We Love the Dogs We Do: How to Find the Dog That Matches Your Personality*. New York: Free Press, 2000.

Daniels, T. J., and M. Beckoff. "Fertilization: The making of wild domestic animals." *Behavioral Processes* 19. 1989: 79–94.

Darwin, C. *The Expression of the Emotions in Man and Animals*. London: John Murray, 1872.

———. *The Variation of Animals and Plants under Domestication*, vol. 1. London: John Murray, 1868.

Davis, S. J. M., and F. R. Valla. "Evidence for domestication of the dog 12,000 years ago in the Natufian of Israel." *Nature* 276. 1978:608–610.

DeMartini-Prince, Malena. *Treating Separation Anxiety in Dogs*. Wenatchee: Dogwise Publishing, 2014.

Diesel, Gillian, et al. "Characteristics of relinquished dogs and their owners at 14 rehoming centers in the United Kingdom." *Journal of Applied Animal Welfare Science* 13. 2005: 15–30.

Dodman, Nicholas, Dr. *The Dog Who Loved Too Much: Tales, Treatments and the Psychology of Dogs*. New York: Bantam Books, 1996.

———. *The Well-Adjusted Dog: Dr. Dodman's 7 Steps to Lifelong Health and Happiness For Your Best Friend*. New York: Mariner Books, 2008.

Donaldson, Jean. *Dogs Are From Neptune*. Wenatchee: Dogwise Publishing, 2009.

———. *Fight!: A Practical Guide to the Treatment of Dog-Dog Aggression*. Wenatchee: Dogwise Publishing, 2004.

————. *Mine!: A Practical Guide to Resource Guarding in Dogs*. Wenatchee: Dogwise Publishing, 2002.

————. *Oh Behave!: Dogs from Pavlov to Premack to Pinker*. Wenatchee: Dogwise Publishing, 2008.

————. *The Culture Clash: A Revolutionary New Way to Understanding the Relationship Between Humans and Domestic Dogs*. Berkeley: James & Kenneth Publishers, 1996.

————. *The Regulation of Companion Animal Services in Relation to Training and Behavior Modification of Dogs*. Cambridge: Companion Animal Welfare Council, 2008.

Dunbar, Ian. *After You Get Your Puppy*. Berkeley: James & Kenneth Publishers, 2001.

————. *Before and After Getting Your Puppy—The Positive Approach to Raising a Happy, Healthy and Well-Behaved Dog*. Novato: New World Library, 2004.

————. *Before You Get Your Puppy*. Berkeley: James & Kenneth Publishers, 2001.

————. *Dr. Dunbar's Good Little Dog Book*. Berkeley: James & Kenneth Publishers, 2003.

————. *How to Teach a New Dog Old Tricks*. Berkeley: James & Kenneth Publishers, 1996.

Faber, Adele, and Elaine Mazlish. *How to Talk so Kids Will Listen & Listen So Kids Will Talk*. New York: Avon Books, 1980.

Fisher, Gail, T. *The New Clicker Training Manual Vol. 2*. Manchester: All Dogs, Inc., 1998.

————. *The Thinking Dog—Crossover to Clicker Training*. Wenatchee: Dogwise Publishing, 2009.

Fox, Michael W. "Behavioral effect of rearing dogs with cats during the critical period of socialization." *Behavior* 35. 1969: 273–280.

Gácsi, M., et al. "The effect of development and individual differences in pointing comprehension of dogs." *Animal Cognition* 12. 2009: 471–479.

————. "Species-specific differences and similarities in the behavior of hand-raised dog and wolf pups in social situations with humans." *Developmental Psychobiology* 47. 2005: 111–122.

Gaunet, Florence, Dr. "How do guide dogs and pet dogs (*Canis familiaris*) ask their owners for their toy and for playing?" *Animal Cognition* 13. 2010: 311–323.

Grandin, Temple, and Catherine Johnson. *Animals in Translation: Using the Mysteries of Autism to Decode Animal Behavior*. New York: Harcourt, 2005.

Hare, Brian, Dr., and Mike Tomasello. "Domestic dogs [*Canis familiaris*] and human infants' comprehension of various forms of pointing gestures." *Animal Cognition* 12. 2009: 621–631.

Hare, Brian, Dr., and Michael Tomasello. "Human-like social skills in dogs?" *Trends in Cognitive Sciences* 9. 2005: 439–444.

Hare, Brian, Dr., and Vanessa Woods. *The Genius of Dogs: How Dogs are Smarter Than You Think.* New York: Penguin Group, 2013.

Hare, Brian, Dr., et al. "The domestication of social cognition in dogs." *Science* 298. 2002: 1634–1636.

Hauser, M.D., et al. "What experimental experience affects dogs' comprehension of human communicative actions?" *Behavioral Processes* 86. 2011: 7–20.

Hepper, Peter. "Long-term retention of kinship recognition established during infancy in the domestic dog." *Behavioral Processes* 33. 1994: 3–14.

Horowitz, Alexandra. "Disambiguating the 'guilty look': Salient prompts to a familiar dog behavior." *Behavioral Processes* 81. 2009: 447–452.

———. *Inside of a Dog: What Dogs See, Smell, and Know.* New York: Scribner, 2009.

Horowitz, Barbara Natterson, and Kathryn Bowers. *Zoobiquity: What Animals Can Teach Us About Being Human.* London: Virgin Books, 2012.

Hunt, M.M. *The Story of Psychology.* New York: Anchor Books, 2007.

"Inhibitory control may affect physical problem solving in pet dogs." *Science Codex.* 10 Feb. 2016.

Johnston, Bruce. *Harnessing Thought: Guide Dog—A Thinking Animal with a Skillful Mind.* Harpenden: Lennard, Publishing, 1995.

Kaminski, J., J. Call, and J. Fischer. "Word learning in a domestic dog: Evidence for 'fast mapping.'" *Science* 304. 2004: 1682–1683.

Keim, Brandon. "Brain scans show striking similarities between dogs and humans." *Wired.* 20 Feb. 2014.

Kratochwill, Lindsey. "Dogs know to look away when humans are angry." *Popular Science.* 29 Jan. 2016.

Lakatos, G., et al. "Comprehension and utilization of pointing gestures and gazing in dog-human communication in relatively complex situations." *Animal Cognition* 15. 2012: 201–213.

London, Karen, and Patricia McConnell, Ph.D. *Feisty Fido—Help for the Leash-Reactive Dog.* Wenatchee: Dogwise Publishing, 2009.

———. *Feeling Outnumbered?—How to Manage & Enjoy a Multi-Dog Household.* Lakewood: First Stone, 2009.

———. *Love Has No Age Limit—Welcoming an Adopted Dog into Your Home.* Black Earth: McConnell Publishing Ltd., 2011.

————. *Play Together Stay Together—Happy and Healthy Play Between People and Dogs*. Black Earth: McConnell Publishing Ltd., 2008.

————. *Way to Go!—How to Housetrain a Dog of Any Age*. Black Earth: McConnell Publishing Ltd., 2003.

Lorenz, Konrad. *Man Meets Dog*. New York: Kodansha America, Inc., 1953.

Luescher, Andrew, and Ilana Reisner. "Canine aggression towards familiar people: A new look at an old problem." *The Veterinary Clinics of North America: Small Animal Practice*. 2008: 1115–1116.

McConnell, Patricia, Ph.D. *Cautious Canine—How to Help Dogs Conquer Their Fears, 2nd Edition*. Black Earth: McConnell Publishing Ltd., 2005.

————. *For the Love of a Dog: Understanding Emotion in You and Your Best Friend*. New York: Ballantine Books, 2006.

————. *I'll Be Home Soon!—How to Prevent and Treat Separation Anxiety*. Black Earth: McConnell Publishing Ltd., 2000.

————. *Tales of Two Species—Essays on Loving and Living with Dogs*. Wenatchee: Direct Book Service, 2008.

————. *The Other End of the Leash: Why We Do What We Do Around Dogs*. New York: Ballantine Books, 2002.

————. and Aimee Moore. *Family Friendly Dog Training—A Six Week Program for You and Your Dog*. Black Earth: McConnell Publishing Ltd., 2006.

————. and Brenda Scidmore. *Puppy Primer, 2nd Edition*. Black Earth: McConnell Publishing Ltd., 2010.

Mech, L. D. *The Wolf: The Ecology and Behavior of an Endangered Species*. Ed. American Museum of Natural History. Garden City: Natural History Press, 1970.

Miklósi, Ádám, Dr., and Krisztina Soproni. "A comparative analysis of animals' understanding of the human pointing gesture." *Animal Cognition* 9. 2006: 81–93.

Miklósi, Ádám, Dr. *Dog Behavior, Evolution, and Cognition*. New York: Oxford University Press, 2009.

Miklósi, Ádám, Dr., et al. "Intentional behavior in dogs-human communication: An experimental analysis of 'showing' behavior in the dog." *Animal Cognition* 3. 2000: 159–166.

————. "Use of experimenter-given cues in dogs." *Animal Cognition* 1.1998: 113–121.

Miller, H., et al. "Imitation and emulation by dogs using a bidirectional control procedure." *Behavioral Processes* 80. 2009: 109–114.

Miller, Pat. *Do Over Dogs—Give Your Dog a Second Chance for a First Class Life*. Wenatchee: Dogwise Publishing, 2010.

———. *How to Foster Dogs—From Homeless to Homeward Bound*. Wenatchee: Dogwise Publishing, 2014.

———. *Play With Your Dog*. Wenatchee: Dogwise Publishing, 2008.

———. *Positive Perspectives—Love Your Dog, Train Your Dog*. Wenatchee: Dogwise Publishing, 2004.

———. *Positive Perspectives 2—Know Your Dog, Train Your Dog*. Wenatchee: Dogwise Publishing, 2008.

———. *Power of Positive Dog Training, 2nd Edition*. Hoboken: Howell Book House, 2008.

Mogel, Wendy, Ph.D. *The Blessing of a Skinned Knee: Using Jewish Teachings to Raise Self-Reliant Children*. New York: Scribner, 2001.

Morrel, Virginia. *Animal Wise: How We Know Animals Feel and Think*. New York: Crown Publishing, 2013.

———. "Dogs can read human emotions." *Science*. 12 Jan 2016.

Nagasawa, Miho, et. al. "Oxytocin-gaze positive loop and the coevolution of human-dog bonds." *Science* 348. 2015: 333–336.

Nelsen, Jane, Ed.D. *Positive Discipline: The Classic Guide to Helping Children Develop Self-Discipline, Responsibility, Cooperation, and Problem-Solving Skills*. New York: Ballantine Books, 1981, 1987, 1996, and 2006.

Pal, Sunil. "Urine marking by free-ranging dogs (*Canis familiaris*) in relation to sex, season, place and posture." *Applied Animal Behavior Science* 80. 2003: 43–59.

Pappas, Stephanie. "What do dogs dream about?" *Live Science*. 17 Feb. 2016.

Pierson, Melissa. *The Secret History of Kindness: Learning from How Dogs Learn*. New York: W. W. Norton & Co., 2015.

Prothmann, A., et al. "Preference for, and responsiveness to, people, dogs, and objects in children with Autism." *Anthrozoös* 22. 2005: 253–278.

Pryor, Karen. *Clicker Training for Dogs*. Thomastown: Sunshine Books, 2005.

———. *Click to Win: Clicker Training for the Show Ring*. Thomastown: Sunshine Books, 2002.

———. *Click! Tricks: 10 Fun and Easy Tricks Any Dog Can Learn*. New York: Sterling Innovation, 2010.

———. *Don't Shoot the Dog: The New Art of Teaching and Training*. Lydney: Ringpress Books, 2006.

———. *How to Teach Your Dog to Play Frisbee*. New York: Simon & Schuster, 1985.

———. *On My Mind: Reflections on Animal Behavior and Learning*. Thomastown: Sunshine Books, 2014.

————. *Reaching the Animal Mind—Clicker Training and What It Teaches Us about All Animals.* New York: Scribner, 2010.

Riedel, J., et al. "Domestic dogs [*Canis familiaris*] use a physical marker to locate hidden food." *Animal Cognition* 9. 2006: 27–35.

————. "The early ontogeny of human-dog communication." *Animal Behavior* 73. 2008: 1003–1014.

Rosalind, Arden and Mark James Adams. "A general intelligence factor in dogs." *Intelligence* 55. 2016: 79–85.

Ryan, Terry. *The Tool for Building a Great Family Dog.* Dogwise Publishing, 2010.

Safina, Carl. *Beyond Words: What Animals Think and Feel.* New York: Henry Holt and Co., 2015.

Schilder, Matthijs, and Joanne van der Borg. "Training dogs with help of the shock collar: Short and long term behavioral effects." *Applied Animal Behaviour Science.* 2000: 319–357.

Serpell, James. *Thinking with Animals: New Perspective on Anthropomorphism.* New York: Columbia University Press, 2005.

Shettleworth, S.J. *Cognition, Evolution, and Behavior.* New York: Oxford University Press, 2009.

Skinner, B. F. "A case history in scientific method." *American Psychologist* 11. 1956: 221–233.

————. "How to teach animals." *Scientific American* 185(12). 1951: 26–29.

————. *Science and Human Behavior.* New York: Macmillan, 1953.

————. "'Superstition' in the pigeon." *Journal of Experimental Psychology* 38. 1948: 168–172.

————. *The Behavior of Organisms: An Experimental Analysis.* New York: Appleton-Century, 1938.

Soproni, K., et al. "Comprehension of human communicative signs in pet dogs (*Canis familiaris*)." *Journal of Comparative Psychology* 115. 2001: 122–126.

Téglás, E., et al. "Dogs' gaze following is tuned to human communicative signals." *Current Biology* 22. 2012: 209–212.

Tomasello, Mike. "Cultural learning." *Behavioral and Brain Sciences* 16. 1993: 495–511.

Tomasello, Mike. "Having intentions, understanding intentions, and understanding communicative intentions." *Developing Theories of Intention: Social Understanding and Self-Control.* Psychology Press, 1999: 63–75.

Topál, József, et al. "Differential sensitivity to human communication in dogs, wolves, and human infants." *Science* 325. 2009: 1269–1272.

Townsend, E. *Darwin's Dogs: How Darwin's Pets Helped Form a World-Changing Theory of Evolution*. London: Frances Lincoln Ltd., 2009.

Trut, Ludmilla. "Early canid domestication: The Farm-fox experiment." *American Scientist* 87. 1999: 160–169.

Udell, M., et al. "Domestic dogs [*Canis familiaris*] use human gestures but not nonhuman tokens to find hidden food." *Journal of Comparative Psychology* 122. 2008: 84–93.

VonHoldt, B., et al. "Genome-wise SNP and haplotype analyses reveal a rich history underlying dog domestication." *Nature* 464. 2010: 898–902.

Wade, Nicholas. "New Finding Puts Origins of Dogs in Middle East." *New York Times*. 18 March, 2010.

Warren, Cat. *What the Dog Knows: The Science and Wonder of Working Dogs*. New York: Touchstone Books, 2015.

Wells, Deborah, and Peter Hepper. "Prenatal olfactory learning in the domestic dog." *Animal Behavior* 72. 2006: 681–686.

Wolko, Lindsey. "Center for Pet Safety 2013 harness crashworthiness study summary report." *The Science of Pet Safety*. 2013: 1–14.

INDEX

Page numbers followed by "t" indicate tables.

Coccidia, 272
Collars, 53, 56–57, 240
Color vision, 47
Come (command), 179–181, 182
Come (games), 182
Comfort Wear, 56–57
Comforting people, 108, 113, 113t
Comic people, 107, 111, 112t
Commands. *See* Learning
Communication
  ears and, 34–35
  everyday words and routines and,
    147–148, 148–149t
  eyes and, 35–36
  importance of, 31–32
  initial meeting and, 33
  mouth and, 33–34
  in people vs. dogs, 32–33
  perspective and, 147
  posture and, 41–45f, 41–46
  tail and, 36–37, 37f
  as type of intelligence, 30
  vocabulary for, 160t
  vocalizations and, 38–40
Compulsive behaviors
  fly snapping, 247–248
  lick granulomas, 247
  overview of, 247–250
  pica, 247
  shadow and light chasing, 247
  tail chasing, 248
Conditioning, 152t, 153t
Confusion, posture and, 44f
Copycat barking, 233–234
Coren, Stanley, 17, 52, 72, 120
Cortisol, 16
Cotton swabs, 275
Counter cruising, 217–218
Counterconditioning, 143–144, 153t,
  242–243, 255
Country life, 95
CPR, 279
Crates, 55
Crawl (trick), 194
Criteria, 156
Critical socialization period, 73

Crotch sniffing, 19, 244–245
Cunning, 30
Curiosity, 19, 24, 42f

D

Daily needs
  elimination, 26t, 29
  food, 25t, 26–27
  overview of, 25, 25–26t
  play, 26t, 29
  sleep, 26t, 27–28
  water, 25t, 27
Dance (trick), 193–194
Darwin, Charles, 71
Declarative memory, 30
Deconditioning, 242
DEET, 269
Defensiveness, 43f, 45f, 81
Definitions, 152–156t
Delayed imitation and declarative
  memory, 30
DeMartini-Price, Malena, 256
Demodectic mange, 269
Demodex mites, 269
Dental health, 272–274
Desensitization, 153t, 255
Detail-oriented people, 106–107, 111,
  112t
Dewormers, 271
Diets, 280–282
Digging, 205t, 234–235
Direction words, 159, 160t
Discouragements, 221, 222
Discrimination, 154t
Displacement activities, 57–59, 245
Distractions, 139, 165
Dizzy Waiter (game), 252–253
Dodman, Nicholas, 28
Dogality
  determining, 71–80
  overview of, 71
  types of, 80–84
Dogality test, 71–80
Doglish, 8
Dognition.com, 30
Dominance, 12–14